# The Householder's Guide to Plumbing

James M. Haig

revised by M. A. Hewitt

STANLEY PAUL
London Melbourne Auckland Johannesburg

Stanley Paul & Co. Ltd
An imprint of Century Hutchinson Ltd
62–65 Chandos Place, London WC2N 4NW

Century Hutchinson Australia (Pty) Ltd
PO Box 496, 16–22 Church Street, Hawthorn, Melbourne,
Victoria 3122

Century Hutchinson New Zealand Limited
PO Box 40–086, Glenfield, Auckland 10

Century Hutchinson South Africa (Pty) Ltd
PO Box 337, Bergvlei 2012, South Africa

First published 1961
Reprinted 1963
Revised edition 1974
Reprinted 1977, 1979
Revised edition 1984, 1987

© James M. Haig 1961, 1984
© M. A. Hewitt 1984, 1987

Photoset in Linotron Sabon by
Deltatype Ltd, Ellesmere Port, S. Wirral

Printed and bound in Great Britain by
Anchor Brendon Ltd, Tiptree, Essex

ISBN 0 09 173467 3

# Contents

# Acknowledgements

The author acknowledges with thanks the help he has received from the Copper, Lead and Zinc Development Associations, the Electrical Association, British Gas Corporation, Marley Plumbing Limited, Wednesbury Tube Company, Le Bas Tube Company Limited and Barking Brassware Company Limited, in the compilation of this book.

J. M. H.

This is the second revision of this book that I have undertaken and by far the more onerous because of the innovations now admissable following the reform of the legislation which controls the pumbing and building industries.

Without the very generous cooperation which I have received from organizations, manufacturers, and individuals this task would have been a very long one indeed. I wish to express my gratitude to those who gave so willingly of their time, and who allowed me to reproduce, in these pages, from their technical material:

Barking-Grohe, the Electricity Council, Ideal Standard, Hunter Building Products, Thames Water, The National Water Council, the Department of the Environment, Grundfos Pumps, the Institute of Plumbing, John Hazzlewood, ex-editor of the IOP journal *Plumbing*, Medic-Bath Ltd, E. A. Molyneux Ltd, Hamworthy, Transbyn Ltd, Belco, Chaffoteaux, and Ms Peggy Andrews, without whose tireless efforts this work would not have been completed on time.

M. A. HEWITT

# Foreword

This book is intended to help householders to acquire a sound knowledge of the functioning of the plumbing and central heating installations in their homes and enable them to undertake minor repairs and maintenance work. Every householder has a responsibility to his family and the community in being able to control the water and gas services within his home if only because of the safety factors involved. Apart from this he should know that inspection and maintenance can prevent deterioration which could lead to costly repairs and replacements.

*The Householder's Guide to Plumbing* is also aimed at the potential houseowner, knowing what to look for is all important as so many plumbing faults and inconsistencies are either hidden or virtually inaccessible. Thus anyone intending to purchase a new home should pay particular attention to the arrangement of pipework and the provisioning and positioning of stopvalves, and before making a final acceptance of the property, should closely inspect the surfaces of the bath, washbasin, w.c. pan and kitchen sink.

The materials and appliances used for plumging and central heating and the skilled labour required to install them are very costly. The extent and complexity of plumbing and heating have also increased with the introduction of more sophisticated appliances and accessories and by the improved standards of living enjoyed by everyone. Particular attention has been given to the increasing use of plastics in plumbing and the development of microbore copper tubes in central heating.

*Torbay, Devon*                                          JAMES M. HAIG

There have been many changes in the plumbing industry since this book was first published in 1961 and, indeed, since I did the last revision in 1984. Even as I write, new products are coming onto the market that will succeed some of those listed in these pages, which is, of course, inevitable in our ever-changing world.

Consequently, I have dealt in detail with fundamental issues, such as the new Water Bye Laws, new Building Regulations, pressurized hot water and heating systems, legionella, water contamination, provision for the disabled, sanitation plumbing, drainage, and basic safeguards for householder when employing contractors, etc, which ensures that this volume is as up-to-date for both craftsmen and lay persons as it is possible to be.

In all aspects this book deals with working principles which, if properly understood, will enable all readers to determine, without difficulty, the appropriate fitting, system, or design for their, or their customers', needs.

Much of James Haig's original script remains for it is still applicable to countless numbers of installations throughout the country and will remain so for many decades; just as this book will stand as a lasting memorial to a man who did so much for the plumbing industry and those who work in it.

*Thornton Heath, Surrey*                                M. A. HEWITT

# 1

# Cold-Water Supply Explained

## Requirements

In this country every dwelling must have a water supply that is fit for drinking. That is a requirement of the Public Health Act. For the vast majority of houses that means a connection piped into the building from a water main in the road. Just about everybody realizes and accepts that; what isn't so apparent to many householders is the set of rules that goes with it.

The byelaws are the rules, and they are made by the water company not only to protect their main water supply but also to safeguard the water delivered to each individual dwelling which, in turn, protects every user of the water.

Because water is on tap and simple to draw it is easy to take it for granted and to accept that at all times it is fit for every purpose for which we use it, from washing the car and watering the garden to the preparation and cooking of food, and drinking. It is certainly wholesome when the water company pump it out of their stations; whether it stays that way depends upon the users along the route: you and me and the people next door.

The byelaws are designed to prevent contamination, misuse, undue consumption, and waste. This year new byelaws will be made under the Water Council's Model Byelaws to reinforce these objectives while taking account of the many recent developments and innovations in the plumbing industry. For our own benefit, each and every one of us must observe these requirements.

Why? How does it affect you? Is it going to be expensive? These things usually are. Sometimes that seems to be the sole purpose. Well, just for once, money isn't the reason for this change, and no, it doesn't have to be expensive, but it can affect you, and you may cause it to affect others.

Let's have a look at a basic cold-water plumbing system in a dwelling supplied from a water company's water main. (There are many properties, particularly in remote country areas, that get their water from deep wells, rivers, or springs, and are, therefore, not affected by the water authority's byelaws. Nonetheless, owners of such properties will be well advised to follow the principles expressed in these pages.)

## Service pipe

The piped connection from the company's main in the road to the dwelling is a service pipe. The water board install the length of pipe from their main to the boundary of the property and terminate it with a stopvalve. This pipe, called the communicating pipe, is laid at a minimum depth of 750 mm, which is generally accepted to be below the depth to which frost will penetrate. (Underground water pipework must never be shallower than this depth or greater than 1.35 m.) The valve is usually encased by a vertical length of 100 mm-diameter earthenware drain pipe which is terminated at ground level with a hinged, or lift and turn, cover. They are a familiar sight along the pavements of our streets.

Each dwelling should have a valve, which is primarily an isolating valve to disconnect the property from the main supply

Figure 1    *Crutch-head stopcock*

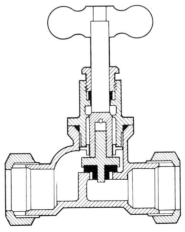

BS 5433 underground stopvalve
BS 1010 above ground stopvalve

pipe, but there are many instances in which one valve controls two or more properties where a service pipe is shared.

Depending upon the area, the valve may be a crutch-head stopcock (Figure 1) or a square-shank-spindle stopcock. The latter type is fitted to deter householders from using this valve to turn off their supply. The valve belongs to the water company, and only they should operate it. Too many spindles have been broken by over-zealous residents armed with water keys. Water boards will respond to householders' requests for the water to be turned off.

The crutch-head stopcock can, of course, be operated by hand, providing you lie flat on your face on the pavement with your arm stretched down the hole, or by using a piece of wood with a deep V cut in one end. But this is not the intended use of the stopcock, and the householder should use his own control valve, which should be located at low level on the main supply pipe where it enters the property.

Happily, these days designers have at last recognized the need to route pipes on internal walls, unlike yesteryear, when water pipes were habitually run on cold external walls. Most of us can remember the problems of burst pipes during bitter winters: the damage caused and the inconvenience of having no water or, equally bad, of storing it in pots and pans or, if you were lucky, the bath.

If any reader is the possessor of that type of archaic plumbing then he will be well advised to alter it. Certainly if the original bad plumbing is still in use, do have it taken out without delay and replaced with copper or plastic pipes. In most areas councils will pay a grant towards the cost of this work, especially in soft-water districts, where the water will attack and dissolve the lead. Hard-water areas were generally regarded as safe because of the limescale deposit with which the water coated the internal walls of the pipe and which effectively prevented any possible attack.

Recently, however, it has been observed that electrolysis, the galvanic action between dissimilar metals in the presence of moisture (dealt with more fully in Chapters 2 and 7) can affect the pipe wall protective coatings, and may change the water characteristic to aggressive. Whatever the situation, it makes sound sense to remove all lead pipes from any plumbing system.

Similarly, aggressive water can attack the solder in capillary copper fittings, and the lead content may be leeched into the water that may be used for drinking or food preparation.

Pipework laid in the ground may also be subject to attack from the acids in the soil: wet ashes and clinker in made-up ground, red marl clay, wet decomposing organic matter, and wet ironstone can have a harmful effect on all metals. Where serious corrosion occurs it is usually due to a combination of poor drainage and high sulphate and/or chloride content in ground that generally has a high water content.

Where these conditions exist the service pipe (or any metal pipe laid in the ground) must be protected by wrapping it in water-repellent adhesive tape or laying it in a bed of limestone chippings, which will effectively neutralize the acidity of the ground. To allow for ground movement the service pipe should be 'snaked' in the trench and not run in a straight line. The bending route provides a degree of elasticity in the pipe which will avoid stress fractures.

Because of this need for flexibility underground water pipes must not be bedded on, or surrounded in, concrete. In any situation, contact between any metal pipes and materials that contain cement must be avoided as the chemical action that occurs in maturing cement may cause a destructive reaction to the metal of the pipe. Where such contact cannot be avoided in passing through concrete foundations or slab floors, the pipe should be sleeved, or wrapped in a durable water-repellent tape.

In many constructions it has been common practice to lag pipework within the depth of a concrete floor slab or in a vertical column. This situation must be avoided at all costs even if it means finding an alternative route on a wall surface above floor level. If pipework must run in a concrete slab, then it should do so in a properly formed pipe duct which is provided throughout its length with a removable access cover.

Underground water pipes must not be laid through manholes or drains, and definitely not in the same trench. Drains are liable to leak, and the effluent may pond in ground cavities or on clay strata; and a fracture in the water pipe at that point could result in back-siphonage into the supply pipe if there were a sudden loss of pressure in the pipe.

Problems are encountered where water pipes have to cross drains to enter buildings. If the drains are deep the service pipe may cross above them, but usually the drains are at comparatively shallow depths. In these instances alternative routes must

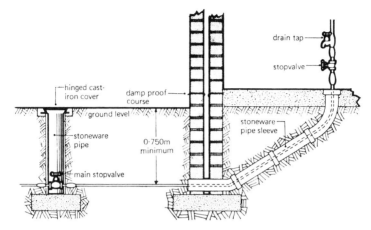

Figure 2    *The service pipe to the house*

be found. Nor must any water service pipe be laid in any form of cesspool or rubbish tip or the like.

Where services are run in ducts, or travel through basements, care has to be exercised in positioning those pipes which may be permeated by gases. Some plastic pipes are susceptible to permeation, and they should be sited at least 350 mm away from any pipe carrying gas.

Service pipes entering buildings should do so through a pipe sleeve, as illustrated in Figure 2. Both ends of the sleeve must be stopped to prevent the entry of insects and vermin.

It must by now be evident that the prime considerations in the installation of pipework are the protection of the pipes and the safeguarding of the quality of the water. These must be paramount objectives at all times in every part of all plumbing systems.

## Stopvalve inside the house

The byelaw states '. . . every service pipe supplying water to any building shall be fitted with a stopvalve inside, and as near as practicable to the point of entry of such pipe into the building'.

There are hundreds of thousands of houses without a stopvalve on the service pipe within the house. To the owners of such houses the key point of the cold-water system remains the stopvalve outside. A stopvalve also fitted inside is an obvious advantage, for if a stopvalve is readily accessible and a drain-off cock is provided immediately above it (Figure 2) the valve may be shut down and the pipe drained at night in inadequately heated dwellings in frosty weather.

However, in these days when so many houses are equipped with an effective system of heating, and both pipework and building fabric are properly insulated, it has become a largely superfluous precaution unless the premises are left vacant during winter months.

Drain-off cocks should be provided at the lowest points on all water service pipes within the house to enable the whole, or part, of the system to be emptied so that repairs, alterations or additions to the pipework or fittings may be carried out.

## The rising main

The service pipe within the house is usually referred to by plumbers as the rising main. This is because it is the pipe conveying mains water, and it rises up through the house to feed the storage cistern in the roof space.

The rising main provides drinking water and, in some areas, cold water to the bath, washbasin and w.c. cistern. The local byelaws should be consulted because many water undertakings do not permit direct connection of sanitary and ablutionary fitments with main water.

The rising main should be fixed to an internal partition wall, but in many houses it will be found on the inside of the perimeter wall of the kitchen and bathroom, and in some cases will be close to the ventilator in the bathroom or w.c. and right in the line of icy draughts in wintertime.

The wise householder will trace the run of his rising main and take steps to ensure that it is protected from frost. Advice on this subject is given in the section of this book dealing with frost protection.

## The storage cistern

The question is often posed 'why must we have a tank in the roof when everything could be supplied from the main?'

First, the difference between a tank and a cistern must be made clear. Far too many plumbers call a cistern a tank and this is both confusing and incorrect.

A *cistern* is a container for water which is under atmospheric pressure (i.e. an open top). A *storage cistern* is any cistern other than a flushing cistern. A *feed cistern* is for supplying cold water to a hot-water apparatus.

A *tank* is a closed container for water under more than atmospheric pressure. The term is used in household plumbing for the hot-water tank (or cylinder).

The container in the roof space of a house is a *storage cistern* and it has a threefold purpose: (i) It provides a reserve of water if for any reason the main supply is cut off. (ii) It limits the pressure of water on pipes and fittings within the house thus reducing noise in the pipes, wastage of water, and enabling pipes of a lighter weight (and less costly) to be used. (iii) It reduces the maximum rate of demand on the company's mains supply.

Further to these points, everyone should know that water undertakers must take every precaution to prevent contamination of the main water supply. It is for this reason that many undertakings do not permit mains water to be connected directly to w.c. flushing cisterns, baths, washbasins, bidets, or to certain types of mixing valves. There are recorded cases of mains water being contaminated by what is technically known as 'back-siphonage', or, in simple terms, fouled water being drawn back into the main supply pipe following a drop in working pressure. The Model Water Byelaws made by the Water Council in 1986 under which water undertakers make their own byelaws in 1987 extend this protection against back-siphonage to all distribution and cold-feed pipes within any building, and make special provision for such sanitary fittings as bidets. Thus water undertakers are enacting the long-overdue precaution against transfer of water from one pipe to another irrespective of whether it is intended for drinking or domestic use.

## The position of the storage cistern

The customary practice is to place the storage cistern in the roof space. There are two points in favour of this: (i) The roof space is the highest part of the house and a cistern fixed there will ensure a good pressure of water at the taps below. This is of particular importance if a shower is to be used in the bathroom. (ii) A cistern can be rather noisy when it is refilling and in the roof space it is more or less out of hearing – and certainly out of sight. There is an increasing tendency to place the cistern as high as possible but not actually in the roof space. It can be fixed in a cupboard on the landing directly above the hot-water storage tank. The 'head of water' which governs pressure will be reduced, but it will scarcely affect the supply of water at the various taps in the house.

If it is decided to fix the cistern in a cupboard, it should be as high as possible but with a minimum 350-mm space between the top edge of the cistern and the ceiling, or frame of the access door, to permit the cistern to be inspected and cleaned, and the ball valve to be maintained.

The cistern should be supported on strong bearers and base board because when filled with water its weight will be considerable – possibly 150 kg – and should be distributed across as many supporting joists as possible.

The water content will also lower its temperature which, in a warm space, usually above the hot-water storage cylinder, will result in condensation. This can be prevented by lagging the cistern with a 75-mm fibreglass paper-covered wrap, not forgetting the underside and the lid. Never use uncovered fibreglass on open-top storage vessels: should any fibres get into the cistern they can play havoc with ball valve, stopcock and tap seatings and, very often, cause blockages in small-diameter pipes.

For cisterns located in the roof space, ensure adequate bearers and base-board support spanning several joists, and, if possible, locate the cistern over an internal wall. Lofts are usually the coldest spots in a house, especially if insulation has been laid across the joists, preventing heat gain from the warm air below. The loft insulation should be removed from the area under the cistern and the cistern must be lagged as described in the previous paragraph with the exception of the underside. It is advisable to ensure that gaps around the eaves are filled to prevent through-draughts of icy air in the winter, but take care not to exclude all ventilation, as it is essential in roof spaces.

One factor that is frequently overlooked when lagging cisterns is the overflow pipe, which connects directly from the top of the vessel just above the water line to the outside air. This is the most common cause of freezing of the top of the water in the cistern; when this occurs the ball valve is locked in the shut position and with normal demand the storage will soon be exhausted. To prevent this, fit a bend to the screw-thread of the overflow connection on the inside of the cistern and extend a piece of pipe to just below normal water level so that no cold draught can enter.

Storage cisterns should have rigid and tightly fitting access covers which exclude light and prevent insects, etc., getting into the cistern, but which are not airtight. There must be ventilation.

## Capacity of the storage cistern

The amount of water required to be kept in storage varies according to the type of building in which the water is to be used. The demand in a hotel will not be the same as in a hospital, a school, or a factory.

For dwellings a minimum storage of 115 litres for cold-water cisterns and 230 litres for hot- and cold-water services (in Scotland 100 litres and 200 litres respectively) is required, but it must be stressed that this is a minimum capacity and does not reflect the likely demand of the users.

As the storage is intended to provide a reserve in the event of a breakdown of the main supply a realistic capacity should be provided. Though the problem is determining the amounts likely to be used by individuals the following are the generally adopted figures:

Dwellings up to four bedrooms     120 litres per bedroom.
Dwelling more than four bedrooms 100 litres per bedroom.

During normal usage water drawn off will be automatically made up through the ball valve. The main supply pipe and ball valve, therefore, must be properly sized to replenish the cisterns at a rate at least equal to the rate of draw-off. If this isn't achieved the cistern may be effectively drained during periods of peak demand.

The ball valve should be checked regularly to ensure that it is working smoothly and is not 'sticking'. Lime scale deposit on the piston of the valve will often cause it to wedge. This may happen when the valve is in the open position, causing the cistern to overflow – and, if the warning pipe is too small to cope with the full-bore inlet discharge, water will spill over into the roof space; or when the valve is in the closed position, when the contents of the cistern will be drained.

Ball valves are reliable fittings and because of this, and the fact that they are normally out of sight, householders generally take them for granted and react only when disaster strikes. Twice a year is sufficient to check them, with a general clean and piston grease every third inspection. A fine file should be used to clean the piston; on no account use wire wool or any abrasive, descaling, or cleaning agents.

When calculating the cistern size remember that the actual capacity of the cistern will be less than the nominal capacity (which is the amount of water the vessel will hold when filled to the brim), because connecting the necessary pipes to it – warning pipe, cold-water down service, cold feed – will not permit you either to fill it to the brim or to drain off its entire contents.

## Cleaning the cistern

Like the ball valve, cisterns are taken for granted until they give trouble. The problem is that very often when trouble comes it is not always readily identifiable. Water can support microbial growth; animal organisms can get into storage cisterns; strange insect-like creatures can appear in water drawn from taps.

Much of the trouble arises from cisterns that are not properly covered or, often, from cisterns that are covered with wooden lids. (Water condensing on the underside of the timber can produce mites which will proliferate in these circumstances.) In many roofs several cisterns are 'married' together incorrectly, creating a reservoir of stagnant water which is ideal for many organisms to breed in.

Cisterns must be inspected regularly and cleaned at least every two years (more often if you can manage it). This is no more difficult than defrosting your freezer, especially if the cistern is plastic. First switch off the boiler or immersion heater, then simply turn off the water supply to the cistern, open the taps on the lowest fittings and drain the contents to the level of the distribution pipework connections. The remaining 54 mm depth of water in the cistern will have to be bailed out and, finally, swabbed up.

Once the cistern is empty the sediment can be cleaned from the bottom and any loose debris swept and cleaned from the sides. The outlets from the cistern should be plugged off or covered with plastic bags during this operation.

Chlorine, which can be purchased from builders' merchants in liquid form, should be diluted in water in strict accordance with the instructions on the container, and the cistern's base and sides scrubbed with a bristle brush.

Plastics cisterns will require little effort, and galvanized steel cisterns should be examined carefully for signs of rust on the internal faces. If the corrosion is well advanced it will be prudent to renew the cistern as soon as possible.

Plastic liners may be fitted to cisterns to prolong their life, and providing they are properly installed – preferably by a specialist – they are satisfactory. There are also many proprietary preparations on the market for coating the insides of storage cisterns, but under no circumstances must any material containing coal tar be used. Many bitumen products contain coal tar. If you intend to coat the inside of a water cistern you should first consult the local water authority for advice on a suitable product.

Once scrubbed, rinse the walls and base of the cistern and bale and swab out. Remove the bungs from the outlet pipes, turn off the control valves, open the main stopcock and fill the cistern, adding chlorine as directed in the manufacturer's instructions. The dosage must not exceed 50 parts per million.

The water should be left to stand for as long as possible, preferably at least four hours, after which time the main supply should be turned off and the control valve in the outlet pipes opened and the water drained down through all taps except the mains drinking water. Turn on the main supply and turn off the taps to fittings. Fill the cistern and open the taps to fittings in turn until water runs clear.

The cistern is now cleaned and chlorinated, and the pipes have benefited by being washed through with chlorinated water. For the pipes in the system to be treated properly they must first be treated with detergent to remove all scale and sludge before chlorination. In domestic properties this need only be done in extreme cases, for instance where the water discharge from taps is discoloured, has offensive odour, has a poor taste, is cloudy and slow to clear, and so on.

Householders suffering any of these symptoms in their water

systems should employ the services of a professional, as bacterio-
logical and chemical tests will need to be taken and the correct
dosage of suitable biocides applied.

Cistern cleaning is important as it maintains a healthy environment for clean water and inhibits the development of many
harmful organisms, including legionella.

### Arrangement of cisterns

There are many dwellings with more than one cold-water storage
cistern in the roof space simply because replacement of an

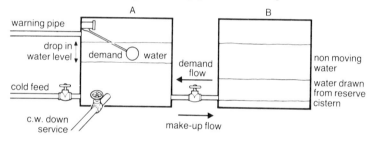

Figure 3  *Two cold water cisterns incorrectly connected*

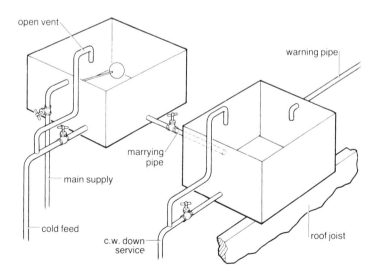

Figure 4  *Two cold water cisterns correctly connected*

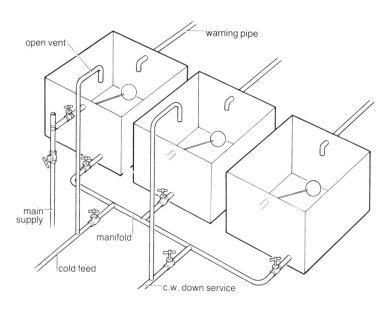

Figure 5   *Three cisterns-manifold connection*

original cistern with one of like size was not possible because of restricted access. It is quite common to fit two, three, or four small cisterns in place of one large one. Too often the supply and distribution pipes are taken from one cistern, leaving the other purely as additional storage. This practice must be avoided. The effect is to draw the bulk of demand water from the one cistern while the top two-thirds of the storage in the other cistern doesn't move and, therefore, stagnates. (This is illustrated in Figures 3, 4 and 5.)

As the water level falls in cistern A, water is fed through the marrying pipe from the lower part of cistern B. As the make-up water comes into cistern A the process is reversed, and water is replaced through the marrying pipe into the lower part of cistern B.

Cisterns should be arranged so that they can be married by a common manifold pipe. This is a pipe of suitable diameter to which each storage vessel is connected by a short, valved pipe. The manifold must be vented. (See chapter on back-siphonage.) All distributing pipes are taken from the manifold pipe, thus ensuring equal demand upon each cistern (Figure 5).

Each cistern must have its own main supply connection and ball valve and its own warning pipe to provide make-up water from the top and so prevent the up and down movement of water in the upper sections of the cistern that is so liable to become stagnant. This system has the added advantage that cisterns can be easily isolated for cleaning without interrupting the cold-water services to the household.

# Heat gain

Roof spaces, with insulation across ceiling joists, may be cold during the winter months but, with anything like a decent summer, the temperature under the tiles soars. Excessive heat build up in the enclosed roof space is common on hot days, and stored water that is static for any length of time in these conditions will increase in temperature. Cold water must be stored and distributed at a temperature not exceeding 20°C (except for storage serving only a hot-water closed-circuit system). Heat gain from solar-heated roof spaces has been known to raise cold-water temperature to over 30°C.

This in itself may be of little consequence to many house-holders other than causing the annoyance of having lukewarm water, instead of refreshingly cold water, delivered from taps and showers. However, most readers will have heard of legionnaires' disease, usually reported widely when it affects hospitals and hotels. It is generally accepted that domestic plumbing systems are not a risk, but the organisms can and do exist in these systems just as in the systems of other buildings. The organism legionella is endemic to many natural waters. It thrives and multiplies in temperatures between 20 and 50°C, with an optimum of 35°C.

There are several other conditions necessary to promote the growth of legionella, and these are discussed in more detail in Chapter 4. However, one certain precaution against legionnaires' disease is to maintain water supplies at safe temperatures, which is why legionella is mentioned here in the context of stored cold water.

# Shared responsibilities

This book is called *The Householder's Guide to Plumbing*, but clearly the subject is not confined to plumbing systems in houses. These days many more people are buying or leasing flats or sharing divided houses, and of course, under the Right to Buy Act, many are purchasing properties in blocks of council flats which were never conceived, or designed, for shared ownership.

Any form of flatted development in which units are owned by individual parties has a maintenance and repairs contract to which all owners are bound. Basically this means that all shared responsibilities are met from a communal fund administered by the managing agents. It is very important that all owners and those leasing who are responsible for repairs make sure that all aspects of shared plumbing, particularly storage cisterns and common pipework, are included in any agreement. It is even more important to obtain assurances that the work, when carried out, is properly supervised.

## Ball valve

The ball valve, usually 15 mm for domestic cisterns, should be a diaphragm valve to comply with BS 1212: Part 2 (brass), or Part 3 (plastic). A large-diameter rubber diaphragm acting against a seating and activated by the ball and arm controls the flow of water. Even if this valve is submerged, and the main supply pipe is subjected to a pressure loss, the valve will not allow water to pass back into the main. Thus it is an effective check against back-siphonage. An additional benefit is that the delivery port is raised above the top of the valve, which provides an adequate air gap even when the valve is submerged (see Figure 6). The traditional

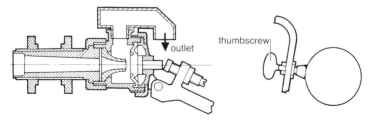

Figure 6    *B.S. 1212 Part 2 or 3 ball valve*

valve, the piston and washer, Portsmouth pattern BS 1212: Part 1, has an underside delivery port which, if subjected to reverse pressures, will not prevent back-siphonage.

The valve should be fixed as high as possible in the cistern without perforating any reinforcing rib, and low enough to prevent the ball from hitting the lid when lifting to the 'off' position. The valve should be equipped with a screw-thread adjustment to position the level of the float, rather than bend the arm to achieve the water line. The arm must be of adequate length for the size of the valve and the cistern, and the ball float of suitable diameter. An arm which is too short does not give the correct lift leverage to overcome the pressure of incoming water and may, indeed, submerge the float before lifting suddenly with a concussive effect. This is a common cause of water hammer. For larger diameter valves the BS 1212 Part 1 may be fitted providing there is an adequate air gap between the delivery port of the valve and the level of the overflow in the cistern.

## Overflow/warning pipes

It is important to understand the difference between a warning pipe and an overflow.

A warning pipe indicates an overfilling cistern which requires instant attention. It may not necessarily cope with a full-bore-inlet discharge. In an emergency, turn off the control valve and check the valve for sticking. If it is free, get it re-washered without delay.

An overflow should be sized to cope with the full-bore discharge of the inlet pipe. On storage vessels of over 1000 litres' capacity an overflow and a warning pipe must be provided, the warning pipe at the lower level and both discharging where they will be readily seen.

## Warning pipe only

The vertical distance between the lowest point of any pipe or fitting discharging into a cistern and the spill-over level of the cistern must not be less than the dimensions in the following table:

Table 1

| Bore of outlet | Vertical distance between valve outlet and overflow |
| --- | --- |
| Not exceeding 14 mm | 20 mm |
| Exceeding 14 mm but not exceeding 21 mm | 25 mm |
| Exceeding 21 mm but not exceeding 41 mm | 70 mm |
| Exceeding 41 mm | Twice the bore of the outlet |

This gap is called a Type-A air break, and is an essential precaution against back-siphonage from storage cisterns. This air break must not be bridged by any rigid-pipe 'silencers'; that is, silencing tubes of rigid material capable of conducting water back through their lengths must not be fitted to the delivery portion of any ball valve. In the event of a drop in pressure to below that of atmosphere in the main supply pipe the contents of the cistern to the depth of the silencer tube could be siphoned back into the rising main (see section on siphonic action). Householders with silencers fitted to ball valves should remove them.

There is no specific diameter for a warning pipe, but it should not be less than 22 mm. However, it should be large enough for any discharge to be immediately conspicuous. Obviously any householder, or plumber, installing a warning pipe in any storage cistern that does not require an overflow will ensure that it is of adequate size to carry away the full-bore discharge of the ball valve.

The warning pipe must be of rigid material (self-supporting), and there must be no hose pipe or other flexible material within its length. It must be laid to the maximum fall possible and not flatter than a gradient of 1:10.

The warning pipe must be at least 25 mm above the normal 'full' level of the cistern.

## Services

Normally at least two pipes will be connected near the bottom of the cistern: a 'down service', which should be fitted 75 mm above the bottom, supplying non-drinking cold water to ablutionary fittings; and a 'cold feed', which should be fitted at a slightly lower level, some 50 mm above the bottom, supplying water to the hot-water storage. This is a precautionary measure. In the event of the cold-water storage being exhausted, the supply at the cold-water taps will run dry before the hot-water system is affected, thereby avoiding a possible dangerous situation. If the two pipes in your cistern are at the same level, screw an elbow on to the down service connection within the cistern and leave it looking up.

The 50 mm depth of water below the cold-feed connection is to allow any sediment to collect without affecting the supply to the taps. Cisterns should be inspected and cleaned as already described. Important: in any system the cold feed supplies the domestic side of hot water cyclinders or tanks only. Supplies to taps must *not* be taken from this pipe.

## Materials for cisterns

The majority of cisterns installed in dwelling houses all over the country are manufactured from galvanized iron. These cisterns give excellent trouble-free service for 25 years and more providing they are properly installed and protected. They are even better suited for hard-water districts when a protective coat of lime quickly forms on the internal surfaces. In very soft water areas the effective life of the cistern will be less and an asbestos, glass fibre or plastics cistern would be advisable.

In recent years the development of plastics cisterns has been rapid and these have many advantages over the other forms.

Polypropylene cisterns have a greater rigidity than those made from polythene but this advantage is not so apparent if the cistern is to be used in an existing house, because it cannot be folded to permit its passage through a restricted trap door into the roof space. This factor is not important of course in new buildings when the cistern can be placed in position before the ceiling and trap door are completed.

Some plastics cistern manufacturers now produce sectional cisterns in glass reinforced plastic (GRP) for quite small capacities, and to a variety of dimensions. By shopping around it should be possible to obtain a cistern which, in pieces, will go through most loft trap doors to be assembled once in the roof space. They are made with external or internal flanges and come complete with jointing gaskets and bolts and directions for assembly. A cistern as small as 300 litres should be a stock item. Advice on manufacturers and stockists may be obtained from most builders' merchants, your local registered plumber, or the Institute of Plumbing.

Plastics cisterns are made in various sizes all to conform to regulations. They may be rectangular or circular in shape and are very light and easy to handle. They are unaffected by any type of water and of course there are no problems of electrolytic action.

The glass fibre polyester resin cisterns are also gaining popularity. They are non-toxic, stain resistant and have good thermal insulation properties.

It is very important that the manufacturer's instructions be followed when installing plastics cisterns. There have been failures due to wrongful use and from incorrect installation. This applies particularly to cisterns being used to feed hot-water systems. Under certain conditions, some plastics are affected by excessive heat such as very hot water. The plumber is advised to acquaint himself with the performance characteristics of plastics cisterns and order the right one for the job in hand.

All things being equal, there are distinct advantages to be gained by installing a suitable plastics cistern.

## Distributing pipes

Distributing pipes convey water from the storage cistern to the various fitments in the house. The definition in the byelaws is: 'any pipe conveying water supplied by the undertakers from a storage cistern or from a hot water apparatus supplied from a feed cistern and under pressure from such cistern.'

The distributing pipe system calls for careful design and correct installation technique. The designer – and the plumber – must consider pipe sizing, avoidance of airlocks, noise transmission, contamination of mains water, protection against frost, corrosion and damage, and of course economy in the use of labour and materials. Unfortunately, the tendency is to take the pipes on the shortest route from the storage cistern to the bathroom, regardless of the fact that it might not be the best route. This is done either from ignorance of the correct principles or to cut down costs – perhaps both.

The protection of pipes required in the byelaws includes the avoidance of water contamination. It is important that the householder should know something about this if he is ever tempted to effect alterations to the plumbing system of his house. There must never be any cross connection between a pipe carrying mains water and any pipe or fitting containing water that is impure or liable to contamination in any way.

The hazard of water pollution within a plumbing system is a very serious one and is dealt with more fully in the next chapter.

The householder should trace the run of the distributing pipes in his house and identify their purpose. It is customary for one pipe to be taken from the storage cistern to supply the cold water to the bath, washbasin and w.c. cistern – and any other appliances that may be installed. A separate pipe from the storage

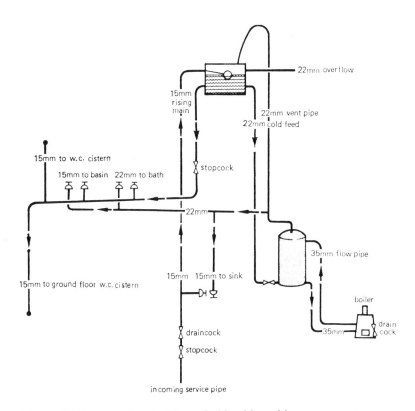

Figure 7   *Layout of typical household cold- and hot-water systems*

cistern supplies cold water to the hot-water system and this is known as the cold feed pipe. It is not a distributing pipe in the accepted sense of the term.

A distributing pipe should be controlled by a stopvalve as near as possible to the cistern but in a position where it is easily accessible to the householder. If there is no stopvalve on the pipe then one should be fixed as soon as possible – it might be the means of preventing flooding in the event of a burst pipe.

In Figure 7, the distributing pipes, hot-water installation and rising mains are shown in diagrammatical form.

# 2

# Cold-Water Installation

## Preliminary considerations

When water supply is obtained from the mains, the water undertaking's byelaws must be observed, so they should be studied before any work is commenced. The plumber, or whoever is responsible for the installation, must submit details of the proposed work for approval by the water undertaking.

Water undertakings provide printed forms for use by the plumber. These include:

(a) Application for a supply of water.
(b) Request to lay a communication (service) pipe.
(c) Notices that whole or part of the service is complete and ready for inspection by the undertaking.

Form filling and submission should be completed in good time in order to prevent delays in obtaining approval for the work and the supply of water to the premises.

There are occasions when the undertaking may require the supply to be taken through a meter, in which case an agreement will have to be completed by the consumer.

It is important to know that the householder is responsible for any alterations or additions made to the water supply in his house. If work has been installed by a plumber who has not previously notified the water undertaking of what he intended to do and when subsequently inspected it is found not to conform to the undertaking's byelaws it is the householder who will have to foot the bill for such alterations as may be required. The householder should therefore ensure that his plumber has complied with the requirements before allowing him to do the work.

## Laying the service pipe

It is usual for the water undertaking to drill the main and lay the service ('communication') pipe, to the stopvalve. The owner of the building pays for this service. When the undertaking permits the plumber to lay the pipe from the main, the actual connection of the ferrule to the main is made by the undertaking, also at the building owner's expense. When the plumber lays the communication pipe from the main he should have it inspected by the undertaking before filling in the trench.

When a house is being built in such a position that it may be necessary to lay a new main or extend an existing main, full details of the house and site should be submitted to the water undertaking as early as possible. The cost of laying or extending the main will be borne by the water undertaking providing the annual income in water rates from the new services to be taken from the mains will be sufficient to reach a prescribed fraction (usually one-eighth) of the total cost. The building owner should be quite clear about his position in this respect well beforehand.

# Design considerations

## Protection against contamination

The water undertakings in this country do everything within their power to ensure that the supply of water to each dwelling served by them is pure and fit for drinking. The water supply in Britain is as good as any in the world and, for obvious reasons, it is important that it is not contaminated in any way at its many points of use. But there is ample evidence of contamination, mainly through installed plumbing systems. Other causes are lack of basic maintenance, and careless use (or misuse) of plumbing appliances.

The main problem is back-siphonage in plumbing systems. This problem has been known about for some years, but now positive measures are being introduced to prevent it.

Back-siphonage occurs when a main service pipe, or main distributing pipe supplying more than one floor, suffers a loss of

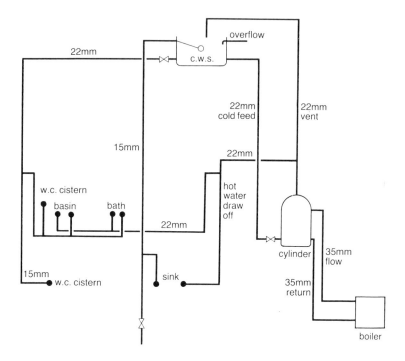

Figure 8    *Figure 7 amended to comply with new anti-backsiphonage requirements.*

pressure at a low point in the system (Figure 8) (for example main-water supply, cold-water down service, or cold feed turned off) and water is drained from a low point (from a tap on the ground flow, or from a leak), causing a partial vacuum in the main rising or falling length of pipework as the water level drops. The force of atmospheric pressure on the surface of say, a wash-hand basin on an upper floor, that is full of water with a hose extension from an open tap lying in the water will push the contents of that basin back through the hose and the tap into the plumbing system in order to fill the partial vacuum (Figure 9).

That is a simplified statement of back-siphonage. Its effects are obvious. What householders must bear in mind is that plumbing pipework suffers constant changes in pressure, some very short lived, others more protracted. All systems need to be protected against such fluctuations.

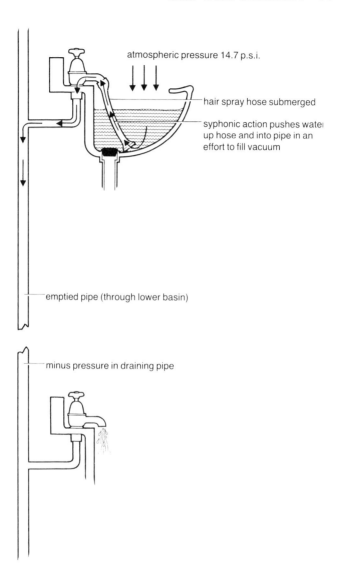

atmospheric pressure 14.7 p.s.i.

hair spray hose submerged

syphonic action pushes water up hose and into pipe in an effort to fill vacuum

emptied pipe (through lower basin)

minus pressure in draining pipe

Figure 9   *Backsiphonage*

The new regulations apply to new systems, but they will also apply to that part of any existing system which is renewed in the course of repairs, and to any alteration or refurbishment of an

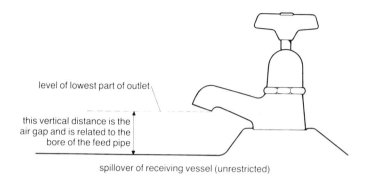

level of lowest part of outlet

this vertical distance is the
air gap and is related to the
bore of the feed pipe

spillover of receiving vessel (unrestricted)

Figure 10   *Type 'A' air gap*

existing system. It makes good sense for householders to check their systems and ensure compliance with the new regulations, especially in respect of such appliances as hoses (garden and shower), washing machines, and bidets.

## Type-A air breaks

Principal protection is at the actual point of use, wherever this can be achieved. A type-A air gap discharges water from a valve into air above the spill-over level of any sanitary fitting or cistern. For example, basin taps have delivery spouts angled upwards so that the outlet of the tap is above the rim of the basin. Even if the basin is filled to overflowing the spout of the tap is still above the waterline, thus preventing any water entering the valve in reverse flow (Figure 10).

It may not be generally appreciated that even if the actual outlet point of the tap is above the water level, but the gap is not sufficient, then water can still be 'pulled up' into the tap if a vacuum is created in the pipework. This works in exactly the same way as a vacuum cleaner picking up objects within a given distance of the suction hose. The distance is determined by the power of the vacuum cleaner and the size and weight of the object.

The dimensions of the air gap are listed in Table 2.

Modern-day baths, basins, and sinks served by standard pillar valves will comply with the requirements of Table 2. They will *not* comply, however, if hose extensions are attached to them,

Table 2

| Size of tap or combination fitting | Vertical distance between outlet and spill-over level of appliance |
| --- | --- |
| Not exceeding ½ in. | 20 mm |
| Exceeding ½ in but not exceeding ¾ in | 25 mm |
| Exceeding ¾ in | 70 mm |

especially extensions that may be submerged in water that has been used. The most common examples are shower attachments which may be dropped into basins or baths while their taps are still open, garden hoses, rubber or plastic anti-splash extensions to tap outlets, hoses for filling washing machines, and copper boilers.

The byelaw states that the type-A air gap must not be bridged. Therefore, flexible hose extensions to taps must not be used. The same fate applies to the anti-splash extensions. Garden hoses must be connected to a tap separate from any sanitary fitting and be provided with an in-line check valve to prevent a reverse flow of water. Washing machines and dishwashers connected to a water service pipe by hoses must be provided with taps specifically for washing machine use only; and the washing machine should be fitted with integral back-siphonage prevention devices such as a pipe interrupter which, if removed, renders the machine inoperable. Those machines not fitted with a pipe interrupter must be supplied from a storage cistern whose supply is protected by a backflow prevention device.

The same problem applies to full-height flexible shower hoses fitted over baths. They should be fixed with ring brackets that allow adjustment of the height of the hose while preventing the shower head from being immersed in the bath water.

The same precaution must be taken with flexible-hose shower connections over shower trays. Though the trays do not have a waste plug and therefore, theoretically, there is no build up of water in the tray, there is the constant danger of the waste grating being covered or blocked.

Most modern shower mixing valves have built-in check valves to prevent reverse flow and the additional safeguard in the event of sudden loss of cold-water pressure of an automatic shut-off device that will close the valve virtually instantly. Householders

purchasing mixing valves should make certain from the manufacturers that the model they have ordered is equipped with these
supply-failure devices.

Water authorities may give their consent to hoses being fixed to
taps, but for showers and the like they will require a combined
check valve and vacuum breaker (air-inlet valve) to be fixed in the
inlet pipe to the appliance.

### Whirlpools

These are often wrongly referred to as 'Jacuzzis', which is a trade
name for a specific bath and does not describe the type of
appliance (illustration and description in Chapter 8). Generally
the bath is filled in the normal way through the taps, and the
hydrotherapy pump merely recirculates the water under increased pressure. Providing that there is no connection between
the water supply pipework and the pump system, and that the
required air gap is maintained between the discharge point of the
taps and the overflowing level of the bath, no additional anti-
back-siphonage precaution is necessary.

### Bidets

These are now a popular bathroom and/or bedroom fitting in a
rapidly growing number of households. There are two types:
those supplied by taps above the rim, and those fitted with
submersible sprays.

The safety precautions against backflow will be satisfied in the
over-rim supply type providing the air gap at the point of delivery
complies with the dimensions listed in Table 2 and the cold-water
service pipe is from a storage cistern with a backflow-prevention
device on its supply. The cold-water service pipe serving an over-
rim supply-type bidet may supply a urinal flushing cistern and a
w.c. flushing cistern on the same level as the bidet and no other
draw-off points except a drain-off cock.

Hot-water supply from a cylinder to this type of bidet must
serve the bidet only except for a drain-off cock. The branch
supply pipe must be a connection to the open vent pipe from the
cylinder made at least 300 mm above the spill-over level of the
bidet (Figure 11).

In the case of bidets with submersible sprays supplied from
vented or unvented hot-water systems both hot and cold water
must be supplied either from the break-pressure cisterns or via

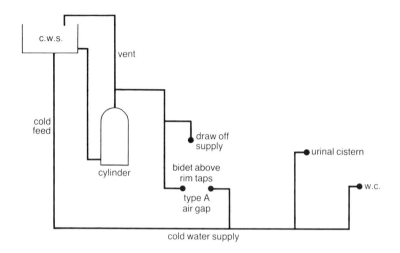

Figure 11   *Bidet supplies*

tundishes which provide the necessary air break between the supply pipe and the bidet (Figure 12).

Supplies to other fittings may be taken from the distributing pipe upstream of the tundish (Figure 13). Both the hot-water and cold-water distributing pipes may connect to the submersible spray bidet (Figure 14). The hot-water branch pipe must be connected to the vent pipe above the cylinder at a point at least 300 mm above the rim level of the bidet and be provided with an additional vent pipe prior to connection with the bidet and downstream of a check valve. The point of connection of this vent to the distributing pipe must be at least 300 mm above the rim level of the bidet.

More than one bidet may be supplied from common hot-water and cold-water distributing pipes providing that the bidets are at the same level. Bidets on different floors will require a separate supply of both hot and cold water to each floor, all run in the manner that has been described here.

### Dwellings

It must be remembered that reference to dwellings must include not only what are described as permanent homes but also caravans, and vessels which will include houseboats, cabin

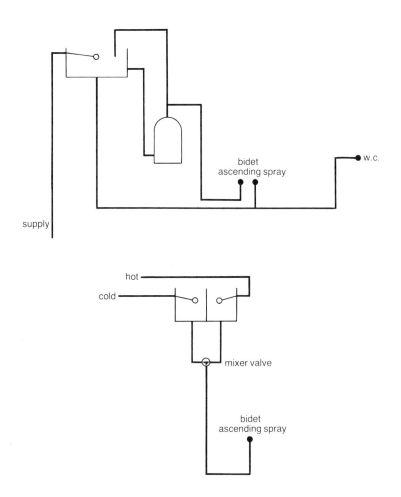

Figure 12   *Bidet supplies*

cruisers, and any craft that may be connected either permanently or temporarily to the water company's mains supply.

Caravans on a regulated site are likely to have a permanent drinking-water supply connected to the water company's main. Domestic water is probably drawn from an elevated common storage tank, and this should be delivered to break-storage tanks

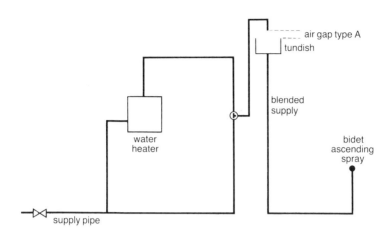

Figure 13   *Bidet supplies via tundish*

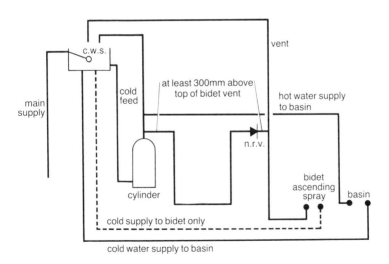

Figure 14   *Bidet supplies separate*

in each caravan. The distributing pipes from the main storage must be vented at their highest point downstream of any control valve.

Charging of water storage on mobile vessels must be by gravity and either via a tundish (type-A air gap) or from an elevated storage tank on the quayside fitted with a type-B air gap or a pipe interrupter and filled through a diaphragm-type ball valve complying to BS 1212: Parts 2 or 3.

Storage capacity in either of the above types of accommodation must be drained and cleaned regularly, and drinking-water supplies must be taken only from main-water-supply taps. All storage cisterns must be adequately covered and ventilated.

### Type-B air gap

This is defined as the gap obtained when water is discharged into a cistern or any other water fitting and there is sufficient vertical distance between the point of discharge and the critical water level of the vessel to ensure that, in siphonic conditions, reverse flow cannot pass from the vessel back into the supply pipe. The vertical distance referred to must not be less than the dimensions listed in Table 1.

Again, as in the type-A air gap, the ball valve in any cistern must be to BS 1212: Part 2 or 3 if 15mm in diameter. The critical water level is that which will be reached with full-bore delivery with all draw-off valves closed, and an obstruction-free warning pipe.

Figure 15   *Pipe interrupter*

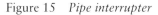
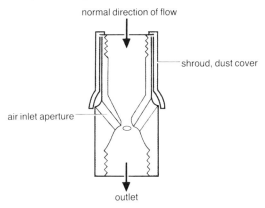

normal direction of flow

shroud, dust cover

air inlet aperture

outlet

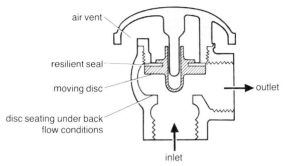

Figure 16   *Vacuum breaker*

## Other anti-back-siphonage devices

Domestic installations for houses are virtually covered by the measures so far described. However, for the many dwellings that are not houses, and particularly for *all* installations of pressurized hot-water systems and, possibly, cold-water supply from the mains to ablutionary fittings, an in-line device may be required to protect a fitting, or a group of fittings, against back-siphonage.

*Pipe interrupter* (Figure 15)
This must comply with BS 6281: Part 3.

*In-line anti-vacuum valve (vacuum breaker)* (Figure 16)
There are two basic types of this device: the 'pressure' type, which will operate satisfactorily even after being subjected to long periods of continuous pressure; and the 'atmospheric' type, to BS 6282: Part 3, which needs to be regularly opened and shut to keep it operable and for this reason needs to be drained down and opened to admit air after use. Consequently there should be no control valve downstream of the 'atmospheric' valve. The 'pressure' type has a spring-loaded air inlet biased to the open position and a spring-loaded check element inclined to the closed position.

At present there is no British Standard for the 'pressure'-type valve, but both valves must be installed at least 150 mm above the highest level of any contaminated water, and neither valve will operate under pressure from reverse flow.

## Terminal anti-vacuum valve

This is the same vacuum breaker valve as described above, but fitted at the highest point of any supply or distributing pipe supplying fittings on more than one level. As stated, no control

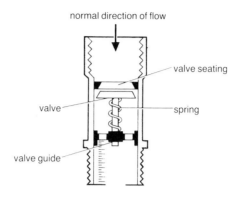

Figure 17   *Check valve*

valve must be installed on the main falling or rising pipe between the vacuum breaker and the lowest fittings served.

*Check valve*
This is usually called a non-return valve (Figure 17). These valves must comply with BS 6282: Part 1. Generally, they are required to be installed in pairs with a drain-off cock (which acts as a test valve) between them.

A combination of one check valve and an in-line vacuum breaker would be an acceptable alternative to a double check valve assembly providing that:

Table 3

| *Type of backflow prevention device* | *Class* |
|---|---|
| Type-A air gap | 1A |
| Cistern with a 2A, 2B, or 2C device on the inlet | 1B |
| Type-B air gap | 2A |
| Pipe interrupter | 2B |
| Combined check valve and vacuum breaker | 2C |
| Double-check valve assembly | 2C |
| Terminal vacuum breaker | 3A |
| In-line vacuum breaker | 3B |
| Check valve | 3C |

1 The vacuum breaker valve is installed downstream of the check valve.
2 There is no control valve downstream of the 'atmospheric' vacuum breaker.
3 The vacuum breaker is installed on a suitable upstand.
(Item 2 does not apply to the 'pressure'-type vacuum breaker valve.)

These are the mechanical devices that may be used within a plumbing system. All valves must be approved by the local water undertaking.

For their application Table 3 should be a sufficient guide. If the class of protection for any fitting is not known, advice should be sought from the water authority.

Table 4

| Water appliance | Class |
|---|---|
| WC pan | 2A |
| Bidet | 1A |
| Urinal | 1B |
| Dialyser (Home use) | 1B |
| Hose tap connector | 2C |
| Boat supply | 1A |
| Flexible shower fitting | 2C |
| Domestic washing machine and dishwasher | 2A or 2B |
| Feed cistern for domestic hot-water primary circuit | 2A |
| Humidifier (spray jet) | 2A or 2B or 2C |
| Permanent standpipe (main) serving small boat in a marina, etc. | 2C |
| Hot- and cold-water single outlet combination mixer tap (unbalanced installation) | 3C (in service pipe) |
| Water softener (ion exchange type) | 3B or 3C |
| Cold-water storage cistern with gravity discharge | 3A or 3C |
| Proportioning pump in mains pressure operated dilution of dialysis fluid in a home dialysis machine | 3A or 3B or 3C |
| Anti-scale solution doser (domestic) | 3B or 3C |

The above (Table 4) is an extract from a list of fittings and the backflow prevention devices required.

In addition to the devices listed in Table 3 every branch supply pipe to a fitting, or group of fittings, on the same level must have an upstand connection to the main rising or falling length of distributing or main service pipe. The upstand must be determined by the degree of vacuum likely to be encountered at the point of connection, and it must not be less than 300 mm. As an added safeguard a vacuum breaker or a vent pipe which admits air can be fitted at the high point of the vertical upstand.

The purpose of the upstand is to prevent possibly contaminated water being siphoned from an appliance into the supply or distributing pipework should the mechanical devices fail to work properly. A particularly vulnerable point is the ball valve to a storage cistern.

All the illustrations of anti-back-siphonage devices in this section are of fittings produced by E. A. Molyneux Ltd. It must be stressed that all plumbing services incorporating these valves should be undertaken by qualified installers. This is not an appropriate area for the do-it-yourself amateur.

Special provisions to protect the main supply pipe must be made in respect of pressurized hot-water systems, and these are explained in Chapter 4.

## Pipe sizing and discharge rates

Information for determining the size of a pipe for any given purpose is based on the rate of discharge required, the length of the pipe, the head available for loss by friction in that length and the roughness of the internal surface of the piping. This information is available to the plumber in the form of tables, formulae and diagrams, for use in designing water supply. It is necessary to make due allowance to provide against the loss of discharging capacity due to the internal encrustation of the pipes in the course of time.

To keep piping down to a minimum size with a consequent reduction in the cost of installation, the designer must give consideration to layout, and see to it that changes in diameter and direction are gradual rather than abrupt to avoid loss of head. All bends in pipes should be made so as not to diminish materially or alter their cross-sections. The pipes should be as smooth as possible internally, and the methods of jointing be such as to avoid internal roughness and projections at the joints. It might be mentioned here that the effective diameter of a pipe is reduced and severe friction set up if material used for jointing pipes is applied in such a manner that it adheres to the internal surface of the pipe or fitting.

## Choice of materials for piping

In choosing the material of the piping and fittings, apart from the character of the water, there are the considerations of cost, appearance, personal preferences and of course the byelaws. The merits of lead, copper, iron and plastics pipes are dealt with in another section of the *Guide*, but it will be as well to mention at this point important facts which must not be overlooked when a final choice is being made.

Apart from repairs to existing plumbing, lead piping must not be used in plumbing pipework installations for water supplies. Until recently it has been held to be a safe material in hard-water areas – because only soft water is plumbo-solvent (capable of dissolving lead) – and the deposit of lime scale formed over a period of time on the inner surface of the pipe prevents contamination.

To a degree, that is still true, but the possibility of unacceptable levels of lead being absorbed by the body through drinking water from lead pipes has led the Department of the Environment, which formulated the Model Water Byelaws for the country, to discourage its use.

Water undertakings make their own byelaws within the framework of the Model Byelaws, though differences may arise because of local conditions. Consequently, water authorities in hard-water areas may, in their byelaws, still admit lead pipes with the qualification that there is no possibility of contamination of the water supply. Clearly the likelihood of electrolysis makes it impossible to give any such assurance. Generally, no lead piping, or lead lining to any storage cistern should be installed, including extensions or renewal of any existing piping or cistern lining.

Copper, of course, is a popular material, but even here care must be exercised in jointing methods. Pipes supplying water for drinking or cooking must not be jointed by lead-tin solder end-feed fittings. This does not apply to pipes delivering water for other uses.

Copper pipe must not be used to renew any section of an existing lead pipe unless corrosion through electrolytic action is unlikely to occur. It is best to renew the whole run of lead pipe with new copper pipe.

Lead is not the only material frowned upon: wrought iron, mild steel and, in some areas, stainless steel are prohibited by some water undertakings as unsuitable for use with the type of water supplied. Copper can be dissolved by certain waters and, although water containing a small amount of copper may be quite wholesome, it is likely to react to soap by producing green stains.

## Electrolytic action

Electrolytic action occurs between dissimilar metals in the presence of moisture – exactly the same principle as a wet battery, and it does, in fact, produce an electric current which will attack the lesser metal. Frequently, the result of such an attack resembles corrosion and many people think it is rust.

It is usually found in the pitting of galvanized iron cisterns, and perforation to radiators, etc., when metals are mixed in a plumbing system. A common practice has been to paint the inside surfaces of cold-water storage cisterns with bituminous solution to inhibit this action, but its effect is questionable and, in the event, water authorities now prohibit it because of possible contamination.

## Minimum strength of pipes

The byelaws of the water undertakings specify the minimum strength of piping required for service pipes and distributing pipes. It is necessary to comply with byelaws in every case.

## Avoidance of airlocks and noise transmission

Good plumbing does not simply happen – it is designed: a fact which, unfortunately, is often disregarded, especially in older-type houses where pipes have to avoid structural obstructions, and bathrooms are not always sited conveniently over kitchens. Ideally, plumbing units should be stacked (placed one over the other) to limit pipe runs and to isolate the noise from fittings as they fill and discharge.

Airlocks are caused by unnecessary high points in pipe runs where air is trapped and the water pressure is insufficient to overcome the build-up of air.

All pipes should be laid with a fall from the highest point (connection to the cold-water storage cistern, etc.) to the drain-off cock at the lowest point. Rising branch pipes to fittings are permissible as air is vented when taps are opened.

Figure 7 shows a typical self-draining self-venting system which will operate trouble-free. Problems arise when branches must travel through floors for any length. If in doubt, remember that a level pipe will both drain and vent.

Services run on wall surfaces should be grouped where possible, lagged and cased and clipped with the type of brackets which will allow for thermal movement. When run across floor joists, allow adequate space in the notchings to accommodate expansion. Copper tube, for instance, will expand only length-ways: it does not increase in diameter. Copper tube in notches that are too tight will squeak every time it heats and cools. Never notch more than 26 mm without seeking the advice of the local authority building inspectors, or you may seriously weaken the floor joists. Do not notch the underside of joists.

Some w.c. cisterns are noisy when filling. As rigid silencing tubes are prohibited, fit either the diaphragm-type ball valve with the collapsible plastic silencing tube which will not pass water back up its length, or a BS ball valve with interchangeable seating, and fit the correct orifice seating for quicker operation.

Probably the most common, and by far the most irritating, noise in any plumbing system is water hammer. Its effect is exactly what the name implies: as though someone were striking the pipe regularly with a hammer. It is caused by the abrupt stopping of a moving column of water, and the primary culprits are worn washers and loose jumpers in stopvalves and taps; or ball valves fitted with float arms that are too short, or floats that are too small.

All stopcocks in rising main supplies must be fitted with fixed jumpers. This effectively stops the chatter that can be set up during the closing of a valve when the pressure on the inlet side may be greater than on the discharge side. The same most definitely applies to cold-water taps to sinks.

Quite apart from the noise, water hammer, if allowed to continue unchecked, can cause pipes to fracture. Any pipe conveying water under a hydraulic head (the height of the cistern above the draw-off – or the mains pressure) is under stress. Water hammer, by creating shock waves, dramatically increases that stress.

Occasionally, excessive pressure from the incoming main may cause problems, and the water authority should be consulted on the type of pressure-reducing valve that may be fitted adjacent to your control stopvalve to remedy this situation.

Excessive pressure can cause the ball valve in the cold-water storage cistern to vibrate, which, in turn, sets up concussion throughout the rising main.

One method of combating water hammer at the ball valve of the storage cistern is to install an air chamber (see Figure 18). An air chamber is formed by a pipe of larger diameter than the service pipe and is fixed in an upright position as shown. As it may have to withstand considerable pressure the air chamber must be strongly constructed and must be airtight.

When the water supply is turned on, air in the chamber is compressed and when a tap is opened the pressure on the air is reduced, and the air is able to expand. When a tap is suddenly closed, instead of the pipe bearing the shock of the water hammer, the air is compressed by the blow and gently expands and contracts until the pressure of the compressed air equals the pressure of the water. When air chambers are installed the air has to be periodically recharged. This is done by turning off the water supply, draining the pipes, and allowing air into the chamber by opening a tap nearby.

Ball valves sometimes cause water hammer, due to the float being raised and lowered by waves on the surface of the water in the cistern. One remedy is to solder a piece of sheet copper to the bottom of the ball in the form of a flat fin. The fin remains about one inch below the surface of the water and prevents the ball from oscillating.

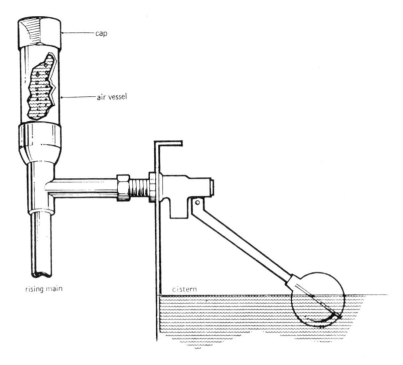

Figure 18  *Preventing 'water hammer'*

## Planning the pipe runs

All pipes should be so placed that they will not be exposed to accidental damage, and fixed in such positions as to facilitate cleaning and avoid accumulations of dirt. Pipework should be accessible for inspection, replacement and repair. Nobody likes to see pipes and if they can be hidden away so much the better. Providing there is sufficient space to work with the normal tools the plumber can usually arrange his pipes to run through, or adjacent to, cupboards or in recesses. Where pipes are run under floorboards the boards should be fixed with screws to facilitate removal at any time.

Pipes should not be buried in walls or solid floors. There is a tendency to provide ducts or chases for pipework in modern homes. These should be properly constructed to prevent the possible entry of vermin.

If it is necessary for a pipe to run in a wood floor it should, wherever possible, be parallel with the joists. Pipes passing through walls or floors should be sleeved to allow freedom for expansion and contraction and other movement.

# Installation precautions

Before any pipe is used for installation work care must be taken to ensure that it is the correct pipe for the job. The pipe must conform to the byelaws with regard to quality and weight.

The pipe should be inspected to see that it is clean internally, and free from particles of sand or soil, metal filings or chips, which, apart from causing obstructions, might well lead to failure by corrosion.

In jointing pipes all internal burrs must be removed and care taken to prevent any jointing material entering the pipes for fear of causing obstruction, corrosion, or giving rise to water contamination.

Only Water Council approved jointing compounds and materials must be used. Such well-known brands as Boss White and hemp are no longer acceptable, as it has been established that these materials promote and support microbial growth within the pipes. Suitable alternatives are readily available, and your qualified plumber will be fully aware of the requirements. Should there be any doubt about the suitability of any material, the local water authority should be consulted.

The joints should be cleaned off externally as should any marks made by tools. The screws of holder-bats or other types of pipe fixing should be checked for tightness.

If sleeves are to be used where the pipes pass through walls they must be slipped over the pipe before it is jointed.

No work should be built-in until it has been fully tested. When testing, care must be taken to eliminate all air from the pipes.

# 3

# Hot-Water Supply Explained

An adequate supply of hot water must be provided in every new dwelling (Building Act 1984 and Building Regulations 1985) and in all older buildings when any improvement works to the properties are undertaken. Nonetheless, there are still many homes in this country without this essential amenity despite the fact that generous grants have been available for years past to assist with the cost of installation.

Ideally the hot-water supply should be piped to all sanitary fittings, but equally acceptable are single-point water heaters to sink, bath, and basin. (These are explained in detail in Chapter 5.)

Most properties that have hot water have a system that is based on a central heat source (a boiler) and a central storage tank (hot-water cylinder) and distributing pipes to all taps. These are traditional systems which, though they have worked well enough over the years, will, in many cases, now be inefficient in comparison with the latest systems presently being marketed and installed. Running and maintenance costs are escalating, and many of those who can afford the cash outlay are investing in the high-efficiency appliances which, if properly installed and run, will repay the initial cost in a comparatively short period.

As there are so many to choose from it will be as well to have a look at some of the options.

## First considerations

There are two:

(a) What duties must the system perform?
(b) Which fuel will be used?

From (a) the householder can decide the full scope of the

installation and, therefore, be in a position to give his plumber precise instructions essential for an adequate design.

1  Will hot water be required to all fittings?
2  Is central heating to extend to all rooms and hallway?
3  Should there be provision for heat in the airing cupboard?
4  Must there be adequate heat in the bathroom?
5  Is a fire to be incorporated in the system for use before the heating season gets under way?
6  What are the temperature requirements for individual rooms?
7  What are the storage and delivery temperatures for hot water?

These seven factors will, in part, be determined by the number of occupants in the dwelling and their daily habits. A household that is empty for most of all working days will not require the amount of heating and hot water demanded in a property that will be occupied during those hours.

Is the dwelling also used as a place of work? Are there frequent staying visitors? (A guest house or hotel will need a more sophisticated system than a two-up, three-down cottage.)

The sum of the answers to these questions will point not only to the boiler and radiators that will be needed but also to the controls that will regulate the system to perform exactly as it is required. The plumber or heating engineer will provide the technical application in producing the design, but to do so successfully he must have all the information.

What is the best fuel? This argument has raged long and furiously over the years, but the choice is invariably decided by availability or the quirk of preference. Gas has a good track record, while electricity is clean, and, with Economy 7, attractively priced. Oil and solid fuel are storable, which is reassuring to people who have suffered the discomforts of power cuts or fear accidents with gas.

If the choice is oil or solid fuel the appliance will need a flue, either integral to the building or as an addition fixed externally on a wall and carried up to above eaves level. Oil and solid fuel systems also require tanks or bunkers for storing the fuel and access for delivery.

The recommended minimum capacity of oil storage tanks is as follows:

Table 5

| Rating of boiler | Tank capacity |
|---|---|
| Up to 18 kW<br>Up to 60,000 Btu/hr | 1250 litres (275 gallons) |
| 18 to 26 kW<br>60,000 to 90,000 Btu/hr | 1360 litres (300 gallons) |
| 26 to 35 kW<br>90,000 to 120,000 Btu/hr | 1820 litres (400 gallons) |
| 35 to 44 kW<br>120,000 to 150,000 Btu/hr | 3000 litres (650 gallons) |

The storage for solid fuel is as follows:

Table 6

| Type of fuel | Volume $m^3$/tonne |
|---|---|
| Coal<br>Anthracite<br>'Phurnacite' | 1.5 |
| Gas coke<br>Hard coke<br>'Coalite'<br>'Rexco' | 2.5 |

Independent gas boilers or those fitted in combination behind gas fires also require flues, but there are 'balanced flue' gas boilers available which discharge straight through the wall to external air. The flue consists of an air intake and exhaust outlet which enables the appliance to be fitted in any room because all of the air required to support combustion is taken from outside and not from within the room.

Some models have independent operation for the heating and the domestic hot-water circuits. One such heating unit is the Chaffoteaux Celtic Combination Boiler, a common output heating unit with automatic isolating valves which operate to interrupt the supply to the central heating when there is a demand for hot water. Thus it works as an instantaneous heater for domestic hot water, and as with every such heater, the delivery temperature is dependent upon the water flow rate to the tap.

When the hot-water tap is turned off the boiler will automatically revert to its central heating duties.

This appliance is explained in greater detail in chapter 7 on central heating.


## Efficiency

Boilers are rated for heat output in BTU/hr (British Thermal Units per hour). A BTU is the amount of heat required to raise 1 pound of water through 1°F. Assuming a 30-gallon storage at 40°F is to be heated to 140°F, the following calculation will give the required rating:

30 gallons × 10 lb per gallon × 100°F temperature rise = 30,000 BTU/hr.

The BTU/hr rating is also given in kW/hrs. If it isn't, it may be calculated as follows:

$\dfrac{\text{BTU/hr}}{3412}$ = kW/hr or kW/hr to BTU/hr: kW/hr × 3412 = BTU/hr

On the boiler should be stated the BTU/hr and kW/hr input rate together with an output rate, which will be a lower figure. The percentage difference when subtracted from 100 gives the percentage efficiency of the boiler.

There is a wide choice of high-performance appliances on the market, one of which will suit your specific needs. They include:

1.  Independent boilers:        gas, oil, solid fuel
2.  Back boilers:               gas, oil, solid fuel
3.  Instantaneous heaters:      gas
4.  Storage heaters:            gas, electric

Only type 2 will provide space heating to the room in which the appliance is sited; the others are designed specifically for the task of heating water. In households where someone is in all day, the solid-fuel boiler with glass front that emits heat to the room can be a comforting companion, but it is essential to obtain the correct grade of fuel as specified by the manufacturer. These boilers can also be connected to a time-clock to increase the rate of burning at predetermined times.

As an alternative to solid-fuel appliances, a wide variety of gas boilers with separately controlled gas-fire room heaters are on the market.

For business people who are out all day the clock-controlled gas boiler is probably the most convenient and, if no flue is available, the self-contained balanced-flue models can be fixed to most external walls without the need to increase room ventilation for combustion purposes, or to provide piped exhaust. These models draw their own external air supply at the same rate that they discharge waste products.

Instantaneous heaters work on demand from taps, with the advantage that you pay only for the fuel used while hot water is running. The multi-point heater can serve several taps, including showers, but only one draw-off at a time. Single-point heaters (gas or electric) are convenient for sinks and can deliver either through a swivel spout or, if the spout is required to be longer than 0.6 m, can be piped to an open nozzle fitted over a sink. Under no circumstances must they be connected to a tap.

Storage heaters (electric) are heated by immersed elements and are either pre-insulated units or copper cylinders fitted with immersion heaters. These are particularly suitable in properties where it is difficult to site a boiler and cylinder combination; they, and gas heaters, are explained in more detail in Chapters 5 and 6.

Having selected the type of boiler it is next necessary to know exactly what it has got to do. How much hot water does your family require and in what time span? Demands from a family with three teenage daughters each clamouring for a bath, or to wash their hair before going on a date several evenings a week, will differ considerably from those of the household with all boys who follow different sports and want to bathe at different times. Many working wives will want to use the dishwasher and washing machine around the same time, perhaps when husbands want to take a bath.

Clearly everybody cannot do everything at once; it takes time to have a bath, and even washing machines do not draw hot water continuously. Try to assess the peak demand in any one hour and rate your boiler accordingly. Allow 181 litres of water for an average bath, with at least 114 litres of hot water: enough to exhaust a 136-litre cylinder.

Incidentally, it makes good sense to fit a shower. They are very economical, far more so than a bath, and they are refreshing.

Houses with more than one bathroom will require more

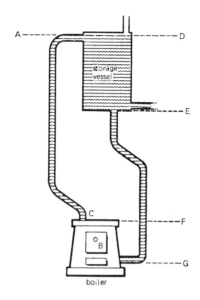

Figure 19    *The circulation of hot water*

storage than the average dwelling, but, assuming a typical family of four in a single-bathroom house, a 136-litre storage vessel should be adequate. It is an advantage to fit a boiler with a higher rating than you have calculated as this will speed temperature recovery in times of high demand.

## Primary circuits

The hot-water storage vessel (either a tank or a cylinder) is connected to the boiler by means of flow and return pipes (Figure 19) which are known as the primary circuit. The flow is connected from the top of the boiler to the top of the cylinder; the return from the bottom of the cylinder to the bottom of the boiler.

Water heats by convection, a term with which most people are familiar. Water heated in the boiler expands and becomes lighter than cold water, bulk for bulk. Then the colder water in the cylinder, because of its greater density, drops by the force of gravity, displaces the hotter water and pushes it up to the highest point. This process is continued until the thermostat temperature is achieved and the burner or element is shut off, or, in the case of solid fuel, the damper closes down.

The speed at which the water circulates is dependent upon the difference in the temperatures between the flow and return pipes and the height of the cold-water storage tank (which is known as the circulating head). The larger the pipes (28–35 mm), the more water will pass along them quickly and therefore, in a gravity system, the greater the temperature differential. Primary circuits of small-diameter pipes will have a greater loss of circulation velocity through friction.

In Figure 19 imagine that the water in both the boiler and storage vessel is cold. It will be quickly realized that circulation cannot occur because the two columns of water AB (consisting of the flow pipe AC and the boiler itself CB) and DG (consisting of the vessel DE and the return pipe EG) are at the same temperature, have the same weight and thus balance each other.

When heat is applied to the water in the boiler it becomes lighter than the water in the corresponding length FG of the return pipe so that on the whole column DG is heavier than the column AG. The water in the heavier column falls and forces the heated water from the boiler up the flow pipe AC and thus circulation commences. The circulation will continue until both columns are at the same temperature.

It will be seen that the flow and return pipes are connected to the top and the bottom respectively of the boiler. If they were both taken from the top of the boiler it would be uncertain which pipe became the flow and which the return. If both pipes were taken from the bottom of the boiler, no circulation would take place as the heating of the boiler would not put the two columns out of balance.

If both flow and return pipes were taken to the top of the hot-water storage vessel, the hot water would circulate across the top of the vessel and the lower part would remain cold. If both flow and return pipes were taken to the bottom of the storage vessel, the whole of the contents would be ultimately heated, but the entering hot water would mix with the cold water in the vessel and a gradual heating of the whole contents would take place.

When the flow pipe is taken to the top of the hot-water storage vessel and the return pipe from the bottom, as in Figure 19, the hot water from the boiler will tend to remain in a layer on top of the colder water and the depth of the layer will increase until the whole vessel is filled with hot water. The effect is that hot water is available for draw-off from the top of the vessel in the shortest possible time.

## Energy conservation

We live in an age of high-priced fuel requiring energy conservation, so systems should be designed to obtain the maximum benefit from the minimum heat input. Very basically, the longer water takes to heat, the more fuel it consumes, because the system is allowing heated water to cool before reaching storage and returning to the boiler.

An efficient system cuts out unnecessary waste, and therefore the cylinder must be placed as close as possible above the boiler. Flow and return pipes should be vertical with a minimum number of bends. Horizontal runs should be avoided, and if this is not possible, kept to the barest minimum and laid with a continued rise to the cylinder. Neither flow nor return pipe should exceed 3 m in length. Other than a safety device and drain-off cock, no valves that can be closed or in any way restrict the bore of the pipe must be fitted to either pipe. Never use elbows to change direction: always bends.

## Arrangement

Usually the bathroom is situated above the kitchen. In many modern home improvements it is located beside the kitchen in a back extension, which is particularly convenient for households with physically handicapped or infirm members. Any other room arrangement will involve extended primary circuits so, if possible, should be avoided. Where long flow and returns have to be used, it is a good idea to fit a circulatory pump to the system to speed the circulation. In these circumstances the size of the primaries may be reduced to 28 mm or 22 mm. In practice, 15 mm is too small.

Site the cylinder in an airing cupboard to obtain the benefit of heat given off by the vessel. It should be lagged with an 80-mm-thick insulating jacket to prevent heat loss; but there will still be sufficient warmth to air clothes arranged on slatted shelves. The airing cupboard should be separate from the bathroom, but as close to it as possible.

## Pressure

The cold feed from the cold-water storage cistern connects to the cylinder on a tapping some 75 mm from the bottom. It should be at least equal in size to the largest draw-off from the cylinder (22 mm minimum, though preferably 28 mm) and controlled by a gate valve adjacent to the cylinder.

Increasing the size of the cold feed ensures that the hot-water supply taps do not run dry when other taps are turned on. Always connect to the side, near the bottom, of the cylinder or tank and not vertically through the bottom, which can cause turbulence and wasteful mixing of cold water with heated contents. The connection in pre-tapped cylinders is always above the concave bottom to avoid deflection of inlet water. It is essential that incoming cold water is layered at the lower part of the storage vessel.

All gravity installations work under pressure exerted from the storage vessel at the highest point of the system. Apart from pumped supplies head alone gives pressure equal to 9.81 KN/M$^2$ for each vertical metre of static water. Therefore, if your cistern is 6 metres above your kitchen tap, the pressure will be 58.84 KN/M$^2$ which, when the tap is opened, is converted to velocity, or the speed of flow from the tap. Conversely, if the pipe rises to the floor above, say 3 metres, the pressure will drop accordingly by 3 × 9.81 KN/M$^2$.

The greater the head at the tap, the faster will be the flow of water when the tap is opened. The flow of water from the tap at the washbasin in the upstairs bathroom will be less than that from the ground-floor kitchen-sink tap, which has a greater head of water.

More water will flow from a large tap than a small one because there is less resistance to water flow. The same applies to the piping and fittings leading to the tap. The actual flow of water at the tap thus depends upon the head of water and the resistance (or frictional loss) of the pipes and fittings connecting that tap to the cold-water cistern.

The resistance of a length of pipe or a pipe fitting is not

constant. In fact, the resistance increases as the flow of water increases, so that for the same pipe run, a larger flow will mean increased resistance. Conversely, a pipe run of increased resistance will give a proportionately smaller flow for the same head.

The resistance of a pipe is expressed in 'loss of head per metre run of pipe' and, to avoid confusion, the resistance of fittings and the tap itself are calculated to an equivalent length of pipe run and a consequent reduction in the effective hydraulic head.

These calculations are important when deciding on ball valve types (high, medium or low pressure), shower roses fitted at high level on top floors, or in positioning combination hot- and cold-water storage units in self-contained flats.

# 4

# Hot-Water Installation

The basic problem in any domestic hot-water installation is to convert the incoming supply of cold water into a constant supply of hot water at the kitchen sink, bath and washbasin – and to any additional points so required.

The planning stage has already been discussed and in this chapter a typical installation will be discussed, assuming that there will be a combination of a boiler and an electric immersion heater in the hot-water storage vessel. There are a great many variations of this combination but only the basic principles will be explained. The installation will be of the gravity type. An accelerated system combined with space heating by hot water is dealt with in the chapter on 'Smallbore Heating'. Electric water heaters and gas water heaters are also dealt with separately.

## Positioning the boiler and cylinder

Having discussed the basic principles, we now come to the practicalities. The sad fact is that the houses in which we live, especially the older ones, are seldom, if ever, designed to allow for the most efficient plumbing system.

Maybe the wife decides on a combination boiler to go in the living room where the family will get the maximum comfort from it. But the bathroom and airing cupboard upstairs are metres away over the kitchen.

The ideal solution is an independent boiler in the kitchen and a gas fire or (if you are going to add central heating) a radiator in the living room. But is there space in the kitchen for a boiler? And what would the effect of the ideal solution be on initial capital cost?

A common reaction is to shrug and bear the inefficient system: but remember your costs in wasted fuel, year after year, will continue as long as the system is in use – and invariably these wasteful running costs are far greater in the long run than the initial expenditure on extra appliances.

Energy is a valuable commodity. This cannot be overstressed. It is likely that in the near future legislation will be introduced to control its use and prevent is waste. Even if it isn't, escalating costs of fuel make it prudent to conserve wherever possible.

If you are saddled with a bad room arrangement, then it may be practical to put the airing cupboard in a bedroom above the boiler. With adequately sized pipes which are well insulated, the noise should be kept below the nuisance level.

## Summer heating

Today's gas- and oil-fired boilers can be used winter and summer to provide water heating and this is probably the most economical way to do it. This is not the case, however, with solid fuel. Very few people would care to light the fire during a heat wave to obtain hot water, so the most practical solution is to fit an electric immersion heater to the cylinder.

This is easily enough achieved as cylinders are generally tapped for fitting immersion heaters, but care should be taken against possible back circulation into the primary circuit, which is energy-wasting and expensive.

Figure 20　*Connection of flow and return pipes*

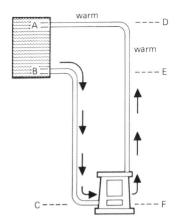

Back circulation is most prevalent where there are extended horizontal pipes level with the flow entry to the storage vessel. Figure 20 illustrates the point. Water heated in the cylinder can set up single-pipe circulation in the horizontal length AD and reach as far as point E, creating a difference in water densities. The heavier water in the lower part of the storage vessel will move to equalize the pressures, down the return pipe, through the boiler and up the flow.

The speed of this circulation will depend upon the temperature achieved in the top section of the cylinder. It will never be rapid, but any significant water movement which transfers heat to the lower part of the system is energy-wasting.

This situation can be prevented by good design, but the reader must appreciate that it is impossible to detail here remedies for the countless existing systems which may suffer from this fault. However, the following are the basic principles, which should be applied in every new installation and adapted wherever possible to suit those that are existing.

Ensure that the flow pipe connecting to the upper part of the body of the cylinder is vertical for its full height and as close as practicable to the cylinder.

Set the temperature control on the thermostat to a maximum of 65°C. Excessively hot water in the cylinder may not only affect the temperature of the cold flow pipe, but will also cause precipitation of lime scale in hard-water areas.

Do *not* be tempted to fit valves to the primary circuit to control any back circulation as it will prove very dangerous if they are forgotten and left shut when the boiler is lit for the winter season.

## Furring

In hard-water districts, furring of flow and return pipes, the boiler (which, incidentally, holds only a few pints of water) and the cylinder can be a major problem. It is caused by water depositing what is termed its temporary hardness, a mineral held in suspension by the water until the temperature exceeds approximately 71°C. A common deposit is lime scale, which quickly coats the walls of the boiler, pipes and, to a lesser extent, the storage vessel.

The greater the mineral content of the water, and the higher the operating temperature, the quicker the boiler and pipes will fur up. There have been instances where systems have ceased to work because boilers have been so clogged with lime that there was less than a quarter of a pint of water in the jackets.

Not only does this prevent circulation, it also effectively insulates the heat-exchange surfaces which, again, is fuel-wasting. For proper efficiency and economy these deposits must be avoided. Many households install water softeners (which are dealt with in Chapter 18) which are an ideal solution if you want the benefit of softened water for all purposes. If your only concern is the hot-water system, then the cure can be quite simply effected by asking your plumber to fit a calorifier instead of the customary direct cylinder.

## Calorifier

The calorifier, or indirect cylinder, is a cylinder with an internal heating coil, or tank. The flow and return pipes from the boiler connect to the internal coil which, in turn, heats the water in the outer cylinder.

As this inner tank, or coil, is entirely self-contained and provided with its own separate cold feed and vent (to a separate feed and expansion tank), and there are no draw-off points on the primary circuit (other than the drain-off valve), the same water is circulated constantly. Consequently there is only the initial deposit of temporary hardness and, providing the system is not drained down for any reason, it will function indefinitely with only the loss from evaporation to be made up from the feed and expansion tank.

This method of heating is efficient, especially when hot water and central heating are run from the same heat source. The temperature recovery time for hot water only is good, because replacement cold water does not enter the boiler every time hot water is drawn from the cylinder. However, when both systems are running the recovery time for the domestic hot water will be extended, sometimes considerably, depending upon the size of the radiator circuit, the efficiency of the design and installation, and the output of the boiler.

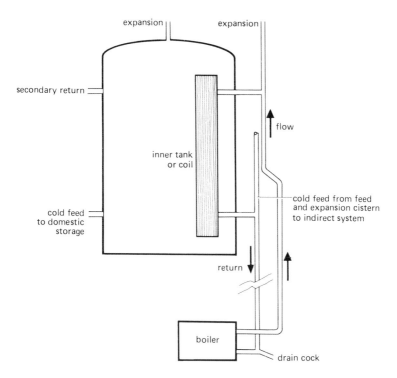

Figure 21 *Indirect cylinder*

## Vent pipe

A vent pipe must be taken from the top of the storage vessel and discharged above the cold feed cistern. Its purpose is to permit the discharge or escape of any air or steam in the system.

This pipe is often wrongfully described as the expansion pipe on the assumption that the expansion of the water in the system when it is heated will be taken up by this pipe and, if necessary, expelled into the cold feed cistern. In point of fact this is not true because the expansion takes place in the cold feed pipe. Reference to Figure 22 will show that in order for water to be discharged from the vent pipe it would have to be lifted the distance AB above the level of the water in the cold feed cistern. The fact that the vent pipe will be hot and the cold feed pipe cold will only account for a difference of about 12 mm/300 mm of vertical distance between cold-water cistern and hot storage vessel. It is

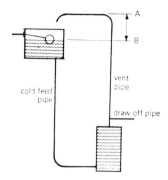

Figure 22    *Vent and feed pipes*

important that the vertical distance between the free surface of
the cold water in the cistern and the turn-over of the vent pipe is
greater than 12 mm/300 mm of vertical distance between cistern
and storage vessel, as otherwise discharge of hot water via the
vent pipe into the cold-water cistern will be liable to take place.
The end of the vent pipe must not dip into the cold water in the
cistern as otherwise siphonic action might feed cold water via the
vent pipe to the top of the storage vessel.

## Draw-off piping

The hot-water supplies to the various taps are taken from the vent
pipe as close to the top of the cylinder as possible. This branch is
the 'high' point of the hot-water service and the distributing pipes
should be laid with a constant fall away, although where they run
on skirting boards or under floors in joists they may be level.

As previously stated, the storage vessel should be sited as close
as possible to the various points to be served. Overlong runs mean
that a considerable quantity of cold water must be drawn from
the tap before the hot water arrives. Then, when the tap is turned
off for any length of time, the hot water in the pipe will in turn
cool, wasting the heat used to warm it. These long runs of pipes
are known as 'dead legs' and because they waste energy they must
be avoided.

The maximum lengths of pipe permitted under byelaws for
supplying hot-water draw-off taps are: up to 19 mm diameter,

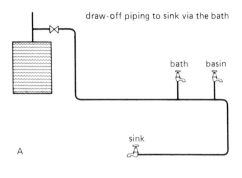

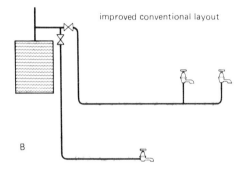

Figure 23 *Draw-off piping*

12.0 m; over 19 mm and up to 25 mm diameter, 7.6 m; over 25 mm diameter, 3.0 m.

For a common pipe run reducing through several sizes the length is determined by the largest diameter.

Clearly it is important to plan pipe routes. A basin and bath within 7.6 m of the cylinder can be supplied from a 22-mm pipe and the sink tap also if it is within the overall pipe length. Some plumbers advocate increasing the diameter of the initial length to the bath to 28 mm to avoid possible starvation at the sink if both taps are used at the same time. This is an unnecessary precaution and limits drastically the permitted length of run. (Though these deadleg dimensions are permitted by the byelaws, they should not, in practice, be fitted for the reasons explained in the chapter dealing with legionella.)

Figure 23A is a fairly typical example of pipe arrangement where importance is attached to running pipes in corners of walls for concealment in casings; possibly pleasing to the eye, but no longer acceptable under Model Byelaw requirement. All branch distributing pipes must connect to the main rising or falling length of pipe at least 300 mm above the spill-over level of the highest fitting to be served by that branch pipe. That being the case, the supply to the ground flow sink must be as shown in Figure 23B.

Full-way gate valves should be fitted to branch supply pipes as close as possible to, but without obstructing, the open vent. This ensures control of the entire lengths of pipework for maintenance purposes. *Under no circumstances must a valve be fitted to the open vent.*

We have dealt with supplies to basic amenities, but these days households will probably have a plumbed-in washing machine, perhaps a dishwasher, and in many bathrooms a bidet.

Hot-water supplies to washing machines and dishwashers may be taken from the supply to the sink and terminated at hose-union taps. These not only control the supply of water to the machines but provide suitable connections for the flexible hose with which these machines are invariably equipped. Cold-water supplies to these machines should be from the storage tank and also terminated with a hose-union tap.

Anti-back-siphonage devices may be required to be fitted to the pipework serving these fittings, as described in Chapter 2. The reader's attention is also drawn to the special provisions that must be made for other appliances, particularly bidets. *It must be emphasized that bidets must not be connected to the cold-water mains supply pipe.*

In general, all hot-water pipes should be lagged to prevent heat loss. Control valves must be full way gate valves. Screw-down stopcocks should not be used on any hot-water pipe because of their high resistance-to-flow factor. Drain-off cocks must be provided at the lowest point of all branch pipework.

## Secondary circuit

The necessity of locating the storage cylinder as near as possible to the draw-off points and within the limit for 'dead leg' branches has been stressed.

Sometimes, however, this is just not possible. In these cases a

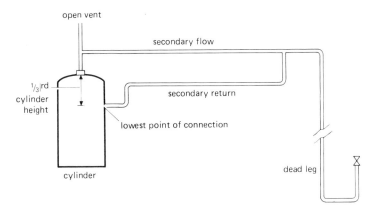

Figure 24   *Secondary circulation*

secondary flow and return which provides a circulation from the vertical vent to a point near the draw-off, and returns to the cylinder, solves the problem. The dead leg is then measured from the return connection to the secondary flow to the draw-off point. This arrangement is suitable only for boiler-fired systems and should not be incorporated in a system designed to be heated by electricity.

The secondary flow pipe (see Figure 24) should fall slightly all the way from the vent and the return back to the cylinder and connect within the top third of the storage vessel (tappings are provided for this connection on calorifiers and also on direct cylinders if ordered). If connected any lower, the water within the tank may be cooler than that in the return and thus, because of its greater density, prevent the return water from entering the cylinder and so stop the circulation.

## Pipe sizing

Pipe sizing and flow rates are a complex subject, too involved to discuss here in basic terms. However, if you are planning additions to your plumbing system it is necessary to know if they will work. Purely for guidance, the following table illustrates the number of smaller-diameter pipes that may be supplied by a larger-diameter pipe in a domestic household, providing a suitable head pressure exists.

| | Taps | | | |
|---|---|---|---|---|
| Pipes | 35 mm | 28 mm | 22 mm | 15 mm |
| 35 mm | 1 | 2 | 4 | 10 |
| 28 mm | | 1 | 2 | 6 |
| 22 mm | | | 1 | 3 |
| 15 mm | | | | 1 |

As shown, a 28-mm cold-water down-service pipe will serve two 22-mm taps or six 15-mm taps. Three 15-mm taps may be connected to a 22-mm pipe.

Remember that the simultaneous use of two taps in the average house is reasonably rare, while three at the same time is very unlikely.

All that now remains to complete the installation is to fit the electric heater. This may be a horizontal immersion heater, a vertical circulator or even twin elements like the 'two-in-one' heater. It should not be forgotten that the effective hot storage capacity is that above the level of a horizontal heater or above the level of the bottom of a circulator, and that no part of a heater should be below the level of the cold feed.

In the case of a horizontal immersion heater, sufficient space between the heater and the bottom of the vessel must be allowed for the accumulation of scale and sludge.

If all the foregoing points are attended to, a simple straight-forward solid-fuel/electric system will result and, providing the hot storage vessel is properly insulated with 75 mm of approved insulating material, the standing losses will be not more than between one and one and a half units a day.

Such a system can be left switched on continuously under thermostatic control, and the full benefit of constant hot water on tap be experienced, without excessive running costs.

## Alternative systems

The boiler–cylinder (or tank) system is traditional in this country, born of the need to store heated water against demand. The design found rapid favour because with its open-vent pipe and low-pressure gravity supply excessive pressures could not develop within the system, and therefore it was safe.

However, since the recent emphasis on the need to conserve fuels, a greater awareness of some of the problems that may occur in stored water, and the development of more sophisticated controls and safety devices, alternative systems to the traditional gravity-fed, boiler-fired cylinder storage are coming on the market.

There are two major problems with the standard calorifier. One is the slow recovery rate when the central heating is operating; the other is the 'dead' area at the bottom of the vessel. Reference to Figure 21 shows that the inner tank, or coil, does not extend to the bottom of the cylinder, and so some 100 mm depth of water remains not only unheated but also unmoving. This is a risk area in respect of legionella.

## Legionnaires' disease

Legionnaires' disease, or legionella pneumophila, is a recently discovered disease, though undoubtedly it has been with us for many years. It swept to prominence in 1976 with the now infamous epidemic in Philadelphia at the Bellvue Stratford Hotel, where the American Legion (hence the name given to the disease) was holding its annual convention. A hundred and eighty-two people were taken ill and 29 died from a then unknown pneumonia.

Since that date there were four further outbreaks at the same hotel up to 1981. Another eight people died and many were taken ill before the cause was traced to the fact that the air conditioning exhaust was next to the air intake at street level.

Continuing research has revealed that legionella is not confined to air conditioning systems but can be equally prolific in many hot-water systems, especially of the storage type.

As it is found widely in hot-water systems as well as air conditioning, it is proper that we examine its implications while discussing the design of hot-water installations.

First the known facts:

1  Legionella is endemic to most natural waters and can be found in the soil, pond water, etc.
2  It is harmless to drink.
3  To become contagious it requires the following conditions:

    (a)  A temperature between 20 and 50°C
    (b)  Stagnation (period not yet known)
    (c)  A host on which to breed
    (d)  To be released into the atmosphere in fine aerosols
    (e)  To be inhaled.

4  Water storage cylinders, even if heated to temperatures above 50°C, are often left to cool into the danger temperature zone (not only can this incubate legionella, but it is also fuel-wasting).

5  Stagnation occurs at the bottom of both direct and indirect cylinders. It also happens when systems are left turned off for holiday periods. Long, little-used deadlegs are another area of stagnation.

6  In a hot-water system there is usually no shortage of host material. The sludge product of electrolysis collects in the bottom of cylinders and is an ideal host. Some jointing compounds, solder fluxes, and rubber washers are also known hosts. The calcium build-up behind shower sprays and in filters makes an ideal breeding ground.

7  Shower sprays emit aerosols which can be inhaled; but then, so does any tap discharging into a fitting such as a basin, sink, or bath. The water hitting the bottom of the fitting bounces up, releasing fine aerosols. Remember, these particles are so small that they cannot be seen with the naked eye. A simple test with a mirror will prove the point. Hold a mirror two feet above a basin and, with the tap running, observe the clouding of the glass as the aerosols in the fine spray condense.

8  Most people using a tap stand over it and are, therefore, in the ideal position to breathe in the aerosols.

Of course legionella may not be present in the water; and if it is, it does not follow that you will get legionnaires' disease, especially if you are healthy, young, and preferably a non-smoking female.

What are the symptoms of legionnaires' disease? And how likely are you to catch it from your hot-water system?

There are many different strains of the disease: some experts say eleven, while others put the total at twenty-three. Of these, serogroup 1 can be fatal ('sero' means composed of serum). The other ten or twenty-two are not fatal, and all have symptoms that can be mistaken for influenza: giddiness, disorientation, aches and pains, nausea, headaches, shivering, vomiting, high temperature, and coughing. Some or all of these symptoms may be present, depending upon the legionella serogroup. In most cases the attack will last for no more than a week, and is likely to be diagnosed as flu.

Serogroup 1 attacks the lungs (legionella pneumpophila – 'lung-liking') as a pneumonic infection and, if diagnosed in the early stages, can be successfully treated with antibiotics.

The chances of catching it in the home from hot-water systems are uncertain because much depends upon the health of the individuals and the type of hot-water system.

It is argued that the rapid turnover of hot-water in domestic dwellings is an adequate safeguard, and to a large extent, this is true. Certainly there is no cause for panic among householders, but it is prudent to insure, as far as is practicable, against any problem. The advice generally handed out is to practise 'good housekeeping', and that is good advice providing you know what is meant by 'good housekeeping'. Cold-water storage water should be regularly checked as previously described (precautions should be taken against all water contaminants and not only legionella).

Hot-water storage temperatures should be maintained at 60°–65°C in dwellings where there is constant occupation. This may seem wasteful if households are in the habit of storing water at a lower temperature, but in fact it is quite the reverse. Less of the hotter water is used at each demand, and consequently less fuel is burned in regaining temperature.

In dwellings that are not in constant occupation, or in any dwelling where, because of low demand on hot water, the boiler is operated on a time clock to fire, say, morning and evening, a positive check should be made to ensure that the water is at a safe temperature before using it.

Let any tap or shower run for a full minute at least before using the supply, and stand away from the area of the fitting. Clean shower heads, any spray fittings, and filters as often as possible. Use only Water Council approved materials when rewashering taps or ballvalves. Check temperatures of coldwater pipes to make sure they are not gaining heat from hot-water pipes or other heat sources. (Cold-water supplies should not exceed 20°C). It is not possible for a householder to clean out the bottom of a calorifier, but the temperatures recommended will inhibit the development of any legionella organism.

These are elementary precautions which, if practised, will avoid the possibility of any member of a family contracting legionnaires' disease in the home (exactly the same care should be observed when using washing facilities away from home, especially at places of work or entertainment and, particularly, in hotels).

People living in flats or places of multiple occupation that have shared water services and a common water heating source who are in any way concerned about the quality of the water may apply to their local water undertaking for water samples to be taken and analysed. Although applicants will have to pay for the service it is good sense to check from time to time the water supplied. After all, few, if any, of us will buy packaged food these days without first satisfying ourselves on the sell-by date. But as with everything else, don't overdo it. There is no need to develop a phobia about it.

However, legionella should be borne in mind when designing and installing new, or replacement, systems. We should also consider energy conservation and, providing efficiency isn't sacrificed, the system that incorporates these two features should be selected.

Ideally, both hot- and cold-water storage capacities should be kept to a minimum. It is quicker and cheaper to heat small quantities of water than to heat larger quantities. It is more economical to locate the storage vessel close to the point of use. It is uneconomical to heat large-capacity storage only to allow it to cool because there is no regular demand on it. Both hot- and cold-water delivery at taps should be at the following minimum rates:

Table 7

|  | Gal/min | L/S |
|---|---|---|
| Wash basin | 2.0 | 0.15 |
| Wash basin with spray taps | 0.5 | 0.4 |
| Bath | 4.0 | 0.30 |
| Shower | 1.5 | 0.12 |
| Sink (½ in taps) | 2.5 | 0.20 |
| Sink (¾ in taps) | 4.0 | 0.30 |

Both the traditional direct and indirect cylinders coupled to a boiler have proved popular over the years for heating water, but from both the legionella and energy considerations they are not

Figure 25 *Hamworthy gas-fired cylinder*

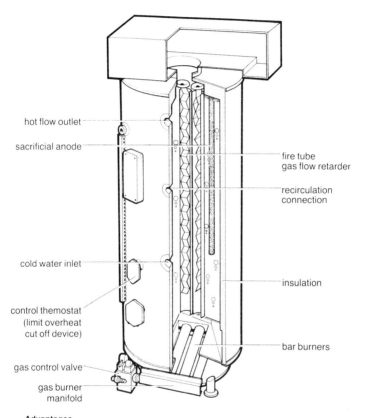

**Advantages**

instant hot water
8 sizes of heater to meet wide range of applications
heat water direct — no primary losses
space saving
can be installed at point of use — reducing distribution losses
high quality glass lined surfaces — up to 5-year guarantee
low capital cost
high level of insulation — low standing losses
simple in design, installation and operation
large inlet, flow and return connections
suitable for firing on LPG
suitable for multi-unit applications
nationwide after-sales and commissioning service

particularly efficient – especially the calorifier, in which water is used to heat water. This is very much like boiling a kettle by immersing it in a bucket of water which is put on the gas ring. The direct cylinder with, often, long primary flow and return pipes to and from the boiler is only marginally better.

A much more satisfactory appliance is the Hamworthy gas-fired direct hot-water storage heater. There are various models, with storage capacities ranging from 130 litres (28 gallons) to 325 litres (71.5 gallons). More interesting is the recovery rate at continuous output. The model DR 90, with a capacity of 57.2 gallons and raising the temperature through 44°C, has an output of 1733 L/h (381 gal/h), which equals recovery of storage temperature every nine minutes.

Figure 25 illustrates the DR model, which operates on natural gas only. The DR-SE model will operate on natural gas and LPG. As can be seen from the section-through illustration the gas burner is located immediately under the water tank, so that the movement of water by convection starts from the base of the vessel and not some 100 mm above the base as with the traditional direct and indirect cylinders. Consequently there is no area of stagnant water in which legionella can proliferate.

The flue passes up through the centre of the water storage, and the restrictor at its top ensures maximum heat transfer to the water from the exhaust. The cylinders are of glass-lined steel and fitted with removable anodes for added protection against corrosion and they are, therefore, not affected by electrolysis or any chemical reaction normally to be found even in aggressive water.

But the real value of these heaters is their versatility. Providing an adequate flue is available they can be fitted close to the point of use. Circulation loops fitted with velocity-booster pumps can be run in exactly the same way as from the traditional cylinder. In large buildings requiring much bigger quantities of hot water the cylinder heaters may be fixed in pairs to work in tandem, or in banks of three or more. Where extra storage is required as opposed to direct heat output an ST storage tank can be combined with a heater (see Figure 26).

The two tanks stand side by side, and circulation from the heater to the storage tank is by temperature-controlled loading pump. The return pipe from any secondary circulation connects to the storage cylinder and not to the heater vessel. When

**Typical schematic pipework arrangement — heater with storage tank**

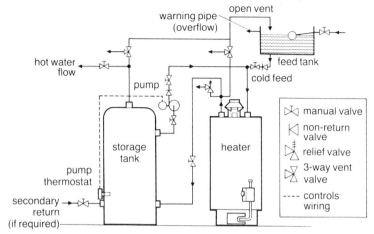

**Typical schematic pipework arrangement — DR heater with storage tank**

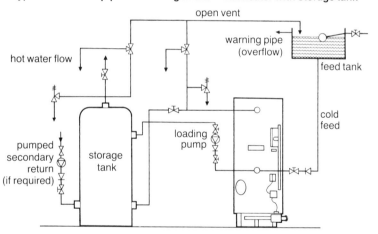

To ensure that the storage tank is brought up to the required outlet temperature a temperature controlled loading pump should be installed between the heater and the storage tank. This enables hot water from the heater to circulate to the tank and the secondary system (if fitted) at periods of no draw off, thus keeping the whole system up to temperature at which point the pump will switch off.

DR water heaters have provision on the terminal block in the heater junction box for the connection of the loading pump, loading pump control thermostat and an additional thermostat to provide pump minimum temperature control. The standard single control thermostat provided with each DR heater should be removed from the heater and fitted into the storage tank, and replaced with a double thermostat unit (obtainable from Hamworthy Engineering)

Figure 26  *Hamworthy gas-fired cylinder and storage tank*

installing this type of system it is important to follow the pipe and valve arrangement shown in Figure 26.

The minimum working head for these heaters is 2 m (6 ft), and this should be measured from the highest draw-off point on the system. The maximum working head is 53 m (174 ft) measured from tank to cylinder.

In common with all hot-water cylinders the cold-feed supply must be equivalent to, or exceed, the maximum possible draw-off rate from the heater.

The DR–SE series heaters do not require an electrical supply as these units have self-energizing controls. The heaters are thermostatically controlled and have the added protection of a high-limit thermostat which is wired in series with the low-voltage thermocouple circuit. All DR model heaters can be controlled by time clocks. For clock control of DR–SE models a conversion kit can be supplied. As with all other gas-burning appliances other than balanced-flue heaters, adequate ventilation must be provided. Details are given in the manufacturer's specification.

For larger households or flats using shared water heating, and for hotels, hostels, and so on, a 'split' or 'separate system' may be used, separating heating and hot-water services. Boilers and water heaters can be used, each sized for a specific duty, rather than the 'traditional' boiler/calorifier system, which attempts to reconcile the conflicting requirements of a seasonably variable heating load with a relatively constant hot-water load.

Split systems overcome the problems that might arise from the use of sophisticated energy-saving controls in large combined systems. They can certainly reduce the amount of stored hot water because, while the boiler/calorifier systems are sized on storage – invariably oversized – direct high-output water heaters are sized to meet a specific demand, which their rapid response enables them to do without excess back-up storage capacity.

## Pressurized hot-water systems

As anticipated, pressurized hot-water systems are now permitted by water authorities (under new byelaws made in 1987 following publication of the Water Council Model Byelaws 1986. In the event of this book's appearing before the enactment of the new byelaws, readers wishing to install a pressurized hot-water system will have to apply to their local water undertakings for a relaxation of byelaw 46.)

'Pressurized hot-water system' means a system in which the primary circulation, the storage cylinder, and all hot-water distribution pipes are supplied directly from the water undertakings main. It has probably provoked more argument within the industry than any other innovation.

The main factor of concern by its opponents is safety; it has frequently been referred to as a 'time bomb', a 'lethal weapon in the hands of cowboy installers', and 'possibly acceptable only when legislation provides for installation by approved installers'. Quite a lot more has been said, but these are the points with which we are concerned here. Let us take them one at a time. Are pressurized hot-water systems safe?

Let's understand that it is the words 'pressure' and 'hot' that are causing the concern. Because these systems are mains water fed, they can have no open-vent pipes – our traditional safety outlet in the event of a system's malfunctioning.

So let's have another look at that 'traditional' system: generally, any expansion would take place through the cold-feed pipe, as the surface area of the cistern is much greater than that of the vent pipe. Pressure relief would be through the vent pipe at a pressure equal to 'X'; and vacuum relief is provided by the vent pipe. Temperature relief is yet another function of the vent pipe which limits the temperature to the boiling point of water which, when subject to the pressure exerted by static head 'X', would be above 100°C.

Figure 27   *Static head*

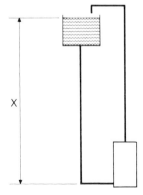

X

Inlet pressure is controlled by height 'X'

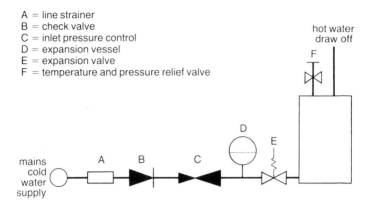

A = line strainer
B = check valve
C = inlet pressure control
D = expansion vessel
E = expansion valve
F = temperature and pressure relief valve

hot water draw off

F

D

E

mains cold water supply

A    B    C

Figure 28   *Control and safety valves*

It is clear that virtually all of the safety functions are carried out by the small-diameter vent pipe in the traditional system. In the pressurized system these functions are discharged by a series of valves and pressure vessels which operate in sequence to provide a protection which is, frankly, superior to an overworked open-vent pipe.

Figure 28 shows a typical connection of a boiler to a mains cold-water supply using E. A. Molyneux Ltd reliance water controls.

The line strainer has a removable corrosion-resisting element with a mesh size small enough to prevent particles of a size that

Figure 29a   *In-line strainer*

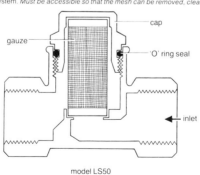

This valve is used to deny access to particles that are large enough to affect the operation of other valves in the system. *Must be accessible so that the mesh can be removed, cleaned and replaced.*

gauze

cap

'O' ring seal

inlet

model LS50
with 100 micron stainless steel mesh

This valve is used to prevent drain down of the heater and to prevent possible crossflow between the water heater and cold water outlets.

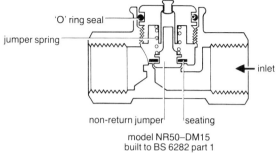

model NR50–DM15
built to BS 6282 part 1

Figure 29b   *Non-return valve*

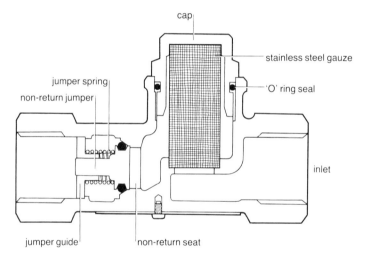

*Figure 30   Line strainer/non-return valve*

would cause malfunction of other components from entering the system. Its primary object is to protect the check valve, because there would be no visible indication if the check valve failed to work properly.

The check valve (or non-return valve) to BS 6282: Part 1 is used for two main reasons: to prevent the water heater from draining down and possibly damaging any heating elements; and to prevent backflow or crossflow, for example the drawing of hot water from cold-water taps.

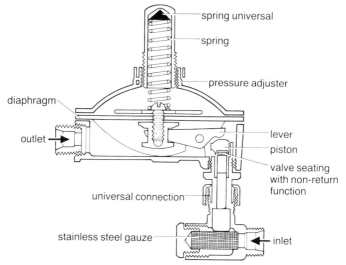

Figure 31   *Pressure reducing valves*

Inlet pressure control valve BS 6282: Part 4 valves fall into two categories:

(a)  Pressure-reducing valves.
(b)  Pressure-limiting valves.

(a)  The maximum inlet pressure to domestic water heaters must be controlled within the working limits of the water heater, and it is important to retain as much of this reduced pressure as possible.

Reliance water valves are designed to give a closely maintained static outlet pressure over a wide range of inlet pressures. If this were not so then the outlet pressure would have to be reduced to compensate for variation.

(b)  The limiting valve does what its name implies and controls the flow of water to the demand point. Such valves do not have, or need, the closely controlled outlet pressure performance over a wide range of inlet pressures required by pressure-reducing valves, but regulate the flow according to demand. The valve will close when subject to back pressure. These valves are specifically designed for use with heaters with high maximum working pressures, usually from 5 bar and above.

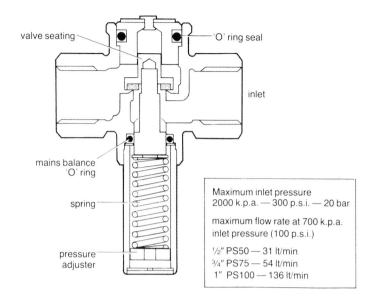

valve seating

'O' ring seal

inlet

mains balance 'O' ring

spring

pressure adjuster

Maximum inlet pressure
2000 k.p.a. — 300 p.s.i. — 20 bar

maximum flow rate at 700 k.p.a.
inlet pressure (100 p.s.i.)

½" PS50 — 31 lt/min
¾" PS75 — 54 lt/min
1" PS100 — 136 lt/min

Figure 32  *Pressure limiting valve*

## Expansion vessel

Relevant standard BS 6144. An expansion vessel is a steel tank divided into two parts by a flexible membrane, or 'bag'. One half of the vessel will contain water, and the other half is charged with air. The air charge pressure is normally the same as the setting on the inlet pressure-control device.

The size of the vessel depends on the volume of water in the heater and any secondary circuit, inlet pressure, the first level of pressure protection, and the water expansion factor.

Obviously water expands when it is heated.

Table 8 gives the percentage factor against degrees centigrade.

A pressure vessel with a bag-type membrane is sized by using the following formula:

$$V = \frac{E \times C}{V \, 1 - \dfrac{Pi}{Pf}}$$

in which:   V  = Expansion vessel size.

Table 8

| °C | Expansion | % |
|-----|-----------|------|
| 50  | 0.0121    | 1.21 |
| 55  | 0.0145    | 1.45 |
| 60  | 0.0171    | 1.71 |
| 65  | 0.0198    | 1.98 |
| 70  | 0.0227    | 2.27 |
| 75  | 0.2580    | 2.58 |
| 80  | 0.0290    | 2.90 |
| 85  | 0.0324    | 3.24 |
| 90  | 0.0359    | 3.59 |
| 95  | 0.0396    | 3.96 |
| 100 | 0.0434    | 4.34 |

$E$ = *Expansion factor (see temperature rise).*

$C$ = *Total capacity of the system in litres.*

$Pi$ = *Static head, or pre-charge pressure in bars absolute.*

$Pf$ = *Maximum system pressure (safety valve setting) in bars absolute.*

*Example calculation*

Quantity of water in system    $C$ = 120 litres.

Initial pressure    $Pi$ = 0.7 bar (1.7 ATE).

Final pressure    $Pf$ = 1.1 bar (2.1 ATE).

Total of volume of tank to be installed

$$V = \frac{0.032 \times 120}{1 - \frac{1.7}{2.1}}$$

= 20.47 litres: take to nearest size above.

This vessel will accommodate any increase in the volume of water due to expansion (the same duty that is performed by the vent pipe in the traditional system) by compressing the air in the tank. As the water cools it will contract allowing the air that has been compressed to expand, thus discharging the water that has been forced into the expansion vessel.

**VESSELS FOR USE IN SEALED SYSTEMS**

| MODEL No. | TANK CAPACITY LITRES | INIT. PRES † NITROGEN BARS | STATIC HEIGHT METRES | AVERAGE TEMP 90°C PLANT LITRES | AVERAGE TEMP 90°C BOILER BTU | SIZES in mm Dia | SIZES in mm H |
|---|---|---|---|---|---|---|---|
| 501 | 4 | 0.5 / 1 | 5 / 10 | 71 / 57 | 23,400 / 18,650 | 228 | 180 |
| 502 | 8 | 0.5 / 1 | 5 / 10 | 143 / 114 | 47,200 / 37,700 | 228 | 295 |
| 503 | 12 | 0.5 / 1 | 5 / 10 | 214 / 171 | 70,600 / 56,350 | 298 | 260 |
| 504 | 18 | 0.5 / 1 / 1.5 | 5 / 10 / 15 | 323 / 257 / 191 | 106,750 / 84,900 / 63,100 | 298 | 365 |
| 506 | 25 | 0.5 / 1 / 1.5 | 5 / 10 / 15 | 446 / 357 / 268 | 147,200 / 117,850 / 88,500 | 328 | 405 |
| 507 | 35 | 0.5 / 1 / 1.5 | 5 / 10 / 15 | 623 / 500 / 374 | 205,950 / 165,050 / 123,400 | 380 | 402 |
| 508 | 50 | 0.5 / 1 / 1.5 | 5 / 10 / 15 | 891 / 714 / 537 | 74,200 / 59,500 / 44,700 | 380 | 537 |

† STANDARD CHARGE PRESSURE 1.5 BAR
THIS SHOULD BE ADJUSTED TO THE REQUIRED CHARGE PRESSURE ON INSTALLATION

**VESSELS FOR USE WITH BOILERS**

| MODEL No. | TANK CAPACITY LITRES | AVERAGE TEMP 90°C (e = 0.035) SYSTEM CAPACITY | AVERAGE TEMP 90°C (e = 0.035) BOILER BTU | SIZES in mm DIA | SIZES in mm HEIGHT |
|---|---|---|---|---|---|
| 531 | 5 | 86 | 28175 | Diam 387 | 75 |
| | 8 | 131 | 43250 | | 105 |
| | 10 | 171 | 55550 | | 120 |
| | 12 | 205 | 67460 | | 140 |
| | 14 | 240 | 79360 | | 155 |
| | 18 | 308 | 99200 | | 205 |
| 541 | 6 | 103 | 33730 | Diam 324 | 100 |
| | 8 | 131 | 43250 | | 130 |
| | 10 | 172 | 55550 | | 140 |
| | 12 | 205 | 67460 | | 170 |

STANDARD CHARGE PRESSURE 1 BAR

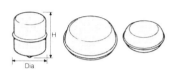

**CONSTRUCTION**
Mild steel casing painted by automatic furnace method, synthetic rubber membrane, steel water connections and brass air or nitrogen air intake valve. Membrane material conforms to physical mechanical requirement of DIN 4807. Water Connections ¾" BSP male, (smaller connections can be made available for models 531 or 541).
Maximum pressure 4 bar (58 psi). Temperature range  10 to + 100° C.

Figure 33   *Expansion vessels – application*

# Expansion relief valve

This valve limits, to a predetermined maximum, the pressure of the water in the system by automatically discharging expansion water in the event of an expansion vessel failure. This valve is always fitted on the cold, or inlet, side of the heater to avoid problems associated with calcareous deposits.

It is essential that no other valves or cocks be fitted between the valve and the heater inlet. Any other control valves must be fitted upstream.

The term 'relief valve' is often taken to mean a safety valve. This is not always so, and certainly isn't the case with this valve, which is a functional control and is designed solely to cope with expansion. However, provision of an expansion relief valve does not eliminate the need to fit safety devices, for they are a safeguard against the failure of functional control devices.

Expansion relief valves must be fitted with a drain pipe of copper that falls continuously from the valve outlet to discharge in a safe place.

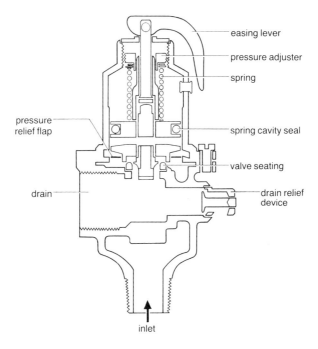

Figure 34    *Expansion relief valve*

*Pressure setting*

The setting at which the expansion relief valve commences to operate must be related to the working pressure of the water heater with which the valve is installed. There are a number of variables associated with the different types of unvented heaters and other controls used in the installation. Such variables are taken into consideration by the system manufacturer.

Because of the importance of the fact, it is reiterated that this valve is *not* a safety device.

It is worthwhile mentioning here the electrical controls that would normally be fitted:

(a) Normal thermostat.
(b) Non resetting thermal cut-out.

(a) would normally be set to a maximum setting of 65°C.
(b) would be set to a maximum of 85°C and would have to

comply with BS 3955: Part 3, so satisfying Provision 1.3 of Building Regulations G3, 1985. It should also have a BEAB certificate. It must be stressed that heated water must not exceed 99°C.

## Safety relief valves

Earlier, the subject of the safety relief valve was briefly mentioned as opposed to the expansion relief valve. To differentiate fully between the two items, it is necessary to appreciate the scope of operation and the category of each product related to the installation of unvented water heaters.

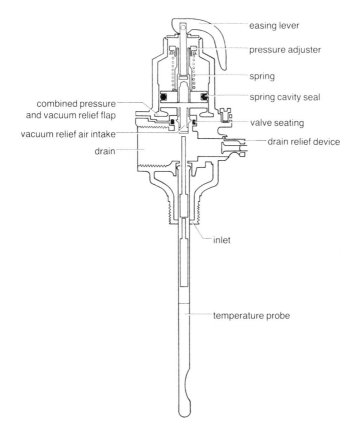

Figure 35a   *Safety valve (temp., pressure, vacuum relief)*

The pressure setting of this valve is determined by the pressure capabilities of the water heater/cylinder to be used and would normally be stated by the waterheater manufacturers. The size of the valve (½″ or ¾″) would be determined by the energy output of the water heater/cylinder used.

The purpose of this component is to act *only* as a safety valve, and it has two functions:
1. pressure relief
2. temperature relief

Function 1 is to safeguard the heater/cylinder from hydrostatic failure to over pressure through failure of valves 'C', 'D' or 'E' (*see Figure 28*). Function 2 is to prevent the water temperature rising above boiling point at atmospheric pressure through failure of the thermostat and over-temperature cut out.

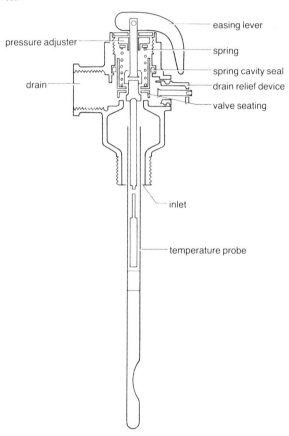

Figure 35b  *Safety valve (temp. and pressure relief)*

Controls for these heaters fall into two categories:
1 Functional controls.

2 Safety controls.

Functional controls may be defined as those controls which protect a water heater against excessive pressure and temperature during the normal operation of the water heater. These would include thermostat, expansion vessel (or expansion relief valve), and reducing valve where fitted.

Safety controls may be defined as those controls which protect a water heater against excessive pressure and temperature in the event of failure of a functional control.

The term 'safety' should be used in connection with the appliance itself as well as people and property. In this context the problems of damage to the water heater must be taken into account. In the terms of the definition, the functional controls must be listed together with possible areas of failure. When these are established, it will be apparent what features must be included in a safety relief valve.

Functional control failures:

1 Inlet pressure control device.
   (a) Failure to close at set pressure.
   (b) Failure to meet draw-off demands.
2 Expansion vessel.
   (a) Loss of vessel charge pressure.
3 Expansion relief valve.
   (a) Blockage of drain line.
4. Thermostat.
   (a) Failure to shut off energy supply.
1 To protect against 1(a), the safety relief valve must have some minimum flow characteristics to guard against an overly high build up in pressure. These flow characteristics are related to the working pressure of the water heater and vary as this pressure increases.

The problem of 1(b) is more likely to occur when the draw-off points are below the base of the water heater. In these instances it is possible for water to be siphoned out of the heater faster than the inlet pressure control valve can supply. A partial vacuum will then be created in the water heater and the cylinder will implode (collapse) if it is of a type susceptible to vacuum.

This collapse can also take place if, after the water has been heated and the content expanded, the power and water supply is closed down. When these conditions occur, the water content contracts during cooling and again a partial vacuum can occur. To overcome these problems, a vacuum valve may be included in the safety valve.

2 (a) With a diminished pressure, the vessel becomes less effective, permitting system pressures above optimum levels.

3 (a) The problem of a blocked drain pipe in the expansion valve could result in a back pressure in the safety relief valve if the drain-pipes from each valve are inter-connected. Alternatively, blocking of the safety valve drain must be avoided. A drain relief device which operates slightly above the operating pressure of the safety valve is included as part of the reliance safety valve.

4 In the event of failure of the thermostat and the over temperature cut-out, energy is constantly fed into the water heater. Eventually the water boils, but as the pressure in the heater is above atmospheric, the temperature of the boiling water is above 100°C, the boiling point of water at atmospheric pressure. The actual temperature varies with pressure, but even at a moderate 1 bar pressure, the temperature is 121°C. If during a period of elevated temperature the cylinder failed (excess pressure) as the pressure dropped, the water content would flash to steam with disastrous results. To overcome this hazard, a safety relief valve must include a temperature function, which opens the valve seat before 100°C and allows the overheated water to be displaced by cold water from the cylinder inlet. When the cold water reaches the temperature probe the valve closes and the cycle is repeated. Normally service is quickly demanded and the faulty thermostat replaced.

Installation is very important, and it is customary for the safety valve to be fitted by the heater manufacturer. The valve should be installed in the top 150 mm or the top 20% of the heater, which is the hottest area.

## Drain lines

The same specification and precautions for drain lines apply as listed for pressure expansion valves.

To sum up, the Reliance safety relief valve for an unvented water heater includes the following functions:

1 It controls over pressure.

2 It overcomes blocked drain lines.
3 It prevents the formation of a vacuum.
4 It prevents temperatures in excess of 100°C.

These valves are covered by British Standard 6283: Part 3 and fulfil the second part of 1.3 of G3 in the 1985 Building Regulations.

Temperature relief valves (BS 6283: Parts 2 and 3) are rated on steam discharge capacity at 1 bar which, in effect, assumes failure of the mains-water supply. Temperature and pressure relief valves only (BS 6283: Part 3) are also tested with the temperature relief probe inoperative at 110% of the valves' set pressure. This gives them a safety pressure relief function. In terms of construction you have to pressure load the temperature probe to ensure correct operation, so it is normal to set this pressure at a level that provides pressure protection for the cylinder. This is the reason why the majority of temperature relief valves are combined with a pressure relief function.

## Vacuum relief valves

As explained previously, one problem allied to unvented water heaters and in particular copper water heaters up to 3 bar working pressure is the formation of a partial vacuum in the water heater.

A water heater which has reasonable resistance to internal pressure (e.g. to bursting) has little or no resistance to implosion – collapse. This collapsing is brought about when the pressure on the outside of the water heater is greater than the pressure on the inside. As the pressure on the outside of the heater is atmospheric pressure, it follows that the condition that must be safeguarded against is the one that would permit the pressure inside the cylinder to reduce below atmospheric.

Two instances of how this could happen were given earlier and are repeated now for clarity:

1 When the rate of draw-off of water exceeds the rate of input.
2 Where the water content contracts, after the power is switched off and the water is turned off.

To prevent the formation of a vacuum or partial vacuum, the simple technique of utilizing the internal pressure in the heater to

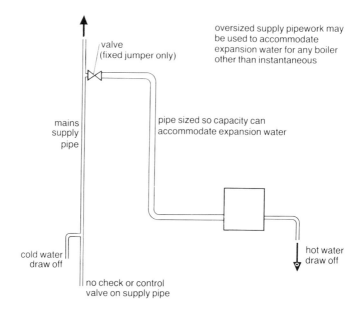

Figure 36a   *Expansion – enlarged supply pipe*

Figure 36b   *Expansion – bubble-top calorifier*

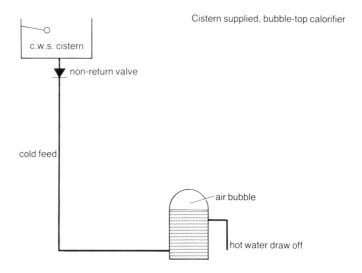

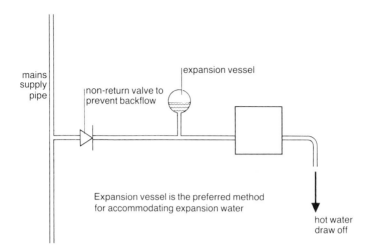

mains supply pipe

non-return valve to prevent backflow

expansion vessel

Expansion vessel is the preferred method for accommodating expansion water

hot water draw off

Figure 36c   *Expansion – expansion vessel*

close a seat which is open to atmosphere on the reverse side is used. This means that as the pressure in the heater is reduced, so is the pressure keeping the seat closed. When this pressure is below atmospheric pressure, the atmospheric pressure on the reverse side opens the seating and allows air to enter the water heater and equalize the pressure on both the inside and outside of the water heater.

Vacuum relief valves are included in the design of the Reliance safety valves specifically designed for use with copper cylinders (see Figure 35A).

There are alternative methods of accommodating water expansion: using increased diameter supply pipe (Figures 36A and 36B) and choosing a cylinder in which air is contained within the top of the vessel (Figure 36C).

However, when you are deciding upon a pressurized system, water heater manufacturers will supply the complete system of control and safety valves. These will be designed to protect their equipment and will be set within the tested pressure safety margins.

All valves and appliances must comply with the relevant British Standards and the system, or package, must carry the British Board of Agreement Certificate. This is a standard for fitness of use and establishes that the package is fit for the purpose for which it is intended. The certificate carries a qualification that the system be installed only by operatives qualified in mains-water supply pressurized systems.

Water heating may be by boiler or by direct, gas-fired cylinders, and Hamworthy, for instance, will supply the valves package to convert their appliances for use in pressurized systems.

*It must be emphasized that this work is not suitable for do-it-yourself or unqualified installers. Incorrect installation of control and safety valves may be dangerous.*

## Unvented storage systems

### Tank-fed high-level storage

These are often mistakenly referred to as pressurized systems or, more correctly, as sealed systems. The installation is fed from a cold-water storage cistern, but the system is sealed in as much as no open-vent pipe is fitted. In the case of Figure 37 expansion will take place through the cold feed, providing no check valve or other restriction is fitted to this pipe.

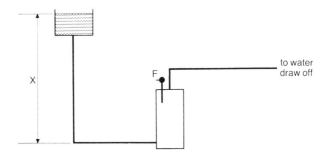

This system is only applicable if there is no restriction in the inlet supply that prevents normal expansion going back to the storage cistern and no other draw off points are served from that supply pipe.
Valve 'F' would be an LTV or HT series valve, pressure set to suit the cylinder being used (approx. ½ test pressure). Height 'X' would normally be a maximum of 50% of the cylinder test pressure. This is a guide only and the cylinder manufacturer should be consulted before proceeding.

Figure 37a   *Unvented storage (high level) systems*

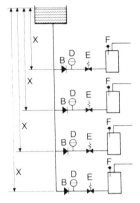

This system is applicable when the cistern feeds more than one cylinder or draw off point.
Height 'X' would be between 33 and 40% of the cylinder test pressure.
The expansion vessel 'D' would be sized on height 'X' and the pressure setting on valve 'E'.
Valve 'E' would be set at approx. 50% of the cylinder test pressure.
Valve 'F' would be set at approx. 50% of the cylinder test pressure.
This is a guide only and the cylinder manufacturer should be consulted before proceeding.

Figure 37b

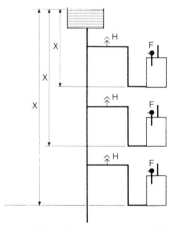

In this system valve 'F' would be pressure set at approx. 66% of the cylinder test pressure.
Valve 'H' would be an in-line anti-vacuum valve to BS 6282, part 3 fitted 150mm above the highest spill over point in the system which it is protecting.
Height 'X' would be a maximum of 50% of the cylinder test pressure.
If height 'X' were greater than the limits given the system would have to be treated as a mains supply system.

There are other variations on system design but every system must obey the following:
- every unvented system must be fitted with a temperature relief valve
- expansion water must be contained within the system without wastage of water
- supply pressure must be controlled to a level commensurate with safe working and long life of the cylinder
- crossflow must be prevented

Figure 37c

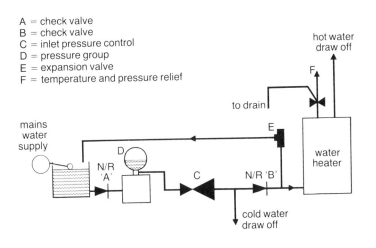

A = check valve
B = check valve
C = inlet pressure control
D = pressure group
E = expansion valve
F = temperature and pressure relief

Figure 38   *Cistern fed, low-level storage*

Valve F should be a temperature, pressure, vacuum relief valve, or a temperature pressure relief valve (Figures 31A and B) set to approximately 50 per cent of the test pressure of the cylinder. The static head from the storage cistern should be a maximum of 50 per cent of the cylinder test pressure.

### Tank-fed low-level storage

Figure 38 shows a typical low-level storage cistern connected to a mains supply with a pumped delivery to the water heater unit. Obviously this system is used mainly in high-rise buildings, but it is also applicable to buildings where provision of high-level storage is not possible.

Both tank-fed systems have the advantage of a storage capacity reserve against a failure of the main supply while enjoying the benefit of pressurized systems: increased delivery pressures to fittings. Systems incorporating secondary returns may have circulating pumps fitted to speed the circulation. There are other variations on system design, but every system must obey the following:

1 Every unvented system must be fitted with a temperature relief valve.
2 Expansion water must be contained within the system without wastage of water.
3 Supply pressure must be controlled to a level commensurate with the safe working and long life of the cylinder.
4 Crossflow must be prevented.

*Layout*

In planning the layout of unvented storage systems, the possibilities of point-of-use water heaters being used in conjunction with storage systems should not be overlooked.

Dwellings with baths (as opposed to showers only) generally need a large amount of water at particular times of the day. The kitchen sink, on the other hand, needs small amounts of water at much more frequent intervals. On larger properties or smaller properties with kitchen extensions, the length of pipe runs to outlets which are in frequent use for small volumes of water could make supply from a central storage system uneconomical. If this is the case the system should be split and a point-of-use water heater installed where it is needed. The hot-water programmer to the main system should be altered to switch on the storage system at those times when it is required.

## Secondary circulation

Cylinders with secondary returns would be plumbed up as normal, but there are constructional limitations on some types of unvented storage cylinders which makes the provision of a conventional secondary return impossible. However, it is still possible to use them on systems where secondary circulation is specified.

The control layout would be as for a conventional unvented storage system but with the inclusion of a special type of non-return valve after the cylinder check valve.

This special type of non-return does not conform to BS 6282: Part 1 as it is not spring-loaded but fitted correctly it would prevent crossflow. The decision whether or not to leave out the BS 6282: Part 1 check valve (B) would be left to the unit manufacturer whose decision, in turn, would be based on Water Research Council testing of the complete unit.

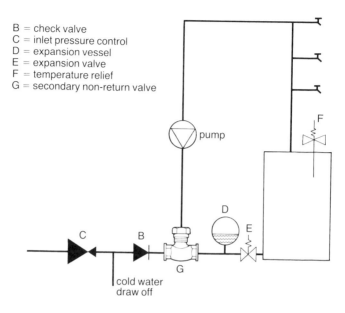

B = check valve
C = inlet pressure control
D = expansion vessel
E = expansion valve
F = temperature relief
G = secondary non-return valve

pump

cold water
draw off

Figure 39    *Secondary return via main feed*

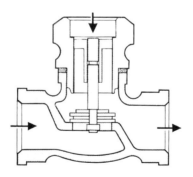

Figure 40    *Non-return valve incorporating secondary return connection*

The volume of the secondary circuit should be taken into consideration when sizing the expansion vessel. Provided a standard type of circulation pump is used, it should not interfere with the operation of the other controls.

## Unvented storage system recommendations

An unvented storage water heater is more versatile than a conventional system and can be located almost anywhere in a house or outside, provided it is protected from the elements and the working pressure is suitable for the application. However, there are a number of points that have to be watched:

(a)  Avoid excessive pressure drop. If the mains pressure is poor, or a number of simultaneous draw-offs are likely, poor flow rates could result.

(b)  Don't mix low-pressure taps and higher-pressure systems and vice versa. Excessive flow or poor flow would result. However, excessive flows can be cured by the use of flow regulators which can be fitted in or to conventional UK low-pressure taps.

(c)  Avoid down-feed installations with larger reticulation pipework than the supply pipework, especially on a vacuum-sensitive cylinder. If this cannot be avoided, ensure that the draw-off rate does not exceed the inlet rate by more than the vacuum relief capacity of the safety valve. If in doubt, fit an additional anti-vacuum valve.

(d)  If the hot-water distribution pipes are higher than the cylinder, airlocks can occur. Fit an automatic air vent at the high point.

(e)  When commissioning an unvented system, turn the water supply on slowly and never turn the supply full on until an outlet in the system has been opened. This should avoid over-stressing the unit and rapid oscillations of the inlet pressure control valve. In tank-fed systems with a high static head and *no* inlet pressure control valve it is possible to split the tank if too rapid an initial fill rate is attempted. If the cylinder distorts on initial fill turn the water supply off, drain the system and refer back to the supplier.

## Discharge/drain pipe recommendations

*The requirement*
Is to ensure that the hot water discharged from safety devices is safely conveyed to where it is visible but will cause no danger to persons in or about the building.

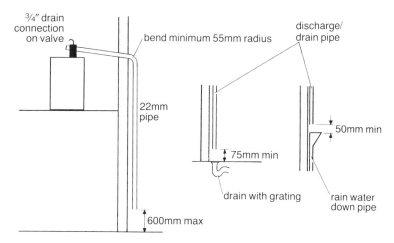

Figure 41   *Example of relief valve drain*

Added to the above is the limitation on drain pipe size and length and the number of bends.

The nominal size of the drain pipe should be the same size as the drain connection of the valve. The maximum length should be 9 metres (see additional notes below). The maximum number of bends should be three, but where it is not possible to meet this limitation the maximum length of the drain pipe should be reduced by 600 mm for each bend. Bends should be made with a radius of four and a half times the diameter of the drain pipe. An important additional requirement is that the relief drain pipe should be installed so that it drains not only itself but the valve to which it is attached, i.e. that it should fall continuously to its outlet.

Where a safe discharge point cannot be achieved within 9 meters of pipe, a drain pipe *one* size larger than the valve drain connection can be used to extend the length. A maximum distance should be no more than 13 metres or thereabouts.

(a) Discharge *not* to a drain but to ground (not a path). Dimension (A) would be a maximum of 600 mm and a minimum of 300 mm.

(b) Discharge to a rainwater down pipe, drain grating or purpose-made conduit including guttering. Dimension 'A' would be 75 mm minimum.

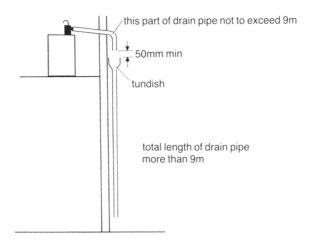

Figure 42   *Example of relief valve drain*

If the discharge/drain pipe is kept close to the wall and does not discharge on to a path (or lawn) where it could be expected that someone would sit or stand, the basic criteria of a safe visible discharge point will be met.

A point which must be borne in mind when selecting the discharge point is that it could be very hot water that is discharged. If it is decided to use the rain water down pipe or guttering, a check should therefore be made to see if the rain water piping is suitable.

(a)  Dimension 'A' as per example (1).
(b)  Discharge criteria as per example (1).

This type of installation would be applicable on taller houses or where the water heater is not against an outside wall.

With external discharges, tundishes freezing under low-flow conditions is a very real possibility. This is not a problem with a combined temperature and pressure relief valve that has a drain discharge relief component fitted in the drain part of the valve. It is, however, a problem if the temperature and pressure valve is of a type that has no protection fitted. In this case an internal airbreak/tundish must be used. The same applies, but more so, in the case of an expansion valve, as a small flow discharge would be the norm for this valve under the most common fault condition.

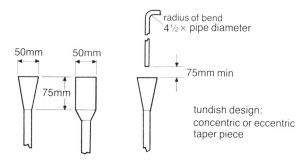

Figure 43   *Examples of relief valve drain via tundish*

In these two examples, the tundishes shown have been used externally to the property. The remaining examples are all based around tundishes used internally, and so it is relevant to give some recommendations on the size of the tundish for use with temperature relief valves.

The following comes from the New South Wales code of practice:

With regard to the location of the tundish in the house it is recommended that it be sited in a regularly used cupboard that is adequately vented. A minimum vapour relief vent would be of 15,000 mm$^2$, which is approx 12″ × 2″.

Figure 44   *Alternative heater and tundish positions*

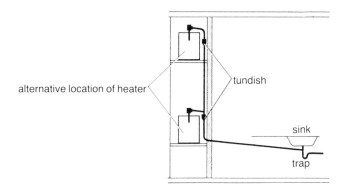

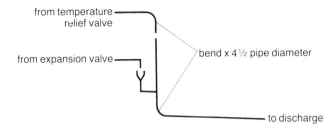

from temperature relief valve

from expansion valve

bend x 4 ½ pipe diameter

to discharge

Figure 45 *Combined drain from temperature relief valve and expansion valve*

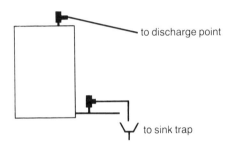

to discharge point

to sink trap

Figure 46 *Separate drains*

The possibility of blockage of the tundish must also be considered when locating the tundish. Blockage is not the only reason why a tundish could overflow. It must be realized that there is a pressure flow from the temperature relief valve and a gravity flow from the tundish. To stop the tundish overflowing, the outlet from the tundish must be one size larger than the pipes from the temperature relief valve.

In this layout the heater is fitted at a height to enable the drain pipe to fall continuously to discharge above the sink trap. The tundish would be sited so as to suit the requirements of visibility, for instance in a regularly used cupboard.

Up to now we have only considered the discharge from the temperature relief valve, which is covered by the Building Regulations. Provision has also to be made for the expansion valve. The expansion valve can be arranged to discharge into the same tundish (if used) as the temperature relief valve provided the rules over continuous fall are obeyed. If a continuous run of drain pipe is used and the discharge is readily visible the drain pipes from the temperature relief and expansion valves may be combined.

As the most likely fault condition calls for the expansion valve to operate and in a block of flats the amount of water discharged by an individual expansion relief valve is minimal and therefore hard to detect, it is advisable to treat them separately. The type of tundish used on an expansion valve can be smaller and neater than that for the temperature relief valve, and so can be permanently visible. Moreover, since it is cold water that would be discharged from the expansion valve, it would be permissible to discharge it into the bath.

This type of installation would be ideal for many normal domestic installations as well.

## Fault finding on unvented systems

*Read the manufacturer's instructions!* The following is intended as a general guide to fault finding on mains connected unvented systems.

*Symptom*
Water discharging from the expansion valve

*Questions*
(a) Is it only discharging when heat is being applied to the storage cylinder
or
(b) Is it discharging all the time?

If the answer to question (a) is yes, the discharge stops almost instantly the power is switched off, then what is happening is that as heat is applied the water expands and, if there is nowhere for it to go, the system pressure rises and operates the expansion valve.

To rectify this fault we must check the method that is used to accommodate the expansion water. Usually it is an expansion vessel which must have a charge pressure equal to the setting of the inlet pressure control device. If this charge pressure is too high or too low the expansion vessel cannot function properly. To check the expansion vessel charge pressure, an ordinary tyre pressure gauge can be used. First of all turn the water supply to the U/V unit off, and open an outlet to reduce the system water pressure to zero. The expansion vessel charge pressure can then be measured from the valve at the top of the unit. If it is too low the vessel can be recharged using dry air or nitrogen. An ordinary car foot pump can be used. If the vessel is overcharged, let the charge pressure down to the correct level.

If the answer to question (b) is yes (the water continues to discharge after the heat has been switched off), the expansion vessel is not at fault. For the expansion valve to discharge continuously there are two possibilities that must be considered:

1 The system pressure is at or above the setting of the valve.
2 The valve is faulty.

Possibility (2) is unlikely unless the system has been operating under faulty conditions for some time. If this is so it would be as well to change the expansion valve as, if the seating is damaged, it is not site repairable. Once the valve has been changed, find out why it operated in the first place.

Possibility (1) is much more likely. A simple check to see if pressure rather than a faulty valve is responsible is to open a tap in the system to discharge a small amount of water equal to the original discharge from the expansion valve. The expansion valve should then stop discharging, indicating that it is pressure rather than a damaged (scale build up) expansion valve seat that is the problem.

Pressure rise, other than through expansion, in a balanced pressure system can only be caused by the inlet pressure control valve ceasing to be drop tight. Some types of inlet pressure control devices allow for the replacement of the seating without alteration of the valve setting. Refer to the manufacturer's instructions for the information.

To rectify the system, replace either the complete valve or the valve seating.

On unbalanced systems it is possible that there is crossflow in the system, for instance higher cold-water pressure feeding through faulty terminal fittings. Shower mixer valves are the most likely culprit. To check this, turn off the cold-water reticulation system or simply open a cold-water tap. The expansion valve should then close.

*Symptom*

Water discharging from temperature and pressure relief valve (valve F).

*Questions*

(a)  Is it a high-flow intermittent discharge?
(b)  Is it a low-flow intermittent discharge?
(c)  Is it a continuous low-flow discharge?

If (a) is the answer, it is a temperature-actuated discharge. Check the energy input controls (thermostat and over temperature cut out). If this has been going on for some time the seating might be bridged by scale and the valve would then not shut properly, giving symptom (c) once the energy controls have been rectified: in which case, see on (c) below.

Symptom (b) is generally associated with systems that have no expansion valve and would indicate that the expansion vessel has an incorrect charge pressure. See first part of this section on expansion valve discharge.

Symptom (c) on a low-pressure system using a Reliance LTV model valve would generally indicate that the vacuum relief component has been breached or that the seating has been breached. Both faults could be cured by lifting the lever on top of the valve and allowing a full-flow discharge. Lower the lever slowly to avoid water hammer problems, and check to see if the discharge persists. If it does, change the valve.

Also in a system without an expansion valve, symptom (c) can be caused by crossflow or failure of the inlet pressure control device: in which case, see the earlier section on expansion valve discharge.

*Symptom*

Water discharging from drain relief device on expansion or T & P valve.

*Action*

For the drain relief device to operate there must be at least two things wrong with the system:

1  The drain line is partially or completely blocked.
2  The reason the valve operated in the first place

It should be noted that if too many bends or too long a pipe run is used in the drain line back pressure in the pipework could also cause operation of the drain relief device under discharge conditions. See drain discharge pipes.

To return to our original question of safety, it must be apparent that, given proper maintenance, pressurized hot-water systems are as safe as the traditional gravity-fed, vented hot-water systems.

Their obvious advantages are the higher pressures that can be obtained at fittings, particularly critical fittings such as showers, including the impulse type, which normally needs a minimum of 1 bar pressure to operate satisfactorily. They are a boon to buildings and dwellings that cannot provide an adequate head for 'normal' gravity working such as bungalows, top-floor flats, or those flats that have combination units of hot- and cold-water storage that are fitted in cupboards on the same level as the fittings to be served.

Cold-water storage for hot-water replenishment is no longer necessary, and this alone may be a major step in preventing legionella and other water-borne diseases. Its main disadvantage is, of course, the very lack of storage in the event of the main water supply's being cut off for any reason. However, it is unlikely that the provided storage would sustain the system for long in the event of heavy demand, so the loss, bearing in mind the number of times the mains supply is affected, is in fact minimal. In the event, for those readers who have cause for concern on this issue the sealed storage system offers the ideal alternative.

Care must be taken with the selection of specific fittings such as water-mixing valves that require a balanced supply to operate satisfactorily. Many mixing valves today incorporate a compensatory device to cope with pressure differences between hot and cold supplies, and only these should be fitted to pressurized systems when the cold water is supplied from storage. An alternative is to fit a local in-line pressure reducing valve in the hot-water supply adjacent to the fitting.

In all cases the minimum and maximum operating pressure for fittings must be checked to ensure that they are suitable for use in any particular system. This is very important with such appliances as washing machines and dishwashers, bidets with submersible jets, copper cylinders, boilers, ball valves, etc. Manufacturers' literature will contain this information, normally expressed in bars. For easy conversion, 1 bar is approximately 15 lb per square inch.

All work must be notified to the local water undertaking, and their approval of both the system design and the materials must be obtained. They will also require to be notified during and on completion of works so that they may inspect.

## Pressurized instantaneous water heater systems

The Chaffoteaux Combination Boiler has been briefly described in Chapter 3. This unit is designed for sealed systems only, and the expansion vessel, circulating pump, temperature and pressure gauges, safety valve, and electrical connection box are included in the appliance.

It is a non-storage heater, and the temperature of the delivery water is determined by the rate of flow as follows:

Table 9

| | | |
|---|---|---|
| Water flow rate raised 50°C (90°F) | 6.5 litres/min. | 1.4 GPM |
| Water flow rate raised 30°C (54°F) | 11.1 litres/min. | 2.44 GPM |
| Maximum temperature | 60°C | 140°F |
| Maximum pressure | 10 bar | 150 PSI |
| Minimum working pressure | 1 bar | 15 PSI |
| Gas rate – hot water | 2.58 M$^3$/H | 90.74 ft$^2$/H |
| Burner pressure | 10 M bar | 3.9 in. W/G |

The combination boiler can be used in conjunction with a hot-water storage cylinder as described in Chapter 6.

# 5

# Electric Water Heaters

In general there are two types of electric water heater: (1) the self-contained type consisting of storage cylinder, heating element, thermostat, and pipe connections, together with thermal insulation and outer case; and (2) the immersion heater or circulator consisting of a heating element and thermostat for fixing into an existing hot storage vessel.

It should be understood that the heating element is common to both types, so that the following information on heating elements applies generally. In the self-contained electric water heater the positions of the heating element and thermostat are fixed by the manufacturer, but the immersion heater or circulator can be fixed in any desired position.

## Electric heating elements

The heating or resistance wire in electric heating elements is almost invariably of nickel-chromium. There are two main types of elements distinguished by the fact that while one type can be withdrawn without the necessity for emptying the storage vessel, the other type cannot be removed without breaking a water joint.

The withdrawable type usually consists of a spiral of resistance wire mounted on a ceramic insulating former, the whole being inserted in a copper sheathing tube. In the other type the resistance wire is solidly embedded in a compressed insulating material within a flat blade or tubular sheath. The tubular sheathed variety usually employs a sheathing tube of about 12-mm diameter and can be bent or formed to almost any shape.

## Loading

The water heating elements that will be encountered in the water heating systems of the small house usually have loadings ranging from 500 to 3000 watts according to requirements.

## Heating surface

If it were possible to keep the heating surface of the water heating element free from scale, a very high loading of heating surface would be possible. In certain hard-water districts, however, where the heater may become covered with scale, a loading density that would otherwise be quite satisfactory will result in the surface temperature of the element sheathing becoming dangerously high, so high in fact that it may exceed the melting point of the tin with which the sheaths are usually coated. The scale does not decrease the efficiency of the heater – with electricity the output of heat must be proportional to the input of electricity – but it does obstruct the transfer of heat from element to water and thus leads to a building-up of the temperature of both element-sheath and resistance wire. Excessive sheath temperatures result in conditions favourable to corrosion of the sheath whilst excessive resistance wire temperatures lead to danger of wire failing by burning out.

The watts density may be as high as 50 watts/645 mm$^2$ in the case of the tubular sheathed variety, but usually lies between 10 and 30 watts/645 mm$^2$ in the case of the withdrawable type.

## Self-descaling elements

The usual shape of sheathed tube type of element shown in Figure 47 is such that its expansion and contraction during heating and cooling is sufficient to fracture and throw off some, if not all, of the deposit of scale. Ample space round and below the element should be allowed for the accumulation of scale which may, with certain kinds of water, fall off in large flakes.

## Action of water on the sheathing metal

Sheaths are usually made of copper and, as certain kinds of water are capable of dissolving copper, are usually tinned in order to prevent such action.

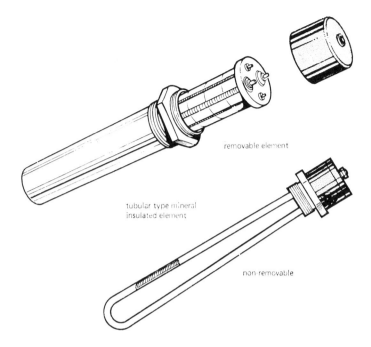

removable element

tubular type mineral
insulated element

non-removable

Figure 47    *Immersion heater*

In hard-water areas, the scale, as it is shed from the element by expansion and contraction, often takes off the tin with it, and in time the element may be completely de-tinned. Such action is hastened by overheating and softening of the tin coating.

The life of a heating element depends very largely upon the type of scale that is formed, and it is consequently advisable to take advantage of the local experience of the Electricity Board in deciding the type of heater to use in any particular area.

## Thermostats

The type of thermostat used in water heating is of quite simple design. It consists of a tube and rod of metals having different thermal coefficients of expansion, and the relative movement of these two pieces of metal is made to operate the switch portion of the instrument.

Thermostats should comply with the appropriate BS DESIGN:

Section 2B, and must be of suitable capacity to deal with the loading of the heating element.

Where the supply of electricity is AC, by far the greater majority of thermostats have micro-gap contacts with some kind of device which gives the contacts a quick 'make and break' action.

In breaking the circuit the contacts are moved only a very short distance apart, hence the term 'micro-gap'. This distance in itself is not sufficient to extinguish the arc that is set up as the circuit is broken. The extinguishing of the arc is done automatically by the alternations of the supply when the pressure during the cycle reaches zero; this happens 100 times a second. The contacts themselves are relatively large in size and thus cool the arc to such an extent that it is prevented from re-striking when the voltage reaches its maximum figure again.

The micro-gap thermostat is sometimes used on a DC supply with a condenser of one or two microfarads' capacity connected across the contacts, but this practice is not recommended by the makers.

Another type of thermostat which is sometimes employed makes use of a mercury tube which is tilted by the action of the bimetallic rod; the mercury in the tube making and breaking contact.

Mercury tube thermostats are suitable for either AC or DC but are not so compact in size as the micro-gap type and must, of course, be installed the proper way up and be in correct alignment.

## Thermostat differential

The word 'differential' is used to describe the number of degrees between the temperature at which a thermostat switches the supply off and the temperature at which it switches it on again. Other things being equal the differential depends upon the length of the thermostat stem. Common values are from 5 to 10°C for lengths up to 300 mm and 3 to 5°C for longer stems. The effect of a deposit of scale on a thermostat is to widen the differential.

There is no particular object in having a very small differential in water heating as there is no need for the temperature to be controlled very precisely. It will, of course, be appreciated that the smaller the differential, the more frequently the heating element will be switched on and off. On the other hand, if the differential is too large the temperature of the water when drawn off just before the thermostat is due to cut in will be unduly low and the output of hot water will thus be reduced.

A thermostat is affected by the average temperature of the whole of its operating length and thermostats that are fitted horizontally in hot-water vessels function rather differently from those that are fitted vertically.

If a long thermostat which extends practically the whole length of a storage vessel is fitted vertically, the temperature at which it operates will be in effect the average temperature of the water in the vessel. A short thermostat fitted vertically will be affected only by the water in the lower or upper half of the vessel, depending upon whether the thermostat is fitted from the top or the bottom. Consequently, with vertical fixing, the longest thermostat that can be accommodated is the best in every case.

If small quantities of hot water are drawn off at frequent intervals from a storage vessel fitted with a vertical thermostat, it is quite possible for the water at the top of the vessel to be boiling, although the mean temperature, which is the temperature that affects the thermostat, is lower than the temperature for which it is set.

When the thermostat is fixed horizontally, it will obviously be affected only by the temperature of the layer of water with which it is surrounded. If used as it normally will be with a horizontally fixed heating element, it will operate as soon as the temperature of the body of water above its own level reaches the cut-out temperature because the horizontal arrangement of the heater tends gradually to raise the temperature of the whole body of water above its level. It will thus be seen that the temperature marked on the dial of a thermostat will be approximately correct if the thermostat is fixed horizontally in conjunction with a horizontal heating element, but if it is fixed vertically the temperature of the water at the top of the vessel will probably be in excess of that shown on the dial.

The setting of a thermostat should always be checked before any installation is handed over owing to the possibility of the instrument having been damaged during transit. In hard-water districts the thermostat setting should not exceed 60°C. Higher settings are permissible in soft-water districts, but the setting should not be higher than is necessary to ensure a satisfactory supply of hot water, in order to avoid unnecessary heat losses.

## Position of the heating elements

Heating elements may be fitted in three different positions in the hot-water storage vessel, i.e.:

(a)  Horizontally through the side.
(b)  Vertically through the top.
(c)  Vertically through the bottom.

In each case the heating element is fitted internally into the storage vessel and the amount of heat actually transferred to the water will be the same however it is fitted. There will, however, be a considerable variation in the way in which the water is heated and in the temperature of the water at various levels in the vessel.

*Horizontal entry*

If the heating element is fixed horizontally from the side (see Figure 48A) there will be a tolerably rapid and general circulation of the water within the vessel, with the result that in a given time a large volume of water is heated through a small number of degrees. This means that there will be a relatively small difference in temperature between the top and bottom of the vessel and there will be a tendency for the whole content of the vessel to be gradually heated. Water that is below the level of the heating element will remain practically unheated and consequently the heater should be fixed low down in the vessel.

With this arrangement of heating element, it is usual for the thermostat to be fixed horizontally and slightly above the level of the heating element. When in this position it will switch off the heating element as soon as the layer of water in which it is fixed reaches the temperature for which it is set.

When the heating element is cut out, the temperature of the water at the top of the vessel will be slightly higher than the cut-out temperature, and the layer of water between the level of the heating element and that of the thermostat will be at a slightly lower temperature.

The water below the heating element will be practically unheated and it would be clearly useless to fix the thermostat below the level of the heater.

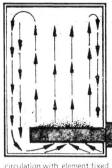

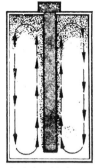

circulation with element fixed
horizontally

circulation with element
fixed vertically from
the top

A

B

Figure 48   *Position of elements*

The mounting of the heating element and thermostat in one head simplifies fixing because only one hole in the storage vessel has to be provided and in practice this arrangement is satisfactory.

### Vertical top entry

If the heating element is fixed vertically from the top as in Figure 48B it must be long enough to extend sufficiently far downwards to heat the required volume of water, as water below the level of the heater will not be heated. In this case, the water heated by the element rises vertically and as it will be in contact with the heater all the way to the top, it is obvious that each portion of the element will heat still further the ascending column of hot water. This means that a relatively small quantity of water is in circulation and that this small quantity of water will absorb the whole output of the heating element with the result that hot water will collect in a layer at the top of the storage vessel, there being a considerable temperature difference between the water at the top and bottom of the vessel.

As time goes on the depth of the layer of hot water increases until the whole of the water above the level of the bottom of the heater is heated. It is thus seen that by this method of fixing, a small quantity of hot water is obtained in a relatively short space of time.

When the heating element is fixed vertically from the top it is usual for the thermostat to be fixed in the same position, and the length of the thermostat should be proportional to the length of the heating element. If the length of the thermostat is much shorter than the heating element, the heating element will be switched off before the water below the level of the thermostat is fully heated.

The thermostat will cut out when the average temperature of the water surrounding it reaches the cut-out temperature, and a high temperature at the top end of the thermostat will be counteracted by a low temperature at the bottom.

*Vertical bottom entry*

If the heater is fitted vertically from the bottom of the vessel, the way in which the water is heated will be a compromise between horizontal fixing and vertical fixing from the top. If the heating element is long and extends nearly to the top of the vessel there will be little difference between this arrangement and vertical top entry. On the other hand, if the heating element is short and does not extend far above the bottom of the vessel, the heating effect will not be very different from that of the horizontal arrangement except that there will be rather more tendency for a layer of hot water to be formed at the top of the vessel.

As in other cases the thermostat will normally be placed in the same position as the heating element and should be as long as possible. If the thermostat is very short, drawing off a relatively small quantity of water will cause the thermostat to cut in and it is possible that the amount of heat added to the water before the thermostat cuts out again will exceed the amount of heat in the water drawn off. If this is so, continual drawing of small quantities of hot water will gradually build up the temperature at the top of the vessel and may lead to boiling.

## Self-contained water heaters

The term 'self-contained' is used to distinguish the complete factory-made assembly of vessel, heater and thermostat together with its insulation and outer case from the installation where an immersion heater or circulator is fixed on site into an ordinary hot storage vessel that is usually part of an existing solid-fuel hot-water supply system.

Self-contained electric water heaters should comply with BS

3456, Section A13, and BS 843 which lays down details of size, performance, and screwed connections for piping.

It is advisable to consult the attractive technical literature issued by manufacturers of water heaters before deciding on the type to use for any specific purpose.

Self-contained electric water heaters can be classified broadly as:

(a) 'Non-pressure' or 'open outlet'-type which are controlled from the inlet side and supply one point only.

(b) 'Pressure'-type heaters which will work under pressure from a feed cistern and are intended to supply one or more taps.

(c) Cistern-type water heaters incorporating a self-contained cold-water cistern arranged for direct connection to the cold-water main and serving one or more taps.

(d) Two-in-one water heaters provided with two heating elements and serving one or more taps. This type is designed primarily for installation in close proximity to the kitchen sink.

## Non-pressure type heaters

Non-pressure type heaters are fitted with open outlets and have the controlling tap on the inlet side so that they may be connected directly to the cold-water mains.

The top of the container is usually vented with the double object of preventing pressure building up should the outlet become obstructed, possibly by scale, and of preventing the formation of a vacuum through the action of the draw-off pipe. Figure 49 shows a typical 'open outlet' sink heater incorporating an anti-siphonic cold-water inlet pipe which prevents the contents of the vessel being drawn back into the cold-water mains.

As water expands approximately 4 per cent in volume when heated through a temperature rise of 80°C, dripping will take place from the open outlet of a non-pressure type heater unless some means are employed to prevent it.

Various forms of anti-drip devices are employed, one being a siphonic trap formed at the top of the outlet pipe as in Figure 50, so that when the tap is turned off, the level of the water in the

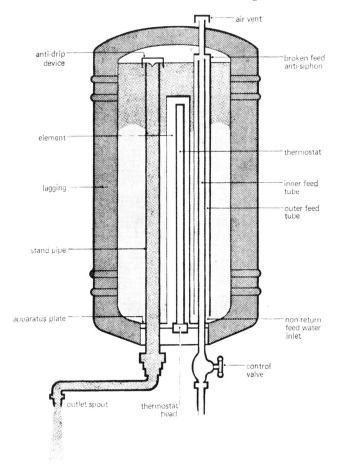

Figure 49   *Open outlet sink heater*

container drops slightly to allow for subsequent expansion without dripping from the outlet. This, of course, means that when the tap is turned on there will be a slight delay before water flows from the heater and that water will continue to flow for a short time after the tap is closed.

The satisfactory working of such a device depends to a great extent upon the flow of water being maintained at a constant figure and consequently it is usual for a restricting device to be fitted to the inlet tap.

Some water authorities insist on a siphonic anti-drip device

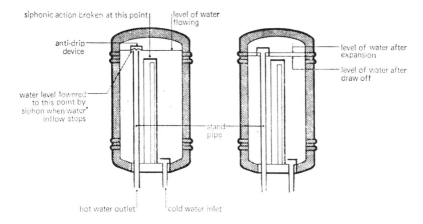

siphonic action broken at this point | level of water flowing

anti-drip device

level of water after expansion

level of water after draw off

water level lowered to this point by siphon when water inflow stops

stand pipe

hot water outlet | cold water inlet

Figure 50  *Anti-drip device*

being provided, but others who recognize the fact that with the siphonic anti-drip device the user cannot draw very small quantities of water from the heater and that the siphon is apt to

Figure 51  *Water heater with air-seal outlets*

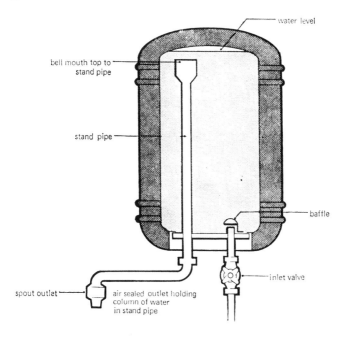

water level

bell mouth top to stand pipe

stand pipe

baffle

inlet valve

spout outlet

air sealed outlet holding column of water in stand pipe

become choked with scale in hard-water districts, permit single-point heaters to be connected provided that they have an air seal fitted to the end of the spout as in Figure 51. This type of heater has a clear waterway at the top of the standpipe and, in action, is completely filled with water up to the spout. The construction of the air seal keeps air from ascending the standpipe and thus prevents displacement of the water.

Another design is made with the ejector device shown in Figure 52 which consists of an anti-drip chamber inside the heater adjacent to the cold-water inlet. When at rest this chamber is filled with water approximately equal in content to the expansion of the whole of the water in the cistern. When the inlet valve is open, the incoming water exerts a suction upon the contents of the chamber and empties it. When the inlet valve is closed, the water in the heater finds its way back by gravity into the chamber

Figure 52   *Water heater with ejector anti-drip*

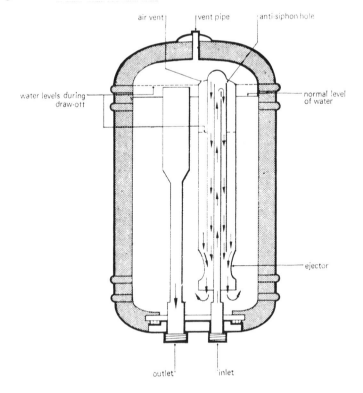

which, when filled, reduces the level of the water in the heater well below the standpipe. It is impossible, therefore, for the water heater to drip, provided the waterways to and from the anti-drip chamber remain clear. As the water in this part of the heater is comparatively low in temperature, there is little danger of scaling even when hard water is used.

## Pressure-type heaters

Pressure-type heaters are designed to work under the head from a cold-water feed cistern at high level provided this does not exceed 18 m and to supply any normal number of taps.

Figure 53 shows a typical pressure-type heater. The smallest multipoint heater in general use is the 55-litre size in view of the

Figure 53   *Pressure-type water heater*

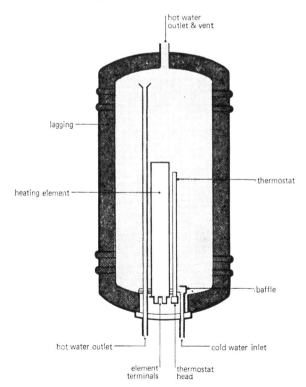

*Figure 17   Pressure-type water heater*

fact that this is the smallest size capable of giving one bath.

Pressure-type water heaters are controlled from the outlet side and, consequently, no anti-drip device is required.

## Cistern-type water heaters

These heaters are also suitable for supplying any normal number of taps. They consist essentially of a pressure-type heater fitted with a ball-valve feed cistern at the top of its casing. A cistern-type heater therefore forms a complete hot-water system in itself, needing no external vent pipe and being suitable, subject to the water authority's requirements, for direct connection to the main. It must, however, be fixed above the level of the highest tap

Figure 54   *Cistern-type water heater*

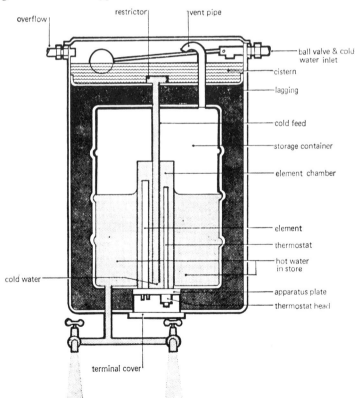

which it has to supply. Owing to the internal pressure being limited to the small head of water provided by the feed cistern, the storage vessel can be made in rectangular shape, thus reducing the projection from the wall, a useful feature where space is limited.

There are two types of cistern heater:

(a)  Constant volume and varying temperature type.
(b)  Constant temperature and varying volume type.

The first, shown in Figure 54, operates in precisely the same way as a pressure type heater.

The second type works on the principle of restricting the flow of cold water into the heater to an amount that can be heated immediately to whatever storage temperature is desired or, in other words, by heating the water to the required temperature as it is admitted. The stored hot water is obtained not by displacement by cold water but by emptying the storage vessel so that the

Figure 55   *Cistern-type water heater*

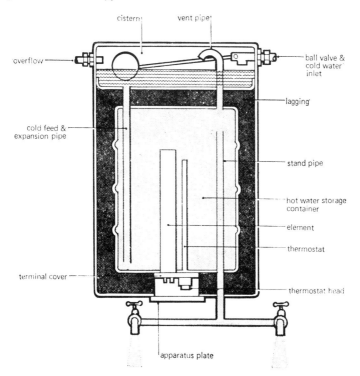

water level in the vessel falls as water is drawn off. With this type of heater the draw-off pipe is taken from the bottom of the storage vessel. Such heaters must be designed so that the heating element is always surrounded with water and an arrangement whereby this can be done without reducing the useful storage capacity of the vessel is shown in Figure 55. The heating element is housed in an inner chamber arranged in such a way that the chamber remains full of water whatever the level of the water in the storage vessel itself. This type of heater never runs cold so long as it is switched on, but when the stored hot water has been drawn off the flow will be reduced to almost a trickle.

## The two-in-one heater

This heater is of the pressure type and is manufactured in two different sizes, 90 and 136 litres. The special feature about this type of heater is that it has twin thermostatically controlled

Figure 56   *Two-in-one water heater*

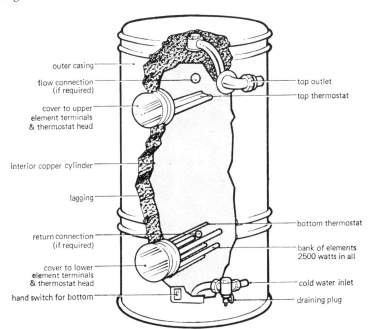

elements, one of which, usually of 2500 watts loading, is placed in the conventional position at low level in the storage vessel whilst the other is fitted at such a level that it heats approximately 28 litres of water. Figure 56 shows a typical two-in-one heater.

In normal operation the upper heating element is kept switched on permanently under thermostatic control while the lower element is switched on only when a larger quantity of water is required for baths or clothes washing.

This arrangement reduces the consumption of electricity in two ways. First, the heat losses from the storage vessel are reduced because of the smaller quantity of water that is kept at the storage temperature and, secondly, economy in the use of hot water is more or less enforced.

With the two-in-one heater constant hot water on tap throughout the house is provided, but the amount of hot water that is normally available at any time is limited to approximately 28 litres. This is ample for general purposes, but it will be appreciated that where the quantity is not restricted there will always be a tendency for more to be used.

## Inlet baffles

All types of water heaters have some kind of device such as illustrated in Figure 57 to prevent the incoming cold water from cooling the storage unduly. The baffle usually employed is fitted at the cold-water entry so as to deflect the incoming water to the bottom of the storage vessel.

Figure 57   *Inlet baffles for water heaters*

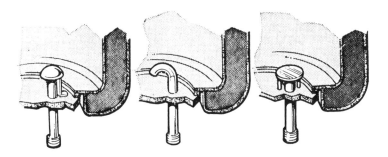

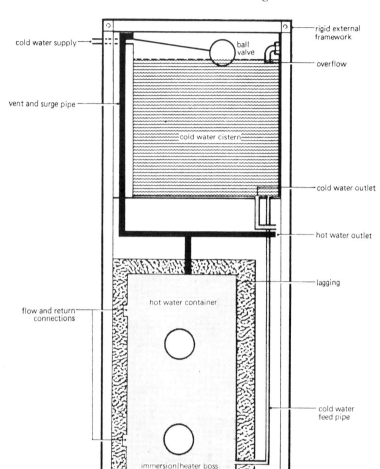

Figure 58   *Packaged plumbing unit*

## Packaged plumbing unit

A self-contained unit for providing both hot and cold water for bath, basin, kitchen sink and w.c. comprises a cold-water cistern, hot-water container and pipework built into and within a rigid framework (see figure 58).

This unit is based on a design developed by the Research and

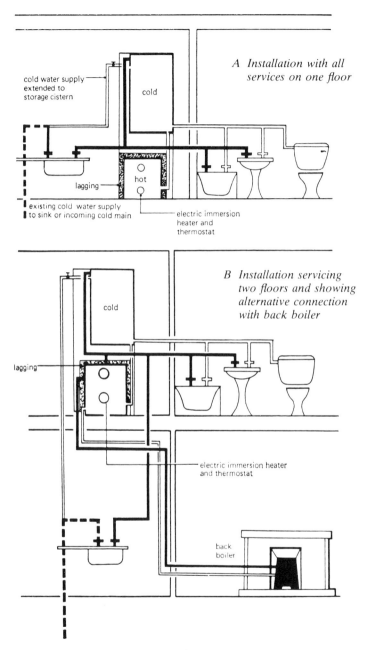

A   *Installation with all services on one floor*

cold water supply extended to storage cistern

cold

hot

lagging

existing cold water supply to sink or incoming cold main

electric immersion heater and thermostat

B   *Installation servicing two floors and showing alternative connection with back boiler*

cold

lagging

electric immersion heater and thermostat

back boiler

Figure 59   *Use of a packaged plumbing unit*

Development Group of the Ministry of Housing and Local Government, and is acceptable for the appropriate Government grants.

It is readily handled up stairs and through doorways. It may be installed in a cupboard, against a wall, in a passage or convenient corner, or incorporated in the structure of new buildings.

The plumbing unit needs connecting only to the mains water supply, electricity supply and services as shown in the accompanying diagrams (see Figure 59A and B). There are alternative capacities available with a basic design of a 230-litre cold-water storage cistern supplying a 115- or 230-litre hot-water storage cylinder.

# Water heating and Economy 7

Economy 7 is a scheme providing cheap electricity between the hours of 12.30 a.m. and 7.30 a.m. It operates on one meter which has an automatic changeover from the normal unit rate to the economy rate at the prescribed time and switches back seven hours later.

There is at present a considerable difference in cost between the two unit rates, and to get the maximum benefit from Economy 7 the customer must be able to heat a substantial proportion of his water on the cheap night-time tariff.

The system should therefore be designed with sufficient storage capacity to cater for the normal needs of the maximum size of family likely to live in the dwelling. An average family uses about 136 to 159 litres of hot water daily.

It is not unusual for new homes which are to use Economy 7 to be provided with a 226-litre storage cylinder. If this supply of water is exhausted during the day some water will have to be heated at the higher daytime rate.

A number of self-contained water heaters designed specially for use with Economy 7 tariff are available.

## Multiple installations

Although it is important to provide sufficient water heated on the night-time rate to cater for the main demand of the following day, it is not essential to provide all this water for the main storage vessel. As with any electrically heated water system, additional 'on the spot' heaters may be placed to avoid long 'dead legs' or difficult plumbing situations.

## Two-heater cylinder

Undoubtedly, the most economical way to provide adequate hot water for a family on the Economy 7 tariff is to fit a cylinder of around 226 litres' capacity. However, there may not be sufficient space to install a cylinder of this size, and it may be necessary to limit the cylinder to a maximum of 159 litres. If the household will not generally require more than 159 litres of hot water a day, this will be quite satisfactory. If it is only necessary to heat the tank on day-time electricity to supplement the night-time charge, say once a week for the extra demand on laundry day, the average cost of electricity per unit will be near the night-time price per unit.

With only one immersion heater at the base of the storage vessel, the whole water content would be heated each time the electricity was switched on. This system would become un-economic if the supply of hot water heated during the night ran out frequently, and day-time boosts became a regular require-ment.

To ensure that only a limited amount of water is heated on the day-time rate, a second immersion heater may be fitted to the tank in a position where it will heat about 56 litres of water, before its own thermostat switches off the supply of electricity. The second immersion heater may also be manually controlled, but it will generally be more sensible for the user to leave it on all the time, since its built-in thermostat will keep it switched off until it is needed. As long as there is more than 56 litres of hot water left in the tank from the previous off-peak night-rate charge this second heater will not switch on.

It is recommended that there shall be a minimum difference of 10°C between the settings of the thermostats of the upper and lower immersion heaters. In soft-water areas the thermostat on the lower immersion heater should be set at 70°C and the thermostat on the upper immersion heater at 60°C. In hard-water areas these settings should be reduced by up to 10°C.

The minimum amount of hot water required for a bath is selected as being 56 litres – the usual last requirement of the day. The following table indicates the approximate proportions of night-time electricity, and day-time electricity used with a two-heater cylinder. The high-level element will be located to provide 56 litres of hot water in each instance. These figures are intended as a guide only, and are the result of practical trials, with the high-level heater under thermostatic control only. It will be seen from the table that even a 226-litre cylinder may sometimes need 'topping up' on day-time electricity. Since the larger cylinder could occasionally heat all of its 226 litres on day-time electricity if it were not fitted with a second heater, it could be said to be the instance where it is most important to install a second immersion heater, if there is any possibility of 226 litres being insufficient.

General Rule: Install a second immersion heater whenever possible in any cylinder if there is any possibility of the total capacity being exhausted early in the day.

| Size of tank (litres) | Low level element % night units | High level element % day units |
|---|---|---|
| 113 | 60 | 40 |
| 136 | 70 | 30 |
| 159 | 80 | 20 |
| 226 | 95 | 5 |

## Immersion heaters for a two-heater cylinder

The upper immersion heater in a two-heater cylinder will need to keep up with demand, as far as possible, and should therefore be rated at 3 kilowatts. This will provide the fastest possible response.

The lower heater, however, has a period of approximately 7 hours in which to heat a tank full of water. In most installations, no water will be drawn off during this time, and it will only be necessary to fit a heater sufficiently large to heat the whole contents of the cylinder in, say, 6 or 7 hours. Some margin of

| Size of tank (litres) | Rating of low level element for Economy 7 |
|---|---|
| 113 | 1.5 kW |
| 136 | 1.5 kW |
| 159 | 1.5 kW |
| 226 | 3.0 kW |

error must be allowed for standing losses during this time.

## Good installation

Because water heated at night on the Economy 7 tariff must still be hot enough for a bath in the evening, a water heating installation for this tariff must be well designed. All losses must be minimized, particularly those from mixing and single pipe circulation. The storage cylinder must be very well insulated.

In any installation where hot-water storage has to stand for a protracted period heat losses are inevitable. These will be accelerated when cold water enters the cylinder following hot-water draw-off. Care must be taken to ensure that the cylinder upper level temperature does not drop below 50°C. This is the minimum. Ideally, as stated before, storage temperatures should be maintained at 60°C to ensure delivery temperatures of at least 50°C at draw-off points.

# 6

# Water Heating by Gas

The main advantages of using gas for water heating are:

1 It is clean, creates no dust or mess in the house and it conforms with the Clean Air Act. As it comes straight from a pipe it needs no storage space.
2 The hot flame of gas properly regulated heats water very fast. The instantaneous heaters provide hot water in an endless supply. The water in storage systems quickly reheats as the supply is drawn from the tank.
3 Automatic controls permit close regulation of the fuel used and allow adjustments to meet the needs of a family.
4 High efficiency of appliances reduces running costs.
5 A gas water heater may be fixed at the very point the hot water is required enabling a certain flexibility in house design and a reduction in the cost of plumbing work.

## Selection of a heater

The output of a water heater is relative to the given rate of water flow and temperature rise, and although the supply of water at any required temperature is continuous, the speed of delivery is limited by the capacity of the heater. For example, although a larger heater will give hot water more quickly than a smaller one the latter will give greater efficiency and at less cost for small intermittent demands. The main consideration in selecting a heater is that it will provide the required amount of hot water to meet the demands of the family at peak times.

### Instantaneous heaters

These heaters will give a continuous flow of hot water at any time within a few seconds of turning on any tap to which the heater is connected. The temperature of the water is variable according to the temperature of the cold feed, most heaters being designed to give a 26°C temperature rise. Models are available which control the water flow to give a constant outlet temperature. The flow is limited at the maximum temperature available at any time but it is usually possible to obtain a greater flow at a lower temperature without any drop in the efficiency of the heater.

Apart from the small consumption of the pilot jet, gas is used only when the water is flowing from a tap. It is the most economical form of heater and the single point type has the lowest running cost of any gas water heater. Capital and installation costs are generally less than for storage heaters giving equivalent service but the high gas rate might possibly require the fitting of larger services pipes and meters.

Since the satisfactory operation of an instantaneous heater depends on a minimum flow of water it is essential that the pressure head of the water supply is adequate. This will vary with each type of appliance and the help of the local gas regional office should be sought.

Thermostatic controls are fitted to some models ensuring that the water is supplied at a constant temperature. The correct adjustment of instantaneous heaters is more critical than that of other types and this means regular servicing is necessary to their functioning.

Some models have balanced flues which eliminate the need for a conventional chimney. Balanced-flue heaters are room sealed and must be fitted to an outside wall. The air enters and the exhaust gases pass out through the balanced flue which is completely sealed off from the room itself. The heater is therefore unaffected by room ventilation and exhaust gases cannot enter the room.

It is important to know that only balanced-flue heaters must be used for new installations in bathrooms.

Single-point heaters over a sink or washbasin must always be fitted within an arm's length (about 0.6 m) of the draw-off point. Where this is not possible the delivery may be piped to an open nozzle fixed over the sink or basin.

Instantaneous water heaters for the bathroom can be provided with an extended swivel spout to serve the bath and the washbasin provided it does not exceed 0.6 m in length. The heater must of course be fitted with a balanced flue.

See Chapter 3 for a description of the Chaffoteaux Combination Boiler for instantaneous water heater duty.

## Storage heaters

These units comprise a heater combined with an insulated storage vessel that will retain heated water over a period of time against a future demand. The volume of hot water they can supply is limited by the capacity, so the size of the unit must be selected carefully to meet peak demands. If it is properly sized it is unlikely that its full capacity will be used at any one time but should this occur, then the good stratification obtained with a gas storage water heater ensures that small quantities of hot water are available again within a short time. This also applies when the heater is first lit. They can be either floor standing or wall mounted and must generally be connected to a cistern supply. Some types are available with an integral feed cistern and provided these are fitted above the level of the highest draw-off tap, it will not be necessary to fit an additional feed cistern.

Sink storage heaters are available for fixing to the wall above the sink and discharge by a swivel spout of not greater than 0.6 m in length.

## Gas-fired direct water storage cylinders

These have been described in Chapter 3. The Hamworthy, or similar, cylinder with underside gas burner is ideally suited to virtually all domestic situations where a hot-water storage capacity is required. Where a cold-water cistern cannot be provided the hot-water cylinder may be fed from the mains supply pipe as previously described.

## Gas circulators

These are in effect miniature gas boilers usually fitted near the hot-water storage cylinder. A circulator is an economical way of converting an existing water system to gas or of providing an entirely new system. Thermostatically controlled, they can also be provided with an economy valve which can be set either to heat the whole tank, or keep a few litres of water at the top of the storage cylinder constantly hot.

## Gas boilers

Several types of gas boilers are available and they are ideal for a busy household needing a great deal of hot water and especially so when the prime purpose is space heating.

The modern gas boiler is a sophisticated appliance being fully automatic in action and capable of being set to follow a specific programme to the clock, making it economical to run.

The boiler indirectly heats the water in the storage cylinder whilst circulating hot water to the radiators around the house.

A modern innovation is the gas back-boiler which is an ideal replacement for the solid-fuel back-boiler. It is possible to install a very modern gas-fire and boiler with the minimum alterations to the existing pipework. The boiler is capable of providing reasonable central heating as well as hot water for domestic usage. The fire and the boiler are separately controlled and they may be used together or independently.

New design principles have enabled gas boilers to be housed in a very limited space without reducing their capacity to provide hot water. They can be wall mounted in the kitchen or anywhere else. They must of course be fixed to an outside wall.

# Installation of gas appliances

The installation of gas piping and appliances must be carried out by skilled men who have a complete knowledge of the technical and safety requirements involved. They must have the proper tools and testing equipment, and the householder should know that under the Gas Safety Regulations 1972 it is in fact specified that only competent persons shall carry out gas installation work.

# CORGI

The Gas Corporation in conjunction with a number of Trade Associations has set up a voluntary organization to maintain proper standards in all gas work. It is known as the Confederation for the Registration of Gas Installers and has assumed the abbreviated title of CORGI. Every plumber who contracts to do gas installation work should be registered under the scheme and householders should insist that any gas work carried out in their homes is undertaken by CORGI members only. Lists of members can be inspected at the Gas Showrooms. Every Registered CORGI gas installing business undertakes to perform gas installation and service work complying with British Standard Codes of Practice, Building Regulations and Gas Corporation requirements.

## The Gas Act

Plumbers and householders should know that the Gas Act became law on 1 January 1973 and Regulations under this Act give powers to designated officers of the Gas Corporation to enter premises and cut off a supply if in the opinion of these accredited officers an installation is unsafe.

## Relevant codes of practice

Reference should be made to the following Codes of Practice when installing gas supply and appliances.

*COP 331 Pt. 2 1974*    Installation of pipes and meters for town gas. Part 2: Metering and meter control.

*COP 331 Pt. 3 1974*    Installation of pipes and meters for town gas. Part 3: Installation pipes.

*BS COP 5871 1980*    Gas fires/boilers not exceeding 60 kw and back boilers with independent gas fire (2nd family gas).

*BS Cop 5376 1976*    Selection and installation, gas space heating (1st and 2nd family gas).

*BS COP 5546 1979*    Gas supply for domestic hot-water systems (2nd family gas).

1st/2nd family gases refer to natural gases (propane, methane/ North Sea).

## Seven points for water heater installation

1 The site should be well-ventilated and convenient for connection to an existing flue where this is applicable. It should be noted, however, that if the appliance is to replace an existing water heater in a bathroom, only room-sealed models should be used.
2 It is preferable to keep the pipe run to the main point of usage as short as possible to minimize heat losses.
3 The existing gas installation pipes should be checked for soundness and adequacy of supply, and where applicable the flue should be checked for sufficient 'pull', correct size and suitable termination.
4 The head of water should be sufficient to operate the appliance as laid down in the manufacturer's instructions.
5 The appliance should be fixed securely, and after connection to the gas and water supplies the installation should be tested for soundness. The gas and water rates should then be adjusted to conform with the maker's instructions.
6 Check that the appliance controls are operating correctly.
7 Finally, instruct the customer on the use of the appliance, referring to the manufacturer's instructions.

## Eight points for space heater installation

1 Before installation, check the chimney (flueway) for 'pull'. This can be done by holding a match near it. The flue is operating satisfactorily if the flame is drawn into the flueway. If it burns steadily, check for restrictions in the flue; if the flame blows back, the flue is subject to down draught and may need modifications.
2 Make sure that the chimney has been swept if the fire is being sited into an open fireplace and remove or wedge fully open any damper, register plate or canopy in the fireplace opening. Make sure that there is adequate clearance at the rear and/or sides of the gas-fire flue spigot (refer to the manufacturer's instructions).

3  Check that the existing installation pipes are sound and are of adequate size.

4  When fixing the appliance a filling-in or closure plate must always be fitted. This is designed to improve the performance of the appliance. It consists usually of two openings, the top one being for the flue spigot and the lower one to provide a flue break and to assist in room ventilation. Plates are usually obtained from the appliance manufacturer or else the type is specified in the manufacturer's fixing instructions.

5  Space heaters must stand on a non-combustible material which extends 152 mm either side of the space heater and 304 mm from the back of the fireplace and is at least 15 mm thick. If the space heater is being wall mounted there should be a distance of at least 228 mm from the burner manifold to the floor level.

6  The space heater must be fitted level using the correct type of fittings and pipe as specified by the local Gas Board.

7  Test the finished installation for soundness and check the gas rate using the meter test dial and a stopwatch, and ensure that this is in accordance with the manufacturer's instructions. The gas rate can be calculated using the following formula:

$$\text{Gas rate} = \frac{\text{Heat input}}{\text{Calorific value of the gas}}$$

8  Instruct the customer on the operation of the appliance.

## Five points for cooker installation

1  The siting of the appliance must be carefully considered, bearing in mind the following points:
   (a) It should be in a well-ventilated position.
   (b) There should be sufficient natural light to ensure that it can be used with safety.
   (c) There should be sufficient clearance to ensure that it can be used without obstruction, in other words there should be room to open the oven door.
   (d) It should be in a convenient position for use by the customer, i.e. near to preparation space.

2  Follow the maker's instructions carefully when assembling the

appliance. Check that the existing installation pipes are sound and are of adequate size.

3 When connecting the appliance use only recommended fittings, ensuring that there is a means of disconnection. The appliance must be fitted level – this is important for all appliances but particularly in the case of cookers where pans of liquid will be placed on them.

4 When the appliance has been connected again test the installation for soundness. Check that the appliance controls are functioning correctly and test any concealed supplies on the appliance for soundness, i.e. the grill and oven supplies.

5 Before leaving the premises ensure that any pilot lights have been relit and, above all, explain the operation of the appliance in detail to the customer. Suggest that the customer operates the appliance after instruction to ensure that he or she understands the explanation; and give the customer the manufacturer's customer instruction leaflet for future reference. It is advisable not to leave the fitting instruction with the customer as this may tempt do-it-yourself enthusiasts to attempt any servicing or repair work.

## Gas supply

The gas meter should be capable of passing the full consumption of the heater, in addition to the requirements of all other appliances, and it is preferable to run in an independent supply from the meter to the heater. If this is not possible it will be advisable to ensure that the heater receives the first delivery of gas from the meter, and that the pipe sizes are adequate to give a full gas supply irrespective of demands. Gas supply pipes which run between joists under floorboards should be in hard metal and not in copper tube or plastic pipes, which could easily be penetrated by a nail.

A full-bore gas cock should be fitted close to appliances to facilitate maintenance without interrupting the gas supply to other parts of the house.

## Cold-water supply

To ensure a constant pressure and flow of water to a water heater it should be fed by a single pipe from the storage cistern of the house. In certain circumstances mains water supply may be used but it is always advisable to consult the local water undertaking on this point.

The most important considerations are to see to it that:

(a) Pipe sizes are adequate to pass the required water flow at the prevailing pressure.
(b) Pipe runs are as short as possible.
(c) A gate valve, or fixed jumper stopcock, of an approved pattern is fitted on the cold-water inlet as close as possible to the heater to isolate it when repairs are necessary.

## Hot-water draw-off

The pipe run should be as short as possible to avoid heat loss and waste of water. The most used draw-off point should have the shortest run. In no case should the maximum pipe run exceed 8 m.

Single point heaters have open outlet spouts and on no account should any additional fittings or other obstruction be connected to the outlet side of the heater. Any such connection could result in damage to the heating body.

## Ventilation

The ventilation requirements for heater compartments and various types of rooms are under constant review by technical committees concerned with gas installation. As knowledge of this complex subject increases, amendments to the regulations are made. It is advisable for the installer to keep himself up-to-date with the regulations issued from the Gas Corporation Research and Development Department.

## Flues

The installer is very much concerned with flues and should have a sound knowledge of their basic principles because of the safety factors involved.

In any fuel-burning appliance the hot products of combustion, being less dense than air, will have a tendency to flow upwards in a flue or chimney. With a modern high-efficiency gas water heater, so much heat is removed from the product of combustion that it is of the utmost importance to plan the flue in such a way to conserve fully the residual heat of the product and to ensure that no resistance is offered to the free flow of flue gases. A permanent state of down-draught can be set up which the heater may be unable to overcome due to the excessive cooling of the flue gases – for example, in a long length of flue exposed outside a building.

*The flue terminal*
The flue terminal should offer the minimum resistance to combustion products and have a free area equal at least to twice the nominal area of the flue.

There should be outlets on opposite, or all sides except where the design is such as to provide extraction under all wind conditions.

It should have effective protection against entry of birds, leaves, rain or snow, and the minimum dimension of any opening should be not less than 6.35 mm or greater than 14.3 mm.

*Construction of the flue*
The material of the flue must be resistant to temperatures up to 95°C. It must have low conductivity and be resistant to acids. This precludes the use of untreated metal flues.

The flue must be run as far as possible under cover to minimize cooling.

The flue must be of the specified size and there must be no reduction in the cross-sectional area at any point. The ideal shape is circular and this should be adhered to as far as is practical.

The interior surface of the flue must be smooth and free from projections, and there should be a rising tendency along its entire length and sharp changes of direction avoided. The horizontal length of the flue should not exceed 1.20 m.

If the flue is of excessive length or if for any reason the flue gases are likely to become cooled below the dewpoint, provision must be made for disposal of the condensate.

Excessive dilution of the products of combustion with cool air should be avoided and this precludes the use of common flues, open tees or any form of extra air inlet.

In the case of persistent down-draught or where static conditions are encountered, the flue installation must be re-designed to conform to the foregoing principles.

*Balanced flues*

The development of the balanced flue has enabled the fixing of water heaters in positions not suitable for the more conventional type of appliance. The balanced-flue heater does not need a draught diverter nor any additional flue equipment inside the room. It therefore presents a neat appearance and is more easily fitted where headroom is limited.

Balanced-flue terminals should not be fitted in any position which would allow combustion products to feed back through adjacent doors or windows. These positions include, immediately beneath eaves or a balcony, at a re-entrant position on the face of the building, or adjacent to any projection on the face of the building.

Other advantages are:

(a) They can be installed in positions not suitable for conventional water heaters.

(b) The terminal is fairly inconspicuous, and a vertical flue pipe is not required. This is particularly important in new housing and has been welcomed by architects.

# Water heaters as auxiliaries

A multi-point heater may be connected to a boiler system as an alternative and continuous source of hot-water supply during the summer months, and is similarly available for immediate use whenever the boiler is inoperative. The combined installation of heater and boiler is simple as the same hot-water draw-off piping may be used for both units, the isolation of one system from the other being effected by the operation of one or more stopcocks or a two-way valve. The heater is not, however, suitable for operation as a booster and must therefore be supplied with cold water. Whichever cold- and hot-water systems of supply are adopted the expansion pipe must always remain open to the atmosphere, and to the hot-water storage tank when the boiler is in use, but must be capable of isolation from the heater when the

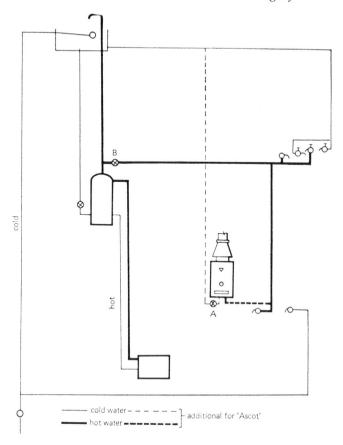

Figure 60  *Water heater as an auxiliary*

latter is in operation. An isolating stopcock ('B' in Figure 60) must therefore be incorporated and a second stopcock ('A' in Figure 60) is required to turn off the supply to the heater when the boiler is in use.

When it is proposed to fit a gas water heater as an alternative to a solid-fuel heating system, a careful study of the existing plumbing should be made and the layout sketched accurately after all the pipes have been traced and their purpose determined.

## Water supply

The cold-water supply to the heater should be taken from the cold-water storage cistern by means of a separate pipe.

If the cold-water feed to the hot-water cylinder is of adequate size then the supply to the heater may be taken from it if the branch connection is made at least 300 mm above the top of the cylinder and an open vent pipe is provided at the highest level of the cold feed and discharged over the c.w.s. cistern.

Similar anti-back-siphonage measures are required if the heater feed is taken from the cold-water down service to the bathroom fittings. This connection should be made only to a falling length of pipe and at a point at least 300 mm above the top of the highest bathroom fitting. Under no circumstances connect to a horizontal run of cold-water down service pipe if it is at a level below the top of the bathroom fittings.

The heater may be connected to the incoming cold-water mains supply pipe providing the following conditions are observed:

(a) That permission of the Local Water Authority is obtained.
(b) That no connection is made between the outlet of the heater and any pipe connected to any tank. This necessitates the fitting of independent taps for the heater delivery.

Whichever system is employed, the existing expansion pipe must always remain open to atmosphere and to the hot tank or cylinder, but the draw-off pipe must be capable of isolation from the expansion pipe and from the whole boiler system.

The correct procedure for the change-over from one system to the other should be fully understood by the consumer, otherwise an incorrect sequence may be carried out, resulting in unsatisfactory operation of the heater when, for example, both stopcocks are left open.

## Simple boiler system for the supply of domestic hot water

The incorporation of a multi-point heater to operate as an alternative to the existing system can be arranged by following the lay-out shown in Figure 60 provided the hot-water feed pipe from the boiler to the kitchen sink is 22-mm nominal bore.

1 The heater is supplied direct with cold water via a 22-mm distributing pipe from the cold-water supply tank.
2 A stopcock 'A' of approved pattern is fitted to this pipe close to the inlet of the heater.

3 The outlet of the heater is connected by a short length of 22-mm pipe to the 22-mm draw-off pipe from the boiler system, but close to the sink tap.

4 A second cock 'B' is fitted to the boiler system draw-off pipe between the expansion pipe and the first branch, thus isolating all hot draw-off pipes from the boiler system when the heater is put into operation.

To change from Boiler to Heater:

1 Close stopcock 'B'
2 Open stopcock 'A'

To change from Heater to Boiler:

1 Close stopcock 'A'
2 Open stopcock 'B'

Alternatively the heater may be connected by adopting the following methods:

1 The 22-mm cold-water supply is taken from the cold feed to the hot cylinder at a point above the level of the top of the hot-water tank.

2 A stopcock 'A' of approved design is fitted close to the inlet of the heater.

The following alternative hot-water draw-off should be utilized where the hot-water feed pipe to the kitchen sink is 15-mm nominal bore.

1 A separate 22-mm pipe is run from the outlet of the heater to a second hot-water tap at the sink.

2 From this point a 22-mm hot-water pipe is run to a two-way cock situated on the hot-water draw-off pipe between the hot-water tank and the nearest draw-off branch. Care must be taken to see that the two-way cock is fitted in such a way as to give the correct alternative paths.

The auxiliary system is still widely used; and there are many dwellings where both a boiler system and a gas multipoint heater are already installed and occupiers may see the advantage of combining systems as described here.

This, however, does raise the question of providing hot-water storage capacity for multipoint water heaters. The comparatively low output from an instantaneous water heater may not satisfy

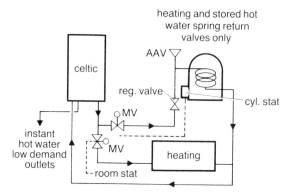

Figure 61    *Combination water heater – cylinder supply*

the demands of a growing household, and there may be space problems preventing the installation of a larger boiler to supply a hot-water cylinder.

Happily, this problem can be resolved by using the Chaffot-eaux Combination Boiler. This balanced-flue heater takes up no more space than an ordinary instantaneous heater and, normally, it has two functions: to provide heating and to provide instantaneous hot water. It can have a third, which is to supply hot water in the case of high demand through the use of an indirect cylinder. This is particularly useful in properties with more than one

Figure 62    *Combination water heater – cylinder supply*

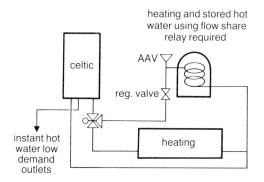

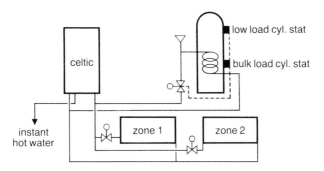

Figure 63   *Combination water heater – cylinder supply*

bathroom and, perhaps, basins in several bedrooms, and, say, a large kitchen. This would indicate a high demand for hot water; some of it in bulk, some in small, but frequent, quantities.

Hot water produced indirectly through the cylinder can be used to satisfy high simultaneous-demand outlets – bathrooms, for instance – while the benefits of the heater's high efficiency in providing small quantities of hot water can be fully utilized in kitchens, cloakrooms, and so on.

Figures 61, 62, and 63 show various layouts for combined heating, cylinder, and instantaneous hot-water installations. It is recommended that only high-recovery cylinders are used and, according to the circumstances, a special saturated heat exchange in an indirect cylinder may be desirable.

Separate time and temperature control over hot water generated by this system can be achieved by the use of either two-port or three-port valves of a flow share, or priority pattern (see notes to Figures 61, 62 and 63).

Tall, small-diameter cylinders should be used where the demand is likely to vary between small and large loads; for instance, when part of the household are away for irregular periods.

When using the instantaneous side of the appliance the use of non-return valves and/or loose-jumpered stopcocks should be avoided. If a non-return valve is fitted to the incoming supply then an expansion vessel with a capacity of at least 0.16 litres *must* be fitted in the domestic hot-water circuit.

If a combination (or instantaneous) heater is to replace an existing cylinder storage system, it is essential that all redundant pipework is stripped out and dead legs eliminated. In properties where there are multiple draw-off points on different levels consideration should be given to the use of non-return valves in the secondary hot-water system to avoid active dead legs. No non-return valve should be less than 1 metre (3 ft) above the top of the appliance and, ideally, should be as close as possible to the terminal fitting.

Whatever the installation, full anti-back-siphonage precautions must be taken, and pressurized systems must be provided with vacuum breakers wherever applicable.

# Metric units for gas

|  | Imperial unit | Metric unit |
|---|---|---|
| 1. *Pressure* | inches water guage (in. wg) | millibar (mbar) |
|  | pounds per square inch (p.s.i.) | bar (bar) |
| 2. *Standard reference conditions for gas volumes* | | |
| Temperature | 60° Fahrenheit (60°F) | 15° Celsius (15°C) |
| Pressure | 30 inches of mercury (30″ Hg) | 1013.25 mbar |
| Condition | saturated with water | dry |
| 3. *Sales unit* | Therm | One hundred megajoules (100 MJ) |
| 4. *Calorific value* | British Thermal Units per cubic foot (Btu/cu. ft) | megajoules per cubic metre (MJ/m$^3$) |
| 5. *Heat rate* | British Thermal Units per hour (Btu/hr) | kilowatt (kW) OR, where information may be required to calculate running costs, megajoules per hour will be given *in addition to* kilowatts – e.g. kW (MJ/h) |

# 7

# Domestic Central Heating

The requirements of human beings vary considerably when it comes to personal comforts and they are influenced by age, sex, state of health, personal preferences and prejudices. The heating engineer must be guided by his customer in deciding the temperatures for the various parts of the house in which he is installing a central heating plant.

However, there are general guidelines and it is accepted by the heating trade that 21°C is a suitable temperature for the living room, 13 to 16°C for bedrooms, 16 to 18°C for bathroom and 16°C for most other areas of the house.

In trying to achieve comfort conditions to his customer's requirements, the heating engineer will take into account the type of house construction, its situation, local climatic conditions, the state of doors, windows and the roof within the house, because all these factors affect his recommendations in the matters of heating form and the appliances to be installed.

The engineer will make a careful survey of the house and from his findings and measurements he will make elaborate calculations. In these calculations he is mainly concerned with heat losses. In this matter, the wise householder will concern himself with insulation before he decides on the installation of any form of central heating. The golden rule is to keep the cold out of the house rather than warm it continuously once it has penetrated the holes, openings, cracks and surfaces. Half the cost of heating in most houses arises from poor or below standard insulation. Anyone who has installed a good double glazing system will understand this all-important point.

The reputable heating engineer will be prepared to advise the householder, and from the results of his survey be able to discuss the best methods of heating the house. He will make recommendations on (1) full-house heating by which every part of the house will be heated constantly to a specified temperature, (2) part-house heating which, as the term implies, will give specific temperatures to selected rooms or parts of the house and (3) background heating by which the whole or part of the house is heated and the temperature maintained at a lower level, supplemented by local heat for bodily comfort.

There is a wide variety of choice today from which to select the type of heating installation to suit individual needs. There can be no 'cheap' installation and householders are advised to seek only the services of qualified installers. Beware of the door-to-door salesman and the man who wishes to work in the evening or at the weekend. People have suffered a great deal from the unqualified charlatans who call themselves plumbers and heating engineers without any right to the titles.

# Small pipe central heating – gravity systems

In this chapter we concern ourselves with those forms of heating commonly known as 'smallbore' and 'microbore' (also known as 'minibore').

It is not possible in this book to cover the subject in detail because central heating in any form is a specialized subject and serious study is required if any plumber is intending to set himself up as an installer. The following is intended as a guide only and would-be designers and installers should read and digest the valuable technical literature obtainable from the British Standards Institution, Institution of Heating and Ventilating Engineers, Institute of Plumbing, British Gas Corporation, Electricity Council, Copper Development Association and others.

The original purpose of developing the smallbore heating system was to heat a dwelling of up to 140-m$^2$ floor area. It is nevertheless possible to install the system in premises having a much larger area, provided the installation can be designed round a centrally placed heating unit, making it possible to design the piping layout to include more but shorter pipe circuits.

Briefly, the smallbore heating system comprises a boiler to which radiators are connected by means of small diameter tubes, and heated water being forced through the tubes and radiators by means of a specially designed pump or circulator.

To ensure proper temperature control, an automatically operated mixing valve is used in conjunction with a by-pass pipe. This mixing valve, which is actuated by the outside air temperature, thus ensures that the heat output from the radiators is controlled under such weather conditions, without affecting the boiler temperature. Such an arrangement ensures that adequate heat is available in the boiler to give an abundant and constant supply of domestic hot water.

## Domestic hot-water supply

On the domestic hot water side, it is essential to use an indirect copper cylinder coupled to the boiler by an independent gravity circuit. This circuit is normally run in 22 mm or 28 mm copper tubing and is entirely separate from the radiator runs, apart from the permissible case of a towel rail being fitted.

The purpose of using an indirect cylinder is that it will act as an accumulator to absorb any excess heat in the boiler, in the event of a sudden reduction in the required heating load and until the boiler damper control in a solid-fuel system slows down the burning rate.

Returning to the heating side of the installation, it is generally only necessary to use 15 mm-diameter copper tubes in the heating circuits apart from where the circuits run into a common flow and return. At such points these common mains would be increased to 22 mm.

The use of small-diameter copper tubes in the heating mains means that there is no need to hide them from view, as they are neat in appearance and can be run so as to blend with the surroundings. The pump allows great freedom in deciding pipe runs, thus permitting easy installation without costly structural work or damage to interior decorations. Furthermore, a considerable saving in pipe length is achieved because it is not necessary to rise above the floor levels on which the radiators are to be fitted; this, in turn, results in lower heat losses from the distribution system and a consequent saving in fuel.

There are now on the market materials other than copper tube which are eminently suitable not only for smallbore central heating but for all water service pipes, both hot and cold. The most notable of these is probably CPVC – notable because it is a plastic which, until recent times, was considered unsuitable for hot water.

CPVC (chlorinated polyvinyl chloride) systems have been extensively used in America since 1965, where the Genova Company led the way. With this background of experience, Hunter Building Products Ltd, in England, began the manufacture of Hunter Genova CPVC at their London factory in 1979. The material has an Agrément Certificate and a British Standard is expected to be published in the near future.

The inertness of CPVC, coupled with the smooth bore of the pipe and fittings, almost completely eliminates scale build-up within piping systems. Because CPVC is not a conductor of electricity, problems of galvanic corrosion do not occur and the piping system will never suffer from oxidative corrosion. CPVC is not recommended for use as gas pipes.

High standards of quality control are enforced in the manufacture of these products and in addition piping assemblies are regularly submitted to hydrostatic and thermocycling test procedures. In these, pipe and fittngs must be able to withstand a sustained hydrostatic pressure of 12 bar (172 p.s.i.) for 10,000 hours (416 days) at a temperature of 82°C without leakage; and pipe and fittings are subjected to a pressure of 7 bar (103 p.s.i.) with the temperature of the water alternating between 82°C and 15°C for 10,000 cycles, taking a total of 55 days.

Hunter Genova pipe is available in 15, 22 and 28 mm sizes and a full range of fittings enables connections to be made easily to other materials, such as copper and iron pipes. CPVC pipe is joined to fittings by solvent welding, a simple technique which gives a bond almost stronger than the pipe itself.

Tests by independent laboratories have shown that the CPVC material and the Nova Weld C solvent cement used in the Hunter Genova system pass all the National Water Council requirements for toxicity, taste, and resistance to microbiological growth.

CPVC, like all organic materials, will burn in a conflagration. However, its flash ignition temperature is some 110°C better than normal uPVC, a material that has wide acceptance in the building industry.

Systems are designed in the normal way, with the following points in mind. Never connect CPVC directly to a boiler or other heat-generating source. Come away from the boiler with a 380-mm (or more) length of copper pipe to allow the intense heat to

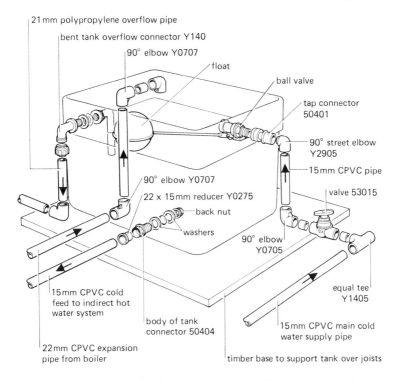

21 mm polypropylene overflow pipe

bent tank overflow connector Y140

90° elbow Y0707

float

ball valve

tap connector 50401

90° street elbow Y2905

15 mm CPVC pipe

valve 53015

90° elbow Y0707

22 x 15 mm reducer Y0275

back nut

washers

90° elbow Y0705

15 mm CPVC cold feed to indirect hot water system

equal tee Y1405

body of tank connector 50404

15 mm CPVC main cold water supply pipe

22 mm CPVC expansion pipe from boiler

timber base to support tank over joists

Figure 64  *How to plumb an expansion tank with Hunter Genova fittings*

dissipate. Similarly, do not let CPVC come close to articles which are likely to become very hot.

CPVC is not a conductor of electricity and so cannot be used for earthing.

CPVC is a pliable material with good insulating properties (water in Genova tube takes four times as long to freeze as water in copper pipes), but even so, care must be taken to protect it by lagging all external pipework or where pipework may be affected by frost.

In general, the strength of CPVC pipe is more than adequate to withstand treatment likely to be encountered in normal installations. However, it is not recommended that attempts be made to bend CPVC pipe substantially, and all changes in direction must therefore be made by using the appropriate fittings. This is easily done with Nova Weld C solvent cement and the appropriate Hunter Genova fittings. Solvent cementing should not be attempted in wet conditions or at temperatures below 0°C or above 40°C.

The pipe runs need not be laid with a constant rise or fall for ventilating purposes. Inverted loop circuits, such as may be met in running round the door casings, may be used, without fear of air-locking the system. Air-cocks fitted at such points are used only during the initial filling up of the installation. Generally, single pipe circuits connecting two or more radiators are used, the temperature difference between the flow and return being of the order of 11°C. With such a low differential the radiators are all maintained at more or less the same temperature. Obviously, the number of circuits used in any given installation will vary according to the type of dwelling involved, the positioning of the rooms and whether it is a house or bungalow. In general, the normal house would have two, or at the most three, major pipe circuits with perhaps a short loop feeding a single radiator as might be required in a hall or cloakroom.

To ensure that the full benefit of a smallbore heating system is obtained, it is advisable to insulate the roof space so as to avoid loss of heat and consequent waste of fuel. The domestic hot-water storage cylinder should be fitted with an insulating jacket and where, as in the case of a bungalow, any pipes are run in the roof space, they must be protected against heat loss.

# Design

In designing a smallbore heating installation the following procedure should be adopted:

1  Decide the required room temperature and then calculate the heat losses through walls, floors, ceilings, etc.
2  Plan radiator positions and pipe runs.
3  Calculate the friction losses in pipe circuits and determine from these the pump size.
4  Size the radiators and boiler.

Room temperature requirements may vary from client to client, but generally the room temperatures recommended in British Standard Code of Practice CP 3006, Part 1: 1969 will find ready acceptance. Thus the following temperatures can be taken as giving comfort conditions:

21°C for living-rooms.
13°C for bedrooms.
16°C for hall and staircase.

Where a room is used only intermittently and for comparatively short periods, such as a dining-room, it is advisable to adopt a design temperature of 21°C, thus ensuring a quicker warming-up of the room concerned. Generally with ordinary domestic premises there is sufficient heat available in the kitchen from the boiler itself and the various hot-water pipe mains and flue pipes to maintain an adequate temperature. Where an outside boiler is used provision must be made to warm the kitchen and in this case 18°C will be found to be a satisfactory temperature.

The foregoing temperatures are those required to give full central heating comfort. Where, however, open fires are to be used with the smallbore heating system providing only background heating, 16°C may be taken as the design temperature for living-rooms. With the room temperatures decided, the heat requirements can now be calculated, starting off by taking the difference between outside and selected inside temperatures to give the temperature difference rise, the outside temperature always being taken as 1°C.

The heat loss through walls, ceilings, floors and windows is then dealt with. The amount of heat lost through these surfaces is known as thermal transmission, which in turn can be defined as the amount of heat in watts (W) which will flow through 1 m² of a particular type and thickness of construction when the temperatures of the air adjoining the inner and outer faces differ by 1°C. This is called the 'U value' and for the convenience of the heating designer complete tables giving the U values for most forms of construction are available from the British Standards Institution and the Institution of heating and Ventilating Engineers.

The formula for calculating heat transmission through a structure is $H = U(ti - to) \times A$, where $H$ is the heat transmission, $U$ the transmission coefficient of the structure, W/m²/°C, $ti$ is the inside air temperature, $to$ is the outside air temperature and $A$ is the area of the structure.

Air changes must be allowed for when calculating heat losses and this applies particularly to rooms with large open fireplaces, which will withdraw air at least three times that necessary for normal ventilation purposes. In houses having central heating it will be found that the room temperature will drop several degrees when an open fire is lit. The use of a modern fireplace with an adjustable restrictive flue throat can keep the flow of air to chimney to a minimum in such circumstances.

In the case of 'open plan' types of houses it is generally necessary to assume a room temperature of 21°C and maintain this for calculation purposes throughout the whole house.

Having completed the calculations for each room they are added together to give the total heat losses throughout the house. The total is defined in watts.

The next step is to plan the radiator positions and pipe runs. This is a matter that requires some care. Wherever possible, radiators should be sited under windows. The advantages gained thereby are as follows:

They make use of areas not normally occupied.

They avoid the soiling of decorations by dust-laden convection currents.

They overcome down-draught.

They provide better temperature distribution through the room.

In some cases, particularly in existing premises, built-in furniture may make siting of radiators under a window impossible, and they may have to be mounted on or against a full wall. Under these conditions, one should always fit a canopy across the full length of the radiator top to prevent staining of the walls and ceilings by dust-laden convection currents.

In preparing a plan of the pipe runs, it should always be borne in mind that the shorter the pipe circuit the better. The plan itself should be drawn to a sufficiently large scale for all pipe runs, with the position of valves clearly indicated. Later as each pipe circuit is sized, the pipe diameter should be marked on the drawing. If an isometric projection is drawn, quantities may be read off from it.

## Friction losses

With the pipe circuit, radiators and valves marked on the drawing, the next step is to calculate the friction losses through the pipe runs, to ensure that they come within the pressure head range of the available and suitable types of pumps. It is here that the choice of copper tube, as a suitable material to use, becomes a major factor. The smooth internal surface, allied to a slightly larger bore than the equivalent iron tube, gives a much lower friction factor. Further, as the manufacturing tolerances for copper tubes are much less than is the case with iron pipes, greater accuracy is obtained in calculating friction losses. Added to this, the copper tube has a slightly smaller outside diameter, making for neater appearance.

To arrive at the friction losses in the pipe circuits, these are each measured separately to give the actual length of pipe in each circuit, to which is added an allowance of one-third to cover the frictional resistance of fittings and valves, etc. While this may seem an arbitrary method to adopt it is indeed one that has been found to give very satisfactory results.

## Heating load

The heating load will be taken by the radiators and it will be equal to the total heat losses, less the heat emitted from exposed pipework in the various rooms. Tables are available to enable calculations to be made of the heat emission from runs of pipe of differing diameters but broadly speaking, emission from pipe and radiator surfaces depends on the difference between the mean temperature of the water in the system, and the room temperature. In forced circulation systems the temperature drop will be between 11°C and 16°C and this differential affects pipe sizing insofar as it determines the rate of water circulation and, consequently, the frictional resistance of the circuit.

By adopting the higher differential of 16°C the water circulation will be lowered thereby reducing friction. On the other hand, this differential means a lower difference between the water temperature in the system and the room temperature, and this could call for larger radiators in certain rooms and the possible need of 22 mm connections. For this reason the 11°C is generally adopted for smallbore systems. This lower differential ensures that the radiators at the extreme ends of the circuit will receive water at higher temperatures, and also allows a rapid heating up of the system from cold.

Frictional resistance is an important factor in pumped circulations and in the event of the resistance of a circuit being greater than the available circulating head, the circuit must be redesigned to give a smaller total length. Alternatively, the designer can regroup the radiators to give an additional circuit, thus spreading the heating load. As already mentioned it might be advisable to increase the pipe size to 22 mm for part of the main circuit. On the other hand, the higher differential of 16°C might solve the problem because the effect of this would be to lessen the frictional resistance in the main circuit.

Where two or more circuits share common flow and return mains, the heating loads of the circuits served must be calculated and used to obtain the resistance of the common mains from the graph. Equally, the heating load of the common mains, by emission and any radiators they feed, must be divided proportionately between the circuits they serve.

The short connecting mains between the various radiator circuits and boiler are usually 22 mm tubes, except where there are four or more separate radiator circuits; in these cases, a 28 mm diameter tube should be used.

## Size of radiators

Finally, it is necessary to calculate the radiator surface area that each room requires and to choose the type most suitable for the purpose. To calculate the radiator surface for any room, first take the actual metre run of exposed pipe in that room and multiply this length by the emission factor. This figure is then subtracted from the total heat requirement of the room, which had previously been found. The remainder is divided by the radiator transmission factor for an average temperature difference between the water in the radiator and the ambient air, to give the total radiator surface required.

With the normal steel radiators, an average transmission factor of 23.8 W/m/°C may be accepted. Working with this factor and knowing the length of exposed pipe in the room, the required radiator area for a room with a heat loss of 2.344 kW and having 6.09 m run of exposed pipe, 3.8 $m^2$ of radiator surface would suffice.

Generally, the choice of the particular type of radiator used is a matter for consultation with the householder. Panel wall radiators are very popular if there is enough space available to accommodate the required length.

## Size of boiler

There is now only the boiler to consider. Whether it be gas-fired, oil or solid-fuel burning depends on the householder's preference but it must be capable of meeting the maximum demand likely to be imposed by the heating system, plus an adequate margin to cover the needs of the domestic hot-water supply. A minimum of 3.517 kW should be allowed for this latter, over and above the total central heating needs. The boiler must be fitted with a thermostat that is reliable in action, to ensure good control of the burning rate. It is recommended that the boiler manufacturer be consulted regarding any particular appliances.

Since the introduction of smallbore heating, a number of boiler manufacturers have devoted considerable attention to reducing the running costs of heating systems. The result is that today there are excellent clock-controlled boilers that are designed to operate separate circuits for day or night only as required. This is achieved by having two separate flow connections, one running to the bedrooms or night areas, and the other to the living rooms or day areas. By pre-setting the separate clocks on each of these circuits they are automatically switched on or off, thus providing heat in the required places at the appropriate times. The result is that with such installations a much smaller boiler is used and it therefore operates at a constant and high efficiency. As a case in point, where under ordinary conditions a boiler of 13.19 kW would be necessary, a clock-controlled boiler of 9.68 kW only would be called for.

## Pump and control equipment

Smallbore copper tube forced circulating heating systems can only work if the correct type of pump is used. There are a number of suitable makes available, and all of these are of the 'canned rotor' type, without glands between the motor and the impeller. The advantages of this form of construction are: (1) no possibility of water leaking out, and (2) as the bearings are water lubricated, no periodical oiling or greasing is necessary. The electric motor itself is of the squirrel cage induction type, powering a 3-speed pump with a wattage consumption depending on pump speed as follows: speed 1, 40 watts; speed 2, 65 watts; speed 3, 105 watts.

Grundfos Pumps market two models for domestic installations: the Standard Selectric Mark 2 UPS 15–50, suitable for the average house smallbore system; and the Super Selectric High Head UPS 18–60, for large boiler and high-resistance systems (low water content, microbore and automatic-valve radiators). The pumps work under a maximum pressure of 10 bar (147 p.s.i.).

Also available with these pumps are fittings to provide connection to iron or copper pipes, and isolating valves and reducers.

The motor and impeller are, to all intents and purposes, silent in operation, which is important when the pump may be required to run at night, though care should be taken in installation to avoid transmitted noise through pipework, which can be a constant source of annoyance.

*Circulator*

The circulator should, whenever possible, be installed in the return main. The reason for this is that it is then operating at a lower temperature than would be the case if it were fitted into the flow pipe and can, if need be, have cork blocks mounted underneath as a stand and to prevent vibration. With installations having heating mains at a level below that of the expansion tank which is less than the pressure head developed by the circulator, it should be fitted in the flow-pipe to avoid the likelihood of sub-atmospheric pressures in the high-level mains. Such conditions may sometimes be encountered in fitting heating installations in bungalows, where the pipe circuits may be run at or near ceiling level.

It is important to note that, because of the close fit between the impeller and the case, all parts of the installation should be thoroughly cleaned and flushed out to remove any swarf or other foreign matter likely to jam the pump or cause damage to the bearings.

*Electrical starting gear*

In dealing with the electrical starting gear, it is imperative that the push-button starter recommended and supplied by the pump manufacturers should be used. This is fitted with the correct current overload release to protect the field coils of the motor from possible damage by over-heating or burning out in the event of the impeller becoming jammed.

*Control equipment*

With a smallbore heating system using only a small amount of water working under forced circulation, a very large degree of flexibility is available. Because of this, individual radiators may be turned on or off to suit any given requirements. With the small amount of water used, and that under pressure, there is no long waiting period between turning on any radiator and that radiator reaching the correct operating temperature. However, it is desirable that some method of controlling the entire system in relation to the outside air temperatures should be fitted to every smallbore heating installation. Such form of control will ensure economic running of the system and at the same time provide a constant and adequate supply of domestic hot water. It may be thought that control by the boiler thermostat alone would be a satisfactory method to adopt. It cannot be emphasized too strongly that such a practice must be avoided, because if such control were used, the closing down of the boiler firing rate would equally cut the heat output to the domestic water side.

## Control methods

The ideal method of control is one that is fully automatic and works through a temperature-sensitive bulb fitted outside the house. A capillary tube runs from the bulb to a three-way control valve fitted to the flow-pipe from the boiler and a by-pass connecting it to the main return pipe. The temperature-sensitive element, being continuously in operation, opens or closes the mixing valve on the heating mains conversely with the outside temperature and thus maintains, within limits, the room temperature at a constant figure. The motive power to operate the control comes from the pressure differential across the pump. By using this type of control unit, all rooms are maintained at the correct temperature and localized air disturbances caused by open doors and windows in some rooms do not affect other rooms. The small additional cost of this piece of equipment should, it is claimed, be recouped over two or three heating seasons by reason of the expected saving in fuel costs.

An alternative method of control is to use room thermostats coupled to the pump, thereby controlling the amount of heat passed to the radiators. There are, however, a number of disadvantages attached to this, such as finding suitable positions for mounting and the cost of installing the necessary switch and electric mains wiring. Similarly, individual radiator thermostatic control would be expensive and would leave the heating mains 'alive' with a consequent waste of fuel.

The only other way of dealing with the problem is to install a three-way by-pass valve connected between flow and return mains, and to adjust the valve manually. This entails the householder altering the setting to meet outside temperature variations.

A variation of the three-way mixing valve is also available. It consists of an automatic three-way mixing valve, with a bimetal spiral in the upper part of the valve casing, controlling the movement of the double clack in the lower part, which either opens the inlet port or closes the return port, so that a mixed flow temperature can be selected and maintained.

## Isolating valves

It is advisable to provide an isolating valve on both the flow and return mains. This will allow the radiators and pipe circuits to be drained without shutting down the boiler and domestic hot-water supply side of the system. The valve on the flow main only may be closed in the event of wishing to shut down the central heating circuits. If the valve on the return were closed, there would be a likelihood of high pressure occurring in the heating system due to the expansion of water.

Lockshield valves should be mounted on the return main of all secondary circuits; this will enable the circulation to be reduced to the required rate and will also prevent 'short-circuiting' of the major circuits. The adjustment of the lockshield valves on the secondary circuits is carried out when the system is first put into use, so that with all the radiators working, the water in the return mains from all circuits is at the same temperature.

# Installation

The technique of installing smallbore copper tubes is a matter with which plumbers and heating engineers are familiar as part of their normal work. Copper tubing used for a heating installation is dealt with in the same way. It must, however, be realized that with a smallbore heating installation, most of the pipes are run on wall surfaces and are plainly visible. Under such conditions, the installing of pipe runs and fittings must be done in the neatest manner, so that the completed job is unobtrusive and harmonizes with the surrounding decorations. In a new house, it is preferable that the pipework should be done after plastering has been finished, but prior to the completion of the painting and decorating.

It is because of this need for neatness that light gauge copper tubes are so suitable. Copper pipes do not rust and painting is unnecessary. In addition, the ductility of the metal allows it to be manipulated with ease, whilst the strength of light gauge copper tube is more than adequate for the service it has to perform.

The smooth internal surfaces are important because of the low frictional resistance they offer to the flow of water.

From the decorative point of view, the smooth non-rusting external surfaces have much to commend them; they can be polished easily and readily take a plated finish, features that can be exploited to fit in with the surrounding decorative treatment.

## Joints

The jointing of the copper tubes may be carried out with either capillary soldered fittings or compression fittings.

In general, the type of joint chosen must not in any way restrict the bore of the tube, and in addition should preferably be so fixed to allow for easy dismantling. This last point is of particular importance where it may be necessary to provide additional circuits or radiators at a later date. It has been found that many people, when having central heating installed, try to save money by cutting down the number of radiators initially installed. In such cases, provision for the additional circuits can always be made by inserting tee-pieces at the required points and blanking off the branches.

## Clips

The stand-off type of clip should always be used and spaced at intervals of not more than 1.25 m. This type of clip holds the pipe off the wall approximately 0.10 mm and thereby prevents possible damage to paintwork through overheating. It allows easy cleaning of the pipes and gives sufficient room for painting the surface behind them.

Where inverted pipe loops are formed in passing over doorways and similar obstructions, experience has shown that it is not necessary to fit open vents at these points. Ventcocks should be fitted on any loop or circuit that cannot be cleared of air through the radiators, for use when first filling up the system. In the same way, draincocks should be fitted in the return main near to the boiler and also on any circuit run at a level below that of the boiler.

## Expansion cistern

As with every other hot-water heating system, a separate expansion cistern must be fitted from which cold-water feed is taken and connected into the return main close to the boiler. The cold-water.feed-pipe should be connected to the bottom of the heating return main by means of a 'U' bend, or taken in at the side. The by-pass connections should be made with swept tees. Expansion pipes should not be smaller than 22 mm diameter.

## Types of radiators

The type of radiator is a matter of individual preference. Consistent with its having the required heating surface, one or other of the many types of the wall, free standing, skirting panel or floorline patterns can be used.

Wall radiators should be mounted above the skirting and have at least 127 mm between the centre line of the bottom tappings and the heating main. It must be remembered that if the radiator is fixed too high on the wall, a higher temperature gradient between floor and ceiling will occur. Connections to radiators may be made either to the bottom tappings or to one top and one bottom tapping. A wheel-head valve should be fitted to the flow connection and a loose key, lockshield valve to the return connection on each radiator. Balancing of water flow through the radiators is achieved by adjusting the lockshield valve, while the wheel-head valve is used to turn the radiator on and off.

In designing an installation, the use of radiators with heat emission greater than 2.05 kW should, if possible, be avoided. Two small radiators to give the required heating surface would be better, otherwise with a large radiator the connections may have to be increased in size to 22 mm.

## Skirting heating panels

If it is desired to use skirting heating panels, care must be taken to see that the connections are fitted in such a way that by turning off the heat it does not interfere with the flow of hot water to heating units in other rooms. Heat emission data for skirting heating, convector heaters or similar units must be obtained from the manufacturers.

Where a pipe has to pass through a wall or ceiling a 28-mm copper or brass sleeve should be fitted after drilling the hole in the required position. Powered angle drills are available which enable clean neat holes to be drilled close in to the corner.

## Connections to the boiler

In connecting the return main to the boiler, it is essential that the stream of water returning under pressure is not injected into the return pipe of the domestic hot-water system. This could give rise to reverse circulation to the indirect cylinder. If there is only one return tapping on the boiler, a twin elbow or pitcher tee should be used and the lead to the heating main reduced to the required pipe size. Where it is more convenient to take both the heating and domestic flow mains from a single boiler tapping, a 35-mm pitcher tee with a reduced branch should be used to ensure an adequate supply to the gravity circulating primary side of the hot-water storage cylinder.

### Thermometers

Thermometers should be fitted, one on the boiler and a second in the flow-pipe past the by-pass and control valve. The latter will give the temperature of the water going to the radiators as distinct from the boiler water.

### Flushing

Finally, before the completed installation is put into service the whole system, boiler, pipework, cistern and radiators, must be thoroughly flushed out at least three times to ensure removal of swarf, filings and any dirt that may be present. This is a most important factor in ensuring a fully successful and trouble-free heating system. In this connection it must be remembered how necessary it is to remove cutting burrs when the tube has been cut to the required lengths.

If, as in the case of cast-iron radiators, it is necessary to paint them, it should be remembered that metallic paints reduce the heat transmission by approximately 15 per cent. With ordinary paints or enamels the efficiency is not affected.

# Micro and Minibore heating

Following development work during the late 1960s the Wednesbury Tube Company introduced their 'Microbore' system in 1968. The Copper Development Association had published details of the system known as 'Minibore' in 1967 and many hundreds of these systems were installed and those in service are said to have fully justified the claims made in the early stages, proving them to be efficient and economical both in materials and labour.

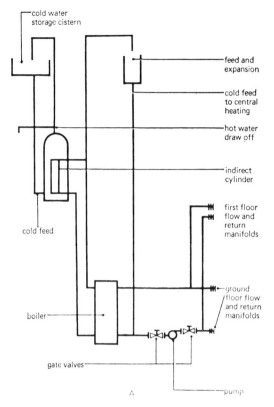

Figure 65    *Layout for a typical open-tank system*

The basic principles of microbore and minibore heating follow closely those of a standard smallbore heating system. In fact, the principles and practices laid down in the Standard Code of Practice for smallbore central heating installation should be followed.

There are two basic systems of this development in small pipe heating: (1) open tank (see Figure 65) and (2) sealed tank (Figure 66).

The low-pressure system is the most frequently installed of the two, although the pressurized system is becoming recognized now because of the higher temperatures that can be achieved using smaller heating units. Both systems employ 8-mm or 10-mm tubes on the radiator circuits and these are connected to flow and return manifolds formed in 22-mm or 28-mm copper tube. It

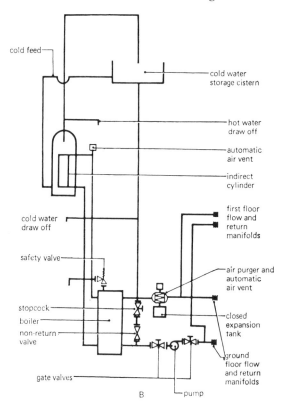

Figure 66　*Layout for a typical sealed-tank system*

is advantageous in a bungalow to connect all the radiators to a single pair of manifolds located close to the boiler. In a house of one or more storeys it will be more convenient to install a pair of manifolds on each floor, siting them in the most central and accessible position so that the length of the 8-mm-diameter copper circuits to the radiators can be kept short to save material and reduce frictional resistance to a minimum.

It cannot be emphasized too strongly that all calculations for microbore (the term most widely used now) must be determined correctly because the design for this system is more critical than for smallbore.

The advantages of microbore can be summarized as follows:

(a)  The installation time is reduced, providing a cost saving.

(b) The disturbance of a household is confined to a minimum during installation.
(c) A reduction in the cost of materials used.
(d) A more flexible installation which permits extension at a later date.
(e) A reduced water content which provides more sensitivity to thermostatic control.
(f) A faster heat recovery is achieved.

## Design and installation of microbore

Copper tubing for microbore installations is manufactured to BS 2871, Part 2 and it is available in 6 mm, 8 mm and 10 mm outside diameter. The tube is supplied in coil lengths of 10 m, 20 m, 25 m, 30 m and 50 m and it is of soft temper which permits easy manipulation by hand, or pipe-bending springs if sharp radius bends are required. The soft-temper tube reduces the noise level in the system which occurs with high velocities.

The manifold could be described as the heart of the microbore system. There are a number of patterns available, one of which is called the 'Microfold' manufactured by the Wednesbury Tube Company. This component is fabricated from a length of copper tube with a disc brazed in the centre, thereby providing both flow and return chambers in one unit. To this length a number of stub bosses are soldered which have compression fittings to which the microbore tubing is connected.

Three patterns of Microfold are available:

WM18 designed for use with up to nine radiators and a maximum capacity of 26 kW.
WM12 for up to six radiators and a maximum of 17 kW.
WM8 constructed of 22-mm copper tube having provision for up to four radiators of 11 kW.

The ends of the Microfold are to half-hard temper to allow the use of compression or capillary fittings. A special spanner is supplied to fit easily between the stub bosses when making connections.

## Double entry radiator valve

The double entry radiator valve is intended to complete the termination of the twin microbore tubes at one tapping on the radiator, making a neat unobtrusive connection. The valve has a BSP taper thread which screws into the radiator. The twin outlets are designed to take 10-mm tube.

During the installation it should be noted that the flow connection is nearer to the radiator and the return is into the valve body. In operation the valve controls the return from the radiator.

When using this valve with standard single panel radiators a length of 10-mm tube is fitted to the valve and inserted into the bottom waterway of the radiator for return circulation. The length of this tube should not be less than 180 mm. In the case of double panel radiators, a special flexible insert is necessary to negotiate the header of the radiator. This flexible insert must be used in all double panel radiators.

When fitting microbore tubing, a length a little more than the distance between the manifold and the radiator is uncoiled and then cut with pliers to ensure that the ends of the pipe are closed together to prevent the ingress of extraneous matter. When preparing the pipe for jointing it must be cut with a fine-toothed hacksaw and the burrs removed with a fine file.

As already stated, the nature of the copper tube facilitates the bending and fixing of microbore. New methods of pipe clipping are being used and a number of clips and cover strips are available. It is sufficient however to restrict the clips to parts where the tube is exposed and needs to be secured down the side of window frames or along the skirting board. The cover strip gives the neatest finish to tubes prominently in view. The flow and return pipes can often be installed without disturbing the normal working of the house, a fact very much appreciated by the householder.

In new houses, a plastic coated microbore tube can be buried in the plaster, eliminating the need for other protective measures. Care must always be exercised in running out the coil of tubing to protect it from sharp edges which could kink the tube and affect the performance of the heating circuit.

On completion of the installation, the whole system should be washed out immediately to ensure that no foreign bodies remain in the tubes. Some form of inhibitor should be added when recharging the system.

# Sealed systems

All wet heating systems are operated by the continuous recycling of water by means of a pump through the boiler and radiators or unit heaters, and it is of paramount importance that only minimum water replacement should take place. However, following the principle of the Perkins system, engineers in America and on the Continent have, for many years, been using a sealed-tank method by which loss of water from the system is virtually eliminated. There is therefore little need for periodic 'topping up' and a mains supply through a ball valve is not required.

## Sealed expansion tank

In a closed system it is essential to install, at a convenient point in the circuit, a sealed expansion tank (sometimes called a flexible membrane vessel) which is just large enough to take up the expansion volume when the temperature rises (see Figure 67). The vessel is normally of a welded steel construction into which is fitted a flexible diaphragm dividing it into two compartments, one of which is filled with nitrogen or air, and the other with water from the heating system: the absorption of air into the water – which occurred with the Perkins system – is thereby prevented. The air or nitrogen cushion is pressurized to support the static head created by the height of the water in the system so that the original gas volume remains unchanged when the system is filled up. When the boiler is fired and the water temperature rises, expansion of the water pushes back the diaphragm and compresses the nitrogen or air on the opposite side, causing an increase of pressure throughout the system.

With all sealed systems, the optimum size for the vessel is dependent upon the water capacity and the working temperature of the installation. A range of flexible membrane vessels is available and the manufacturers should be consulted regarding selection.

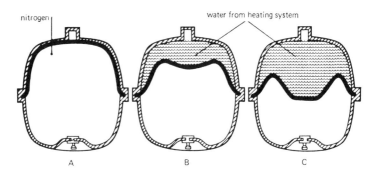

Figure 67   *Expansion tank with flexible diaphragm for sealed system. (A) Before the boiler has been fired the tank contains only air or nitrogen. (B) As the temperature rises the diaphragm moves to accept the increased water volume. (C) Position of diaphragm when water temperature has reached its maximum.*

### Location of sealed expansion tank

As the sealed expansion tank is comparatively small, it can be placed at more or less any convenient point in the system, and this obviously makes concealment relatively easy. Where there is a possibility of tanks being isolated when valves are shut off many installers position the expansion tank close to the boiler. If an air purger fitting, which consists of a simple air separation and float-type air vent, is used, venting can, if required, be a semi-automatic operation. Installation costs can be reduced by fitting a combined sealed tank and air purger unit. If the layout of the pipework is such as to make it more convenient for the sealed tank and air purger units to be installed separately, this will not impair the efficiency of the system, but it is recommended that the air purger should be at the point of highest temperature and therefore as close to the boiler as possible. To gain full economic advantage from the sealed system the average water temperature should generally be higher than for the open-tank system. However, there are many sealed-tank installations in use working at a mean temperature of 78°C, the average for open-tank systems.

# Pressurized heating systems

The principle of pressurized systems has been accepted for both

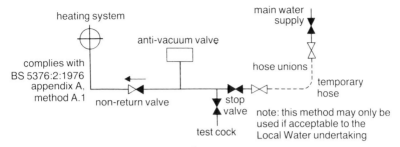

Figure 68 *Mains connection to heating system*

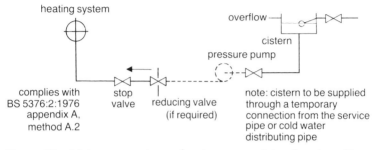

Figure 69 *Mains connection to heating system (via a break tank)*

hot-water supply and heating systems. The one difference between the two systems is that while the hot-water installation may be connected directly to the mains water supply, the heating system cannot. Instead it must make do with temporary connections which must be removed once the system is charged. Figures 68 and 69 illustrate two methods of making a suitable temporary connection.

Because the system is 'sealed' the only loss of water from the system will be from 'bleeding' radiators, possible leaks, or the operation of pressure relief or temperature relief valves. Any drop in pressure must therefore be made up from the main supply after refitting the temporary connections.

The expansion vessels, temperature, relief, pressure relief and safety valves will be fitted either on the heating appliance or close to it in the heating circuit pipework. The domestic side of indirect cylinders incorporated in the system can be supplied from the cold water as illustrated in Chapter 4.

The pipe and radiator layout will be the same as that described for gravity systems except that there will not be an open vent or a feed and expansion tank. Air will be vented from the system through the radiators in the normal way, but vacuum breakers must be provided at the high points of both flow and return pipework to prevent dangerous reduction in pressure within the system from either contraction of cooling water or loss from leaks, etc.

The Chaffoteaux Combination Boiler is ideally suited to heating systems and, with an output of 23.2 kW (over 79,000 Btus), can cope comfortably with most average dwellings. It is specifically designed for pressurized systems and has the added advantage of being able to supply instantaneous hot water without the need of a storage cylinder. Because it is a balanced flue appliance it must be fitted on an external wall, and the flue must be positioned to avoid other openings to the building, or any projection that may cause an obstruction to the flue's operation.

Table 10

| | |
|---|---|
| 1 Directly below an openable window, vent, or any other ventilation opening | 300 mm (12 in) |
| 2 Below guttering, drain, or soil pipes | 75 mm ( 3 in) |
| 3 Below balconies or eaves | 200 mm ( 8 in) |
| 4 Above adjacent ground or balcony | 300 mm (12 in) |
| 5 From vertical drain or soil pipes | 75 mm ( 3 in) |
| 6 From internal or external corners | 200 mm ( 8 in) |
| 7 From a surface facing the terminal | 600 mm (24 in) |
| 8 From a terminal facing the terminal | 1200 mm (48 in) |
| 9 From side of a window | 150 mm ( 6 in) |

The flue can be extended to clear a projection. Where the terminal is fitted within 850 mm (34 in) of plastic or painted eaves, an aluminium shield of at least 750 mm (30 in) long should be fitted to the underside of the gutter or painted surface. Where the lowest part of a terminal is less than 2 m (6 ft 6 in) above the level of any ground, balcony, flat roof, or place to which any person has access and which adjoins the wall in which the terminal is fixed, the terminal must be protected by a guard provided by the heater manufacturer. The terminal must not be closer than 50 mm (2 in) to any combustible material. The appliance must not be fitted in any timber-framed house without

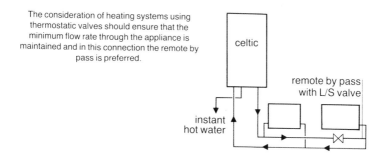

Figure 70    *The remote by-pass*

first consulting the manufacturer and the Gas Board.

Any room in which the heater is installed requires no added ventilation. However, if the boiler is installed in a cupboard or compartment then permanent air vents, one at high level and one at low level, either direct to outside air or to a room, provided both vents connect to the same space, must be provided.

Where the appliance is connected to an existing system all pipework joints and valves should be carefully checked for leaks. An old vented system is likely to have worked on a pressure of no more than 0.4 bar, while a mains supply system may have a running pressure in excess of 1.5 bar. Radiator valves should be replaced with a pattern capable of sealing at the higher pressures.

Only high recovery, indirect cylinders can be used with the Chaffoteaux Combination Boiler. Single-feed and direct cylinders are not suitable for use with this appliance.

Where thermostatic valves are used within a system, a remote by-pass (Figure 70) should be used to maintain the minimum flow rate through the appliance.

# The Economy 7 boiler

The Economy 7 boiler is produced by Heatrac Sadia and marketed by the Electricity Council to be installed either as an initial system of heating or to replace a boiler in an existing system.

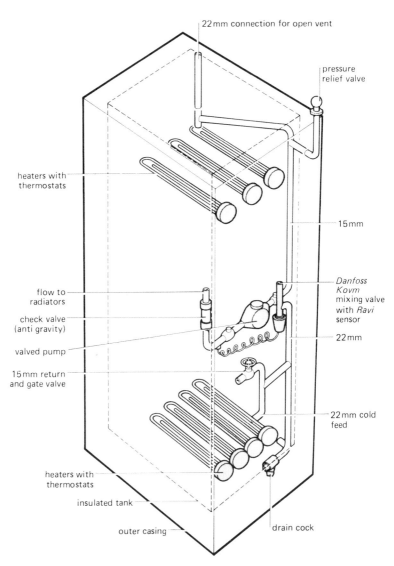

Figure 71   *General view of 680 litre Economy 7 boiler*

Briefly, it is a rectangular water-storage tank with heating elements located in the bottom to heat water using Economy 7 rate electricity. Additional elements are located at the top to boost the heat during the day as necessary. The boiler comes complete with integral pipework, insulation, control box, mixing valves and pump (see Figure 71).

There are three standard sizes (though special requirements are made to order and boilers can be erected on site) as follows:

E7 680 litres' capacity for property with heat loss of 4–6 kW.
E7 900 litres' capacity for property with heat loss of 6–8 kW.
E7 1350 litres' capacity for property with heat loss of 8–10 kW.

Working head is 7.2 m measured from the base of the boiler to the water level in the feed and expansion tank.

Loadings for 680 litres' capacity are 12 kW element for night and 9 kW for day. The temperature controller uses platinum resistance elements and solid-state control circuitry, and temperatures are pre-set to the following:

|  | *House* °C | *Bungalow* °C |
|---|---|---|
| Night store temperature | 98 | 92 |
| Day elements | 70 | 70 |
| Limit temperature | 103 | 97 |
| Return water temperature | 40 | 40 |

The system works by heating the storage during the night-time off-peak period, then heat is distributed in the normal way by pumping hot stored water, mixed with return water, through the radiators (see Figure 72A). The stratification of the water in the storage vessel ensures a stable flow temperature throughout the day. A common-size boiler is one with a capacity of 680 litres, which is adequate for a house with up to about 5.5 kW heat loss.

Ideally the boiler should be fitted within the dwelling where any heat loss from it will be of benefit, but it can be fitted in any practical location – garage, outhouse, etc. – providing it is adequately protected against low temperature and the pipe runs are not over-long.

When using the Economy 7 boiler as a replacement unit it is advisable to disconnect, or valve off, any existing domestic hot-water storage cylinder and primary flow and return pipework as

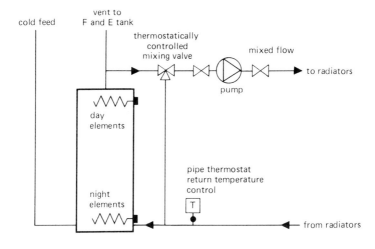

*single storage unit*

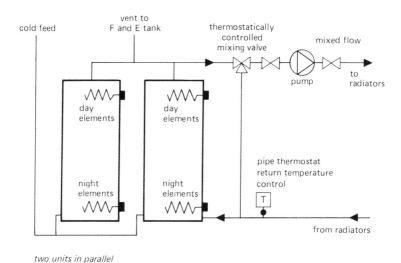

*two units in parallel*

Figure 72A   *Economy 7 single and twin boiler connections*

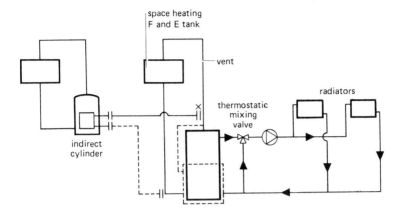

A — Separate the gravity feed HWS from space heating. This could be achieved by valving-off the run of pipe between the coil feed and system expansion (at the point marked X in the diagram). A better method would be to disconnect the feed and return from the indirect coil and then blank off the open ends (marked || on the diagram). Economy 7 water heating can then be installed.

B — Replace boiler with Electric Boiler connecting vent and cold feed directly to unit.

C — Replace F and E tank if necessary.

*NB — broken line shows original boiler and gravity feed HWS.*

Figure 72B    *Economy 7 hot water and heating system*

the heat loss from gravity circulation can be considerable. Furthermore, in summer there would be standing losses from both the main storage vessel and the domestic hot-water cylinder at a time when only domestic hot water is required. These losses would generally absorb more energy than would be used to provide hot water (see Figure 72B). Towel rails connected to the primary flow and return should be disconnected and piped to the pumped circuit.

For domestic supplies an Economy 7 hot-water cylinder should be installed which works on exactly the same principle as the boiler. Hot-water draw-offs should not be taken from the boiler.

Whatever the heating system, it is beneficial to have the property insulated: for heat-storage systems it is essential. Particular attention should be paid to roofs, cavity walls, external doors and windows, remembering always, however, to provide adequate ventilation to prevent (among other things) condensation.

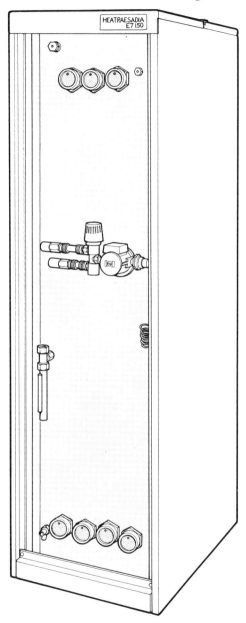

Figure 72C   *With the door off, the long-life Incoloy elements at the top and bottom of the Heatrae Sadia Economy 7 domestic control heating boiler can be seen clearly*

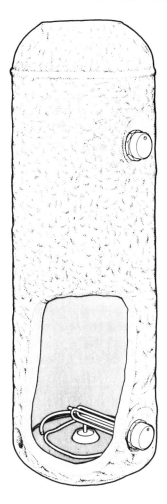

Figure 72D *Superseven cylinder manufactured by IMI Range for Economy 7 operation*

## Feed and expansion tank

The Economy 7 boiler requires a feed and expansion tank exactly the same as any other heating system, apart from the primatic system. It should have a capacity to water line of 18 litres plus 6 per cent of the volume of water in the system. Therefore, a system containing 780 litres (680 litres for the storage unit plus 100 litres in the pipes and radiators) would require an expansion vessel with a capacity to water line of 65 litres.

# Care of the system

Any plumbing system must be maintained. This is especially true of central heating installations, particularly the pressurized type. Gas- and oil-burning boilers should be serviced at least annually, and thermostat settings and control and safety valves checked. It is important that this work is done by a qualified person. Any part of the safety equipment on the system that has a malfunction should be replaced. This work will normally be done on a contract basis by the Gas Board or other appropriate body, or by an approved contractor.

But that's the part that everybody can see. Equally important are those parts of the system that are not readily visible: inside the system, where the major damage can be done.

## Corrosion

Corrosion starts the moment water enters a system. It is still quite a common belief that free and dissolved oxygen in the installation will rapidly be consumed in the formation of a quite small amount of iron oxide and, therefore, providing the water content of the system is not changed, there will be no further problem.

An element of this may be true depending upon the design of the system, the standard of workmanship, the materials used in it, and the quality of the water. For too many installations corrosion is a progressive process and, often, very rapid. The prime causes are electrolysis and the presence of impurities.

### Electrolysis

Two dissimilar metals, one anodic and the other cathodic (more noble) in the presence of water which is an electrolyte results in a positive attack on the lesser metal. Raised temperatures, and impurities in solution in the water, increase the rate of electrolytic attack. In any heating system there is usually a mixture of metals:

copper, steel, aluminium, iron, etc. Common symptoms are pinhole perforations of radiators and metal cisterns, and corrosion deposits in pipes.

*Impurities*

There are many 'natural' and added impurities in the waters of most systems. Mains water may contain sulphates and chlorides and dissolved oxygen and carbon dioxide which, in themselves, would make the water corrosive.

Installation procedures can leave residues of soldering fluxes which attack most metals in systems. Obviously these residues should be cleaned out of the pipework before any system is commissioned but, sadly, this is seldom done.

Then there is the problem of jointing and other compounds in the pipework which contain oil, grease, hemp, and other organic matter upon which bacteria and fungi can feed. Sulphate-reducing bacteria cause the biggest problems of corrosion and, if present in sufficiently large quantities, produce hydrogen sulphide, a toxic and corrosive gas that smells like rotten eggs.

*Pressurized systems*

Any system which prevents the ready admittance of air will stop oxidic corrosion once the free oxygen in the water has been consumed. The problem is that electrolysis will extract oxygen from the water molecule, thereby producing hydrogen. This gas can become compressed at the top of radiators and is a common cause of the top section of radiators becoming cold and the need for frequent venting. As this is a flammable gas, people should not smoke while venting radiators.

It is the presence of this compressed hydrogen gas and the deposits of the thick black sludge which most people have emptied from their radiators at decorating time that can cause loss of circulation pressure in any system, including sealed and pressurized systems. It is also a clear warning that electrolysis is active in the installation.

*Prevention*

What to do about it? Obviously prevention is the best course and, in new installations, not too difficult to achieve. Existing systems are likely to have all the problems inbuilt. But let's deal with the ideal world.

1 Avoid dissimilar metals. Use, for example, copper cylinder, copper tubes and fittings, copper radiators, and glass reinforced plastic cisterns. This will leave only the boiler and the pump to present any problems.
2 Alternatively, use plastics pipes and fittings and cisterns with copper cylinders and radiators.

Copper radiators cost more than steel radiators and, very often, initial installation costs are critical.

Much also depends upon the nature of the water. It also depends upon any aeration of the water, so all users should ensure that their circulating pump is not set too high (or that their non-variable head pump is not rated too high). Excessive velocity in pumping causes aeration in the system, and then we're back to oxidic corrosion.

And if all this fails? Or you're too late because your system is cluttered with different metals and corrosion is well advanced?

Then you must consider a corrosion inhibitor. But be careful. Don't go out and buy the first one offered and tip copious quantities into your feed and expansion cistern. There are numerous inhibitors on the market, many of which do a specific job, while some claim to do all jobs. Some can actually be harmful in certain conditions, especially if overdosed.

The best advice is to read all the literature, then consult a specialist. Whatever is recommended, find out the estimated life of the dosage and the recommended top-up periods and amounts to be added, and get a statement in writing to say exactly what protection you have purchased. Above all, consult the boiler manufacturer's directions, as certain inhibitors may not be acceptable to his appliance.

The sad fact is that plumbing and heating services are largely taken for granted, so even the basic maintenance needs are ignored by many householders. So often it takes a disaster to make people realize that pipes, fittings, and appliances don't last for ever. Regular checks pay dividends. Good design saves trouble. Whatever your system, avoid the obvious pitfalls such as burying pipes in solid floors or walls because they're best unseen – because they are not; such as laying pipes where they are likely to be affected by cold air draughts; such as locating valves where you can't get at them; and, probably the most irritating of all to any plumber, running pipes through the centre of a floor space over which you lay a fitted carpet.

Case in your pipes by all means; secrete them in cupboards and alcoves; but do make sure that they are accessible.

# 8

# Plumbing Fitments in the Home

## The kitchen

### Sinks

The kitchen sink, from the days when it was made from brown earthenware and about three inches in depth, has now become an attractive as well as functional piece of kitchen equipment manufactured in a number of materials and designs.

*Fireclay*
There are several types of kitchen sink. The once popular 'Belfast' sink, which is made of fireclay and enamelled after baking, is still used in certain areas. It is easily fixed on brackets built into the wall, or on leg supports.

*Stainless steel*
By far the most popular is the stainless steel sink and draining board combined, made in various sizes to suit individual requirements. The sink is stamped out of one sheet of metal, is very easy to keep clean and lends itself for use with purpose-made cabinets, giving a smooth streamlined finish (see Figure 73A).

A double-compartment sink with double drainer is made for the larger kitchen, and this is becoming increasingly popular because it enables the housewife to prepare vegetables and, where necessary to keep them in soak in one compartment while the other can be used for washing the glass, china, cooking utensils, etc. One of this type is illustrated in Figure 73B. The sinks and

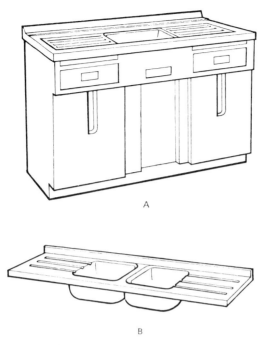

Figure 73   *Types of sinks*
*A   Stainless steel sink unit*
*B   Double compartment sink*

draining boards have a sound-deadening under-skin, and a food waste-grinding machine can be attached. Some stainless steel sinks are now made smaller and round in shape, so that no washing-up bowl is needed.

In most cases the back skirting of the sink is pierced to enable the hot and cold services to be run along inside a cupboard and up through the skirting, finishing with a neat chromium-plated standard and whatever type of taps that may be desired, thus giving a very clean-looking finish.

### Enamelled steel

Another type is the vitreous enamelled steel sink. This is stamped out of one sheet of metal, and after colour is applied the sink is subjected to heat treatment giving the finished product a hard vitreous surface. These sinks can be obtained in various colours and sizes and, to provide the housewife with a complete unit, very attractive cabinets have been designed to match the varying colours of the sinks.

*Ceramic sinks*

Increasing in popularity today are luxury ceramic sinks. There is a growing selection, with choices of attractive colours, from firms such as Ideal-Standard, all theirs being made in a strong and dimensionally stable ceramic body finished in a satin glaze.

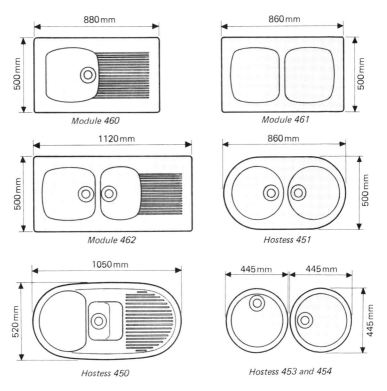

Figure 74    *Types of sinks and dimensions*

# Food waste disposers

In the course of a year over a thousand meals (per person) may be prepared in the kitchen of every home, not counting snacks and in-betweens. There is nearly always some form of waste from every type of food. This is either collected in a sink tidy or put into the bin beneath the sink to be taken out to the dustbin (in all weathers).

There is no doubt at all that modern housewives are anxious to improve conditions in the kitchen and the disposal of food waste is, to some, a particularly nauseating job, i.e. cleaning scraps of food from the sink outlet, scooping peelings from the bowl, scraping congealed food from plates into the pedal bin, etc.

The modern food waste disposer is an electro-mechanical device fitted to the sink to macerate food waste, etc. These machines will dispose of all grades of food waste such as fish remains, fruit skins (including banana skins), vegetable parings, plate waste (including fatty materials), bones, eggshells and tea-leaves.

## Installation

The food waste disposer has a 76 mm opening to the grinding chamber. This entails a 90 mm opening in the sink. Many sinks are now made with this size of opening to take either a food waste disposer or a crumb strainer waste. It is wise, therefore, if installing a new sink to see that it is one with a 90 mm opening.

Fireclay porcelain sinks of various types are now in production, with and without overflows, to take the food waste disposer.

If a stainless steel sink is already installed, it can usually be modified to take a disposer. The manufacturer of food waste disposers will lend plumbing contractors the necessary equipment to enlarge the hole and impress in it the recess for the disposer outlet. This is a simple operation for an experienced plumber.

### Plumbing

All plumbing must be done in accordance with the Water Byelaws in force in the area in which the installation is to be made and in accordance with the British Standard Code of Practice COP 5572.

The proposed work must be notified to the appropriate authority before work begins. If you are in doubt about the regulations, consult the local water authority or employ a qualified plumber to carry out the work.

A deep-seal trap must be fitted to the outlet side of the disposal unit and a 42 mm waste connected with a minimum fall of 7.5° directly to the drain, or to a main discharge stack which connects directly to the drain without an intervening gully or trap. Any bend in the waste-pipe system should be of generous radius and formed without any distortion of the pipe bore.

It is most important that the waste pipe should not impose any strain on the free hanging position of the disposer. This will tend to make it noisy in operation.

*Electrical*

The motor incorporated in the disposer is designed to give the maximum power from a 13 A fused plug. The rating of the motor is over ¼ h.p. and is capable of a higher output over a short period. The control of the unit should be of such a nature that it conforms to I.E.E. requirements.

When running under the full load the motor takes 2.7 A, but in the event of the motor stalling under overload conditions the current taken by the motor will rise to 13 A. The circuit should therefore be fused for this current. The current will only flow for a few seconds until the overload device in the motor cuts it off. The overload protection device is a red button situated at the bottom of the motor on the waste outlet side. It is reset by pressing it firmly upwards and it will re-engage with a slight click.

The reversing feature of the appliance (if specified) is the switch below the point of the cable entry. This switch reverses the direction of rotation of the motor, thus utilizing both edges of the cutting teeth. If the reversing switch is not fitted the motor can be reversed by a qualified electrician removing the terminal cover and changing over two wires which will be exposed in the terminal block. The disposer, whilst earthed through the three-pin plug and socket, should also be earthed independently.

# The bathroom

Perhaps one of the most encouraging forward trends today in home life is the great interest being shown by householders in the furnishing and equipment of the bathroom. This is possibly the result of the consistent – and persistent – publicity by the

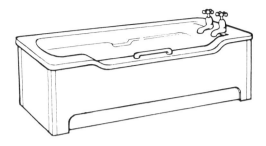

Figure 75   *Shallow bath in enamelled cast iron*

manufacturers of the bathroom fitments from the bath to the tooth-brush rack. The design and quality of their products has improved and they have advertised widely and well. Public response has sharpened competition and today there is a wonderful selection from which the householder can make his choice if he decides to re-model his plumbing installation.

## Baths

### Enamelled cast iron

There is an attractive display of baths to be seen in the showrooms of most plumbers' merchants, baths to suit every purpose, taste and purse.

Most baths are manufactured in enamelled cast iron in various lengths to suit personal preference, available space or the decor of the house. They have flat or rolled rims and the latest shallow type has an almost flat bottom. This has many advantages over the conventional curved bath. First, the shallow 'step' makes it safe for the oldest and for the youngest members of the family. Then, with its flat bottom, it's safer for taking a shower. A shallow bath saves space and makes the bathroom look larger. One such type is shown in Figure 75.

Another new bath available is a porcelain enamelled one-piece apron bath. This bath has no tap holes and is supplied with hot and cold water through a spout outlet controlled by concealed valves. It must be ordered for a left- or right-hand corner as required because it obviously cannot be turned round like the normal bath with the detachable front apron.

*Pressed steel baths*

The modern steel bath is pressed out of one piece of steel and then vitreous enamelled. There are no feet to the bath; it is cushioned into two cradles lined with felt. The bath stands quite rigidly and it will withstand all hot-water temperatures. It is less costly than the cast iron bath.

## Hydrotherapy

Nor are baths designed simply for washing. Today it is possible to enjoy the benefits of technology in the home by fitting a 'whirlpool' bath; massage by water is excellent for athletes, the elderly, and sufferers from rheumatism and arthritis; and fun for children and parents alike.

The smallest by Ideal-Standard measures 170 × 75 cm and will fit into any average bathroom. For more spacious bathrooms there are attractive corner baths and baths to accommodate two people.

The six impulse nozzles are adjustable and operated by a pull cord. Baths come with matching basin, w.c., bidet and shower.

Ideal-Standard whirlpool baths are supplied with the pipework for the water nozzles and aeration controls already fitted (Figure 76), and every bath is individually pre-tested. The pump is supplied ready for the plumber to fit and only two or three pipe connections (according to model) have to be made.

The electrical connections are straightforward and your electrician should provide a pull switch over the bath and a separate isolating switch.

When the pump is on, water is withdrawn from the bath through a suction outlet and recirculated through the pipework to the six nozzles below the water surface.

The aeration controls on the side of the bath may be opened to add air to the streams of water, the bubbles of air adding further liveliness to the whirlpool action.

## Care of the bath

A good bath deserves good treatment before and after installation. Unfortunately, much damage can be caused before the

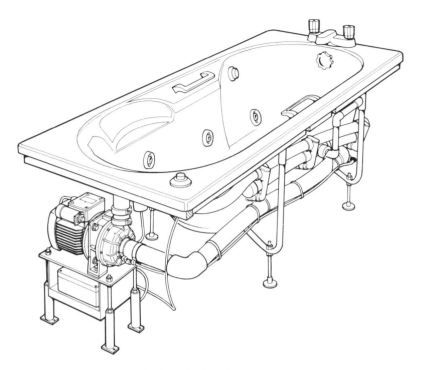

Figure 76    *Ideal-Standard's Whirlpool 2000 system*

bath is fixed. It is delivered to the site usually some time before it is installed and is left out in the weather. It is liable to damage from falling materials and rough handling. When it has been fixed by the plumber it may be scratched by other tradesmen working in the bathroom. Despite efforts by progressively minded people, it still happens that due to ignorance, stupidity and carelessness many baths are damaged. The owner of a new house will be well advised to make a close inspection of all his sanitary fittings before taking over.

## Acrylic baths

Domestic baths made from cast acrylic sheet are produced by several manufacturers, and are stocked by leading builders' merchants throughout the country. Although designs and prices vary, there are some features which are common to all acrylic baths. Where coloured luxury baths are being considered, acrylic baths offer a considerable saving in cost.

Cast against plate glass, they have a superb surface finish with no ripples or blemishes. The colour goes right through the material and will not wear off. It will not stain, rust or corrode. It is unaffected by bath salts, and because it is non-porous its surface will not retain bacteria.

### Light in weight

Acrylic baths weigh as little as 14 kg, saving on handling, transport and installation costs both in private houses and multi-storey buildings. Although these baths are light in weight they are completely stable once installed. A substantial cradle is provided which supports the bath both underneath and round the rim, and

Figure 77   *One man can handle an acrylic bath*

the cradle is included in the price of the bath. Figure 77 illustrates how easy they are to transport.

*Easy to maintain*

The high gloss and good appearance of acrylic baths can be preserved by cleaning with warm soapy water or detergent. When necessary mild scouring powder may be used, but some loss of surface lustre must be expected in time. This lustre can be renewed by polishing the surface with a liquid metal polish or a soft cloth. If a deep scratch is accidentally made, it can be rubbed out with a mild abrasive or, in an extreme case, with wire wool or emery paper, and the polished surface can be completely restored by rubbing with liquid metal polish.

*Economic*

Because acrylic is a good thermal insulator, the water stays hot longer. The material is also warm to the touch. But acrylic baths are affected by extremes of heat, such as are generated by lighted cigarettes and burning matches, and these will cause marks on the surface. Lighted cigarettes should not therefore be placed on the surround or allowed to fall into the bath. Some dry-cleaning agents and paint strippers will also cause damage.

## Installation and plumbing instructions

There are no special problems connected with the installation of acrylic baths, but some allowance must be made for the thermal expansion and contraction. Plumbers should pay particular attention to the fixing instructions which most manufacturers issue. In general the following points should be observed.

*Installation*

An unsupported acrylic bath lacks stability because of its low weight and must therefore be securely fixed to the supporting cradle which the manufacturer provides. The bath should be levelled and secured to its cradle according to the maker's instructions. The cradle should be fixed to the floor via the supporting legs of the cradle and/or to the wall along the top rear member. All surfaces of the bath cradle which are in contact with the bath are lined with felt which should not be removed or

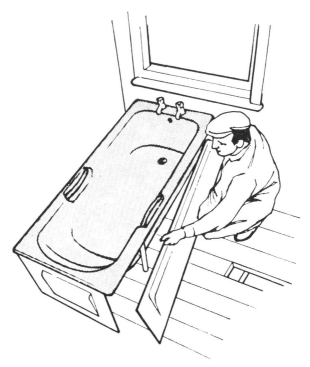

Figure 78   *Installing an acrylic bath*

disturbed. This felt interlayer prevents creaking which could be caused by the bath rubbing against its cradle.

Creaking can also occur when adjacent side panels rub against one another at the corners or against the underside of the bath flange. The rubbing can be avoided by slightly trimming the side panels and binding the edges with cloth tape.

When the side panels are fitted to the bath cradle (see Figure 78), it is important to provide clearance holes through the panels for fixing to allow for thermal movement. Full support must be provided on the underside of the panels when drilling these holes.

When the bath is fitted flush with the wall, the final seal should be made using a silicone sealant. Small tubes of this material are available from most builders' merchants or ironmongers. For trade use there is a gun cartridge grade available – 'Silicone Building Sealant' – which is readily available from builders' merchants. Alternatively most builders' merchants or ironmongers supply a variety of specially shaped PVC strips which can be used to make the final seal.

## Tiling

The walls around an acrylic bath can be tiled in the normal way following the tile adhesive manufacturer's instructions. The tiles should preferably be laid so that the lower horizontal edge of the tiling lies below the rim of the bath. In this case the tiling can be undertaken prior to the installation of the bath.

If the tiling is to be carried out after the bath has been installed, the bath should be protected to prevent accidental scratching of the surface of the bath. Some tile adhesives contain solvents which can damage acrylic and care should be taken to ensure that any adhesive accidentally falling into the bath is quickly removed. The effects of any slight surface damage may be removed by the use of a liquid metal polish.

## Plumbing

When fitting the services to a bath made from acrylic sheet care must be taken to avoid damaging the material and also to avoid fitting the services in such a way that damage to the bath could occur in service.

## Waste pipe

Normal sealing compounds can be used between the flange of the waste-pipe fitting and the bath, but it is recommended that a washer of some resilient material, such as rubber or polythene, be used between the nut on the underside and the bath itself. Moderate pressure only should be used to tighten the nut, care being taken to avoid excessive leverage which would occur if long-handled pipe wrenches or spanners were used.

Where a metal trap and waste pipe are used they must be accurately aligned to avoid imposing a twisting stress on the bath. It is essential to ensure sufficient flexibility in the plumbing to allow the trap and waste fitting to move with slight thermal movements of the bath otherwise there is a danger of cracking around the waste-pipe flange hole in service.

If a short length of iron piping is used, the system will be too rigid. This problem of providing resilience can be overcome by using plastics waste pipe in conjunction with a plastics or metal waste trap. The use of suitably reinforced polythene or flexible

PVC pipe for the overflow connection to the trap is recommended so that the effect of any misalignment is absorbed in its resilience rather than imposed as a stress on the bath.

## Taps

For the normal types of tap no special precautions are necessary other than the provision of a resilient washer between the nut and the bath.

Some types of mixer installations and hand shower fittings are considerably bigger than normal taps and, if used as grab handles by the bath occupant, could impose sufficient leverage to the bath flange to cause damage. When fittings of this type are installed they must be secured through a reinforcing member on the underside of the bath flange.

## Warning

Whenever a blow lamp is being used during the plumbing operation care must be taken to ensure that the flame is kept well away from the bath.

# Washbasins

It is perhaps a sad reflection on the designers of sanitary ware that many of the washbasins manufactured in this country in the past presented both the housewives and the plumbers with problems. The housewife found it impossible to keep the basin properly cleaned because of awkward corners, crevices and the bad siting of the taps, while the plumber had difficulty in fixing the services and waste pipe.

However, in recent years the manufacturers have given the matter attention and sought the help of experts in design, with the result that the new washbasins are pleasant to look at as well as being functional.

Washbasins can be obtained in glazed fireclay, vitreous china, porcelain enamelled cast iron, pressed steel and stainless steel and more recently in plastics. The range of designs is extensive – as is of course the range of prices.

A type which is becoming very popular is the *vanity basin* (Figure 79). The one illustrated has the bowl fitted flush into a plastic top having a moulded back skirting, bullnosed front edge

Figure 79    *Vanity basin*

and shaped ends. The unit has two drawers and is supported on polished beechwood legs. Another type is a basin with a spacious table top formed from square eggshell finish tiles, with a wooden cabinet beneath.

Washbasins are being fitted in bedrooms and guest rooms today as well as in the bathroom and the pleasant modern types with splashbacks and mirrors will grace any room (Figure 80).

Figure 80    *A modern washbasin*

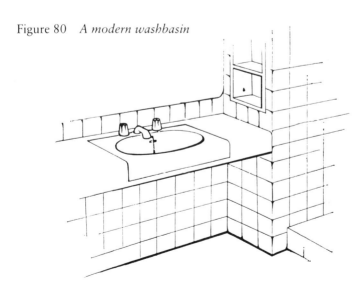

It has been suggested that wherever there is a w.c. there should be a washbasin. Furthermore, it is recommended that the tap of the washbasin should be operated by a foot pedal so that the user of the w.c. can wash his or her hands before flushing the cistern. We believe that with the attractive little washbasins now available, one could be placed in every w.c. compartment, even if it were provided with but one cold-water tap.

## Water closets

The modern w.c. pan is designed to be functional, unobtrusive and easy to clean. They are available in earthenware, fireclay, stainless steel and vitreous china. There are some imported plastic w.c.s on the market.

Figure 81 A, B and C   *Types of w.c.s*

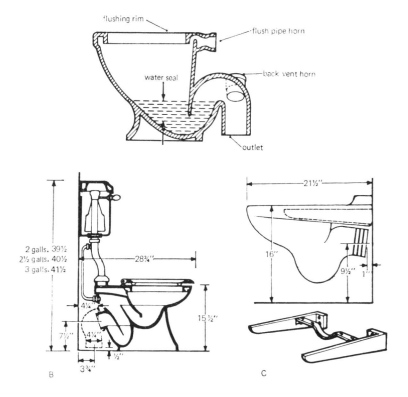

The most commonly used type of w.c. is the washdown pedestal, so called because the flush of water washes and cleanses the whole of the internal surface of the pan. Referring to Figure 81A, the water from the flushing cistern enters the flush pipe horn and is directed round the flushing rim and then washes down the internal surface. The water seal is, of course, the barrier which prevents drain gas from entering the house.

The clanging noise of the w.c. cistern being operated and the rush of water into and out of the pan, especially at night, can be something of a nuisance. If this is a problem, it can be best overcome by the installation of a modern type siphonic w.c. pan. The seal of the trap of this type is much deeper than that of the washdown closet, thus giving a large bowl of water and a limited exposed area. A normal flush would not be sufficient to cleanse down the fittings thoroughly and leave such a large bowl recharged with water. The contents of the pan are therefore removed by siphonic action. The action is started by the impulse of the water flush and the contents of the bowl are removed completely and silently. A typical modern siphonic w.c. is shown in Figure 81B.

Another type of w.c. which deserves more popularity is the bracket w.c. which, as shown in Figure 81C, is fixed on brackets clear of the wall, thus avoiding the joint between the floor and the pan. Because the pan is virtually fixed to the wall there is no chance of it cracking due to movement of the floor. The pan is of the washdown type.

## W.C. suite of advanced design

In Figure 82 a close-coupled w.c. suite is illustrated. It is the combination of a plastic or pottery cistern with a pottery washdown pedestal w.c. pan. It incorporates a silent flush of 'hydromatic' action – a design of ducts and channels which direct the water in correct volume to the right places to effect controlled maximum flushing efficiency. The washdown pan is manufactured with the trap to British Standard specification to eliminate the risk of blockage. It is a free standing unit, only 736 mm high and projecting 710 mm from the wall. Being of low height and short projection it is easy to fit under the window in the average w.c. compartment and can be installed in many awkward places, where previously only a high-level suite could be accommodated.

Figure 82   *A close-coupled w.c. suite*

The suite is available in a variety of colours and has the smooth flowing lines and shape of contemporary design in addition to maximum hygienic qualities. Even the fixing screws are domed to avoid dust-traps and the whole suite can be easily and quickly wiped clean. Two screws at the base of the pan hold the complete suite firmly in position.

The cistern in pottery or plastic is non-corroding; it bolts directly to the pan without need for brackets or flush pipe. An easy pressure on the cistern handle will immediately operate the polythene siphon mechanism to give a positive action flush.

The w.c. is fitted with an attractively shaped seat which has been designed to blend with the contemporary lines of the whole suite. It is made from what the manufacturers claim to be a virtually unbreakable material. The seat is flexible and needs no buffers. It has a light, smooth surface which is very easy to keep clean. The material from which it is made is a bad conductor of heat, therefore the seat is not as chilly as some other types.

It is a simple matter to fix the seat by means of its adjustable sliding bolt with wing nuts and washers. There are no hinge rods to be cut as the fixing bolts are adjustable in the socket.

The hinges are streamlined to make them easy to wipe clean.

The seat has a cover made from strong flexible material which overlaps it, thus completing the streamlined appearance of the suite.

In many dwellings there is a need for extra w.c. or bathroom facilities. Often it is because families are growing up; sometimes it is because the age or illness of a member of the household makes a more conveniently sited w.c. a necessity. If the required, or only available, position for the pan is a long way from the existing plumbing soil pipes then the job may be impossible because of either constructional obstacles or the cost and upheaval of installation.

Happily the new Building Regulations which, among other things, control sanitary installations, now permit the use of pump-assisted w.c. pans. There are various makes on the market, all of them designed to cope with those awkward situations where it would be virtually impossible to fit a w.c. pan to the conventional gravity outlet.

Basically, a standard w.c. suite connects to a sealed tank in which is housed a macerater and a pump (Figure 83) which are operated by the water pressure within the tank as it fills. Both the macerater and pump run at a controlled low speed to avoid unnecessary wear and to minimize the noise level (normally just under 60 DB). The macerater can cope comfortably with normal organic waste and paper discharged from the pan. Solid items such as

Figure 83A   *Sanitop Macerator w.c. pan*

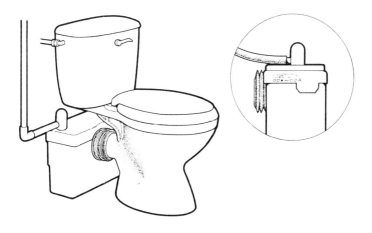

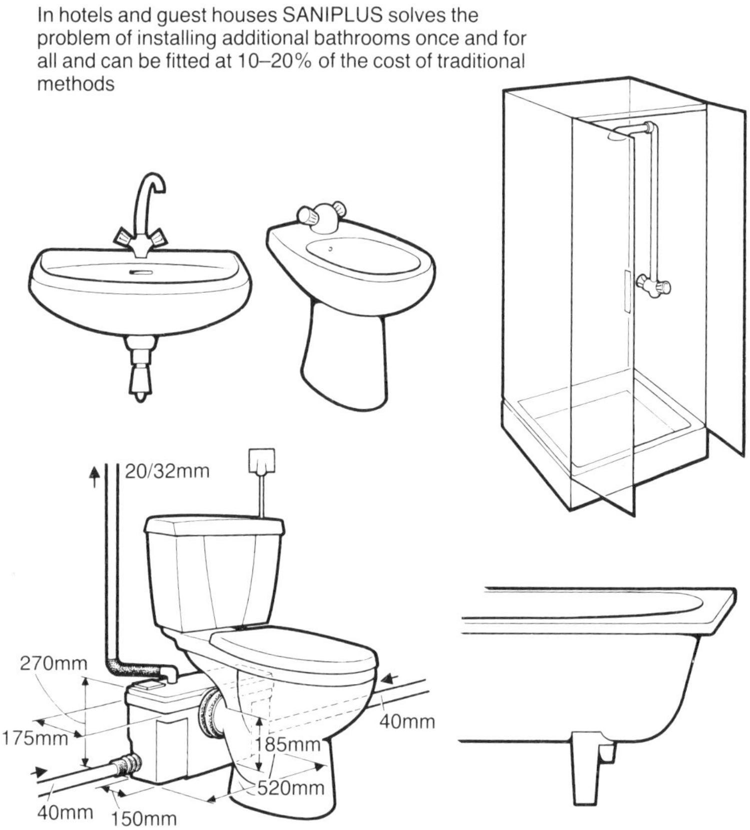
In hotels and guest houses SANIPLUS solves the problem of installing additional bathrooms once and for all and can be fitted at 10–20% of the cost of traditional methods
20/32mm
270mm
175mm
40mm
150mm
185mm
520mm
40mm

Figure 83B *Saniplus Macerator w.c. pan*

metal and plastic must not be passed into the tank, but if they are the machine will cut off automatically to protect both the pump and macerater blades.

The attraction of the Saniflo system is its versatility; it can be fixed virtually anywhere within 20 m of a soil stack, or suitable drain point. (It must not be discharged into a gully, or into any pipe that connects to a gully.) Where the pan is to be fitted in a basement where there is no available drain point, the pump will lift the tank contents two vertical metres (6 ft 6 in), but the subsequent horizontal length of pipework is drastically reduced.

A 20 mm-outside-diameter pipe is adequate for the discharge which should be laid to a minimum fall of 1 in 200 to ensure drainage when the pump stops. This pipe may be run within the depth of a timber floor, or at skirting level, and may be in plastics or copper tube or any other equally smooth-bore pipe. It can also discharge via another waste providing the diameter of the existing pipe is increased by one size at the point of connection, a swept tee is used, and any boss connection to a soil stack is increased, normally to 50 mm (2 in).

The duration of pump running is usually no more than 15 seconds, and will cut off automatically as the water level in the tank drops. An air-inlet vent is provided to the top of the tank.

The Saniflo tank is airtight, so no smells leak into the room, and easy access is provided so that the mechanical parts are easily maintained.

These fittings can be used only in addition to an existing gravity-discharge w.c. pan in any building or dwelling.

Saniflo also produce models with an enlarged capacity tank and extra pipe connections to take the discharge from other fittings (bath, basin, bidet, shower, sink, etc.). These are particularly useful where properties are converted into flats, providing each flat has a gravity w.c. pan, or where hotels and guest houses need to supply extra bathrooms, or for offices, shops, factories, and any other premises that need to increase the sanitary accommodation.

Figures 83A and 83B show the Transbyn models Sanitop and Saniplus. The pumping distance through horizontal pipework for both these machines is up to 50 m or a vertical lift up to 4 m. The Sanitop will also take the waste from a basin in addition to the w.c. while the Saniplus caters for an entire bathroom with tank connections for w.c., bath, basin, and shower wastes.

Each model requires a 220/250 V single phase AC 50 Hz electrical supply. The appliance must *not* be connected to a conventional plug and socket. It must be wired into a fused, unswitched, fixed wiring connector of a type suitable for use in bathrooms.

The appliances should be fitted only by installers who are qualified to do plumbing and electrical work. The installation must comply with the building regulations both in respect of the plumbing and electrical work and the provision of any necessary aerial disconnection lobbies where the toilet opens into an area where food is prepared or stored, or where washing-up is done.

It is very important that the manufacturer's directions are followed at all times; and that before installing any extra sanitary appliance the Building Control Officer is informed.

## Help for the disabled

Slowly, as a society, we are beginning to recognize some of the needs of people who suffer from some form of handicap, mental or physical. Many public and commercial buildings now make provision for physical handicaps but, surprisingly, many households do not. Perhaps it is because so many people are unaware of the assistance available, are put off by the cost incurred, or, just as likely, they have always managed and they always will.

In some respects, of course, giant strides have been made, particularly in home dialysis; but in too many instances people try to cope with the burden unaided. And it is very easy to do the

Figure 84   *Toilet aids for the infirm*
A   *The 'Seabird'*
B   *Bath safety seat*
C   *Bath safety rail*

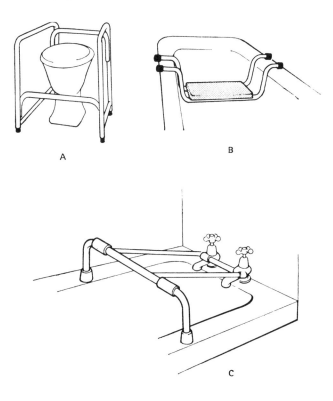

wrong thing: for instance, one unfortunate borough built a public toilet for the disabled – at the bottom of a long flight of stairs. This was an unfortunate mistake that stems from the fact that so many able-bodied people have no conception of the needs of the handicapped. And that applies in the home as well as elsewhere.

### Paraplegics

These sufferers need, above all, room to manoeuvre wheelchairs. Bathrooms and separate w.c.s, therefore, must have wider doors (1 m minimum), and they must be slide-opening (it is very difficult to open a hinged door towards the wheelchair in which you are sitting).

Within the toilet there must be space to turn the chair, room to park beside the pan, and convenient grab rails for support. The w.c. pan must be higher than the normal 400 mm (16 in) rim height – 450 mm (18 in) to 500 mm (20 in). An existing pan can be converted with an adjustable height seat, which is preferable to blocking up the pan to the required height. Do not put a w.c. pan on a plinth, especially for the disabled, because the centre of gravity is altered and the pan is liable to topple as the user slides across from the chair.

A wash basin must be fitted in such a position that it can be used by a person sitting on the pan. Self-adjusting brackets should be used, together with telescopic waste outlet connection to the trap, and flexible water connections so that the height of the basin can be altered with the minimum pressure by the user.

There are many types of disability and it is not possible to detail the sanitary provisions for them all in these pages, but here are some of the fundamental points that should be observed not only for handicapped users but also for the elderly and, indeed, for the young who may be expected to fend for themselves.

### W.c. cistern

The flushing handle must be within easy reach, and require minimum pressure to operate.

### Toilet roll holder

This should be at hand height, and free-running.

### Support rails

Fixed securely at heights and positions as detailed in BS COP 5810.

*Basin taps*

Fit single-lever action, quarter-turn, spray nozzle outlet taps supplied with constant-temperature water from a water-mixing valve which should be 'locked on' the selected temperature. The basin should not be provided with a plug to the waste outlet. (Spray taps are not normally recommended because, unless they are regularly cleaned, the lime scale build up in the filter can support legionella and various bacteria.) However, special provision is needed for handicapped people, bearing in mind that often they need to be protected against things that able-bodied people usually take for granted.

The regulated temperature guards against scalding. The spray delivery and lack of a basin plug are a precaution against the forgetful, who might otherwise leave a tap running on leaving the toilet with the result that the basin fills and the water spills over on to the floor.

Supplies from the mixing valve should be as short as possible and serve only the fittings in one room.

*Showers*

This form of bathing is often preferred by the handicapped because it is more convenient than the traditional bath. Shower trays, however, are not really suitable. Instead the shower area, on the ground floor, should be constructed on the floor level from non-slip quarry tiles with a gully outlet at a low point of a gently graded surface. A drainable hinged seat should be secured to the tiled walls with the shower rose fixed above it. Entry should be through a curtain-protected opening. The space should be large enough to allow manoeuvrability of a wheelchair and, if necessary, someone to assist the bather. The patient may use the hinged seat or, if preferred, remain in the wheelchair to bathe.

With disabled or elderly people hot water should always be delivered through a mixing valve which is pre-set and is not alterable by the user. It must be remembered that a handicapped or elderly person cannot react as quickly to scalding water as a younger, able-bodied person can.

All showers should have rigid stems fitted with self-draining valves operated when the shower is turned off. If they are provided with a flexible hose, anti-back-siphonage protection must be fitted.

The 'Plus 32CM' hinged door comes as an option to the Medicbath XP unit. It provides that extra leg room which may be desirable for patients unable to bend their limbs to the natural seated posture or indeed for 'taller than tall' bathers — the standard XP unit is quite suitable for simply 'tall' people. A cubby hole is built into the hinged door, which itself is removable and inter-changeable with the standard door for baths supplied from January 1983 onwards. The 'Plus 32CM' doors may be 'handed', that is hinged on the right or left hand side viewed from the outside looking into the bath.

Further details from Medic-Bath Limited, Ashfield Works, Hulme Hall Lane, Manchester M10 8AZ

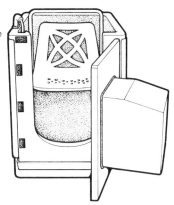

Figure 85A    *Medic bath – XP model*

Figure 85B    *Medic bath – Hybath recliner*

The Medic-Hybath may be regarded as a static unit sited in the usual way in the bathroom, firmly plugged down to the floor; or, fitted with castors, the Hybath is capable of easy manipulation through door openings and along corridors, possibly from bathroom to bedside.
The Hybath is light in weight and is smooth running, thus very little effort is needed to move a patient from point to point.
Future maintenance of the standard Hybath is minimal — no hydraulics, electrics or pneumatics.

Further details from Medic-Bath Limited

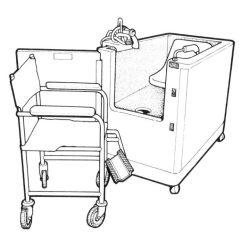

*Medic baths*

Several models of the Medic bath are produced, each specifically designed for ease of operation and the comfort of the user.

The XP model (Figure 85A) is designed to afford more leg room for tall bathers. Reclining seats are optional on most models. Hand shower-spray attachments can also be provided for use by the bather or a helper.

For patients confined to bed the Hybath recliner is an ideal appliance both in domestic dwellings and nursing homes, because it is mounted on castors, is fully mobile and can be used at the bedside provided that hot- and cold-water supplies and a waste point are available (Figure 85B).

There is a 'Mermaid' hip bath in which the user can sit and be in comfortable reach of all the easy-to-operate controls. This bath enables handicapped users to bath themselves: such independence is important psychologically. The Maelström bath is a hydrotherapy bath particularly beneficial to chair-bound users.

Ultimately, there is the Medic 'Shower' bath which incorporates an overhead shower with the normal bathing facilities. These are particularly useful where patients are incontinent.

There is a very full range of appliances to suit virtually every need, and they may be fitted in the home either by the manufacturer or by the householder. All the appliances are DOE and Water Council approved, and are widely used by many organizations who care for handicapped people.

To complement the range of baths there is the Medic Loo

Figure 86   *Medicloo 'Dryad'*

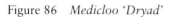
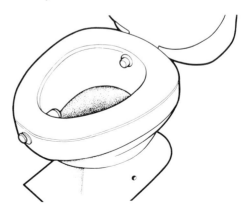

'Dryad': a specially designed w.c. pan which incorporates the douche feature of a bidet and a variety of controls so that it may be operated by most users irrespective of their disability.

## Home dialysis machines

Special care must be exercised in both the supply to the appliance and the disposal of the waste products. The proportioning pump used in mains-pressure operated dilution of dialysis fluid must be protected by a terminal vacuum breaker, or an in-line vacuum breaker. A double-check valve assembly with a drain-off testing point between is an equal safeguard, subject to the approval of the local water undertaking.

The waste pipe must not connect directly to a drain point, a soil pipe, a gully, or another waste pipe because, in the event of a blockage in any one of those, the waste products would back up the waste pipe to the point of discharge with, possibly, damaging results to the patient. The waste pipe from the appliance must discharge through an air break to a tundish or hopper and then to waste so that any stoppage of flow will simply cause the tundish or hopper to overflow. Messy, maybe, but, for the patient, safe.

For all home-treatment appliances regular maintenance is essential and should be carried out by a trained person.

## The bidet

This is a sanitary fitting designed on lines similar to a pedestal w.c. pan, but is intended primarily as an ablution fitment for use by women in matters of personal hygiene. It is used in a great many homes and hotels on the Continent, and is now in demand in this country. It should be used only for ablutionary purposes and therefore may be connected to a waste pipe and not a soil pipe.

Figure 87 shows a modern type of bidet. It is provided with a douche jet in an upward direction for ablution, and this is controlled by hot and cold valves. The bidet does not have a seat and warm water can be used to flush the fitment so that the rim is rendered comfortable to the person sitting on it.

Figure 87    *The bidet*

IMPORTANT: The bidet must be installed in compliance with the requirements described in Chapter 2 in respect of the prevention of contamination of water supply.

# 9

# The Shower Bath in the Home

The shower is the most convenient method of bathing. It is quick, refreshing, economical and, not least important, uses constantly clean water.

Drawbacks are that you cannot soak totally immersed in supportive water, or use bath toiletries. A growing number of people are installing both baths and showers in their homes and enjoying the best that each has to offer. Showers can be fitted separately in cubicles or, if space is limited, a shower spray can be fitted over a bath.

Showers may be fitted virtually anywhere in the house providing there is a convenient hot- and cold-water supply and an accessible waste connection. There are instances of cubicle showers located on landings at the top of stairs; in the kitchens of small, two-roomed flats; and, of course, in bedrooms, where they are very convenient. Manufacturers provide a variety of models to suit most if not all requirements.

The salient advantages of the shower, not necessarily in order of importance, are:

1 It is hygienic and pleasant to use.
2 The shower is much cheaper to operate as water consumption is considerably less than with the traditional bath. This is particularly important with regard to hot water, and where water softeners are installed.
3 It follows that many showers may be obtained in succession without an increase in the heating or storage capacity.
4 The shower takes less time to use, thus alleviating bathroom queues.
5 It occupies considerably less space than a bath.
6 Because it is simple to adjust the water temperature of the shower, the possibility of a person catching cold after a hot

shower is remote, particularly if the mixing valve is turned to cool before finishing.

# First essentials

For a shower bath the hot and cold water must be mixed to give a constant supply at a selected temperature, and it is most essential that a means of varying this temperature between fully hot and fully cold should be provided. This can be done by using a mixing valve which equalizes the pressures of the hot and cold water. An obvious way of doing this with the ordinary domestic system is to arrange that the cold-water supply to the mixing fitting be taken from the same cold-water supply that feeds the hot-water system. It must be understood that byelaws prohibit the mixing of cold water direct from the main with hot water from a gravity system.

It is also essential that there is an adequate 'head', or pressure, of water at the shower itself, and this is determined by the height of the cold-water cistern above the shower outlet. Generally, it can be taken that if the bottom of the cold-water cistern is a minimum 3 m above the floor of the bathroom, a satisfactory shower can be obtained. If a greater height than this is possible, so much the better. If the cold-water side of the mixing fitting is fed from a single pipe from the supply cistern it will avoid the possibility of other draw-off points causing a drop in pressure and a consequent sudden increase in temperature at the shower.

When mains-fed, pressurized hot-water systems are installed it is unlikely that water undertakings will object to the cold-water services being supplied from the water mains providing that anti-back-siphonage precautions are taken. The only reason they may refuse permission is if their mains distributing pipes are unable to cope with direct draw-off peak demand. The water mains in many parts of the country cannot provide the capacity required and, therefore, storage may have to be provided for domestic cold water to reduce the 'instant' demand on the services.

In this event a shower mixing valve capable of compensating for the differential pressures must be selected. If this is not possible then a pressure-reducing valve must be fitted to the hot-water branch supply pipe to the water mixing valve.

# Mixing fittings

These are divided broadly into two classes: (1) the mixer, which consists of a pair of orthodox hot and cold screw-down taps with their outlets joined together by means of a 'breeching' or mixing chamber; and (2) the mixing valve, which combines the two taps or valves in one, is operated by a single control handle, and allows any temperature between hot and cold to be selected manually by moving a pointer round a scale marked 'cold', 'tepid' and 'hot', or calibrated in degrees.

With the mixer fitting no visual indication of the temperature is given, and this, allied to the fact that two valves have to be adjusted, makes it slower and very much less convenient and positive than the mixing valve.

There is a wide selection of mixing valves on the market today, attractively designed with durable, easy-clean finishes suitable for any bathroom.

Ideally, hot and cold supplies to mixing valves should be of equal pressures, but there are valves on the market that can operate satisfactorily with a pressure difference as great as 5 to 1.

All mixing valves should be fitted with a fail-safe device, which will shut off the hot-water supply immediately in the event of loss of pressure in the cold-water supply, to prevent scalding.

Where the hot water is supplied to the mixing valve from a mains-fed, pressurized system, the cold-water supply to the mixing valve should be taken from the main (subject to the manufacturer's recommended maximum working pressures). Connecting the hot-water system to the mains-water supply effectively puts every hot-water tap on the main.

The following specifications and illustrations are reproduced by courtesy of Barking-Grohe.

The Neotherm CP brass shower uses a sealed capsule thermostat to control the hot and cold supplies, ensuring that the shower never varies from the selected temperature. The wax-capsule thermostat is unaffected by corrosion or deposits from hard water. Hot surge is eliminated by the provision of a special metering device. The temperature selector is clearly seen when the user is under the shower, and the Neotherm has special compensating valves for controlling the pressure of hot and cold supplies. It is suitable for use with the Main Severn instantaneous water heater.

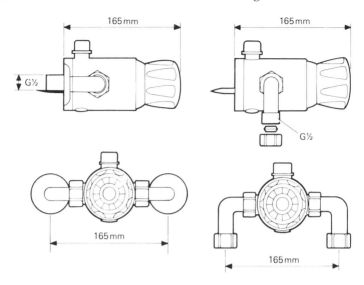

Figure 88    *Neotherm thermostatic shower*

The Euromix CP brass concealed shower mixer has a single lever regulator for precision control of volume and water temperature, provided that the hot and cold supplies are at a constant pressure and temperature. Supplies can come from above, below or from the sides.

The Crystal CP brass deck bath-shower mixer with non-rising headworks has a button for changing to 'shower' which is conveniently positioned on top of the nozzle, and the diverter returns automatically to the 'bath' position when the water is turned off. Accepted by the National Water Council.

## Shower booster

For a normal shower installation a nominal head or gravity pressure of 1.5 m (effective head 1 m at a flow rate of 0.1 l.p.s.) is recommended.

However, in many homes space is not available to install a cold-water cistern high enough to achieve the recommended head and flow. In such cases the Barking-Grohe Flomatic shower booster permits the use of a shower where it would otherwise be impractical. By lifting the water available at the mixer, the

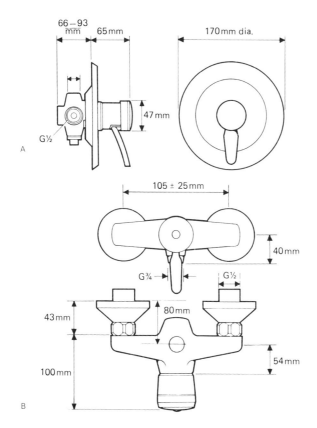

Figure 89  *Euromix single lever shower mixer*

booster can provide a flow of 0.1 l.p.s. with a water supply that would otherwise provide as little as .03 l.p.s. flow at the shower rose. It can accomplish this when the water level in the full cistern is a mere 200 mm above the highest point of the shower attachment.

It does not pressurize the flow (which would require some three times the volume of water than is normally available in British domestic installations). To ensure an effective shower it is important that the Flomatic is not starved of water. The flow of blended water available at the shower outlet of the mixer (with shower attachment) should be at least 6 l.p.m. For bath/shower mixers with self-return diverters the flow should be at least 8.4 l.p.m.

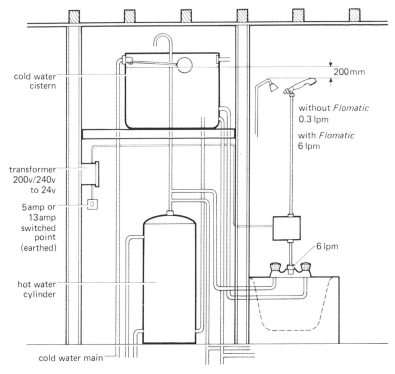

cold water cistern

200 mm

without *Flomatic* 0.3 lpm

with *Flomatic* 6 lpm

transformer 200v/240v to 24v

5 amp or 13 amp switched point (earthed)

6 lpm

hot water cylinder

cold water main

Figure 90   *Flomatic shower booster installation*

Hot- and cold-water supplies to the shower mixer or bath/ shower mixer must originate from a cold-water cistern (see Figure 90): the Flomatic must not be connected to high-pressure mains water. The maximum pressure on one side of the mixer should be 7 metre head.

The temperature of the hot water at the mixing valve (prior to blending) must be a minimum of 50°C. The Flomatic, like all other Barking-Grohe products, should be used only in approved plumbing installations.

## Shower rose or shower spray

The part of the shower fitting from which the water finally issues may be referred to as the shower head and is available in two types. There is the 'rose' type, often referred to as the 'watering can' type. This can take different forms but in each the water comes out in jets from a large number of small holes. The advantages of the rose are that it will operate at a somewhat lower head of water and, if large enough, can give an extremely heavy shower; it is often slightly cheaper in cost than the sprayer.

The other type of shower head is the 'sprayer', which, by utilizing centrifugal force, forms a spray of what might be likened to raindrops. The sprayer makes use of a small number of comparatively large holes. Much more economical in the use of water, its consumption is predetermined. Its centrifugal action has the effect of assisting the mixing of hot and cold water, and its small consumption will damp down sudden variations of temperature that may be caused by 'heavy-handed' manipulation of the mixing valve handle. The spray of aerated drops is extremely pleasant and invigorating. The most popular type passes 7 litres per minute, of which only half is hot and half cold. The sprayer is much less liable to choke up, can easily be cleaned out and is almost indestructible in use. It usually has a cap end that can be changed to vary the volume and size of spray.

## The shower in conjunction with the bath

Practically any type of shower can be used over a bath. For the sake of convenience and safety, the type of bath which has a fairly wide and flat bottom is to be preferred. It is also an advantage if the bath is fixed in a corner or in an alcove, and is of the type which has a flat rim, or roll, over which the walls will project slightly, thus ensuring that water cannot run between the bath and the walls.

In order to prevent water from the shower spraying or splashing over the front of the bath on to the floor, some type of shield is required. This may take the form of a glass panel which can be hinged to swing outwards, or, as is more usual and considerably cheaper, a curtain rail and waterproof curtain can be used. The curtain will need to be long enough to fall inside the bath, and wide enough to cover the whole length of the bath. If the bath is fitted in an alcove, a straight rail of tube with a flange at each end will be required. If the bath is fitted in a corner, the rail will need to be semi-rectangular, and the 'return' end, across the bath, will be secured to the back wall. In this case the curtain must be wide enough to draw across both the front and the return end.

In the case of a bath which stands clear of the walls, a curtain rail of fully rectangular shape can be provided. Curtain rails of circular form are obtainable, but although they permit a person to stand under the shower, they allow insufficient space for soaping and rinsing.

It is usual to fix the shower at the end above the bath taps and to take the water supplies to it from the service pipes feeding the latter. Both mixer fittings and mixing valves are made in 22-mm size, and arranged for the double purpose of filling the bath and feeding the shower, as required. It is more common, however, to provide a separate 15-mm mixing valve for the shower and a pair of 22-mm taps, or a 22-mm mixer fitting, for the bath.

Whatever the arrangement may be, it must be remembered that, so long as mixing takes place and the hot water comes from a low-pressure storage system, the cold-water connection must not be made direct to the main.

NOTE: Flexible hoses to shower heads from bath mixer taps must be fixed in such a way as to prevent the spray nozzle from falling into the bath below the spillover level of the fitting.

### In-line showers
Available on the market are electric in-line heater units for shower heads connected to a mains water supply. Before considering the use of this type of heater, both the local water authority and the Electricity Board should be consulted.

## The shower bath as a complete unit

Where the shower is to take the place of, or is to be separate from, the slipper bath, a shower cubicle can be built in as an annexe to the bathroom (see Figure 91), or in any other suitable place in the house. The essentials here are a receiving tray at floor level, which can be obtained in fireclay, enamelled iron, stainless steel or fibreglass. The tray may also be of tiled construction or built from timber and lined with a suitable material. A 42-mm waste and trap and an overflow connection will be required. Three walls can be tiled or rendered waterproof by other suitable means, and the fourth, or front, side can be provided with a waterproof curtain

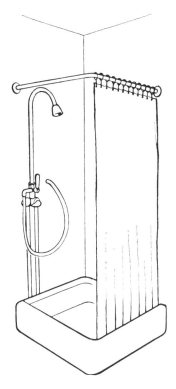

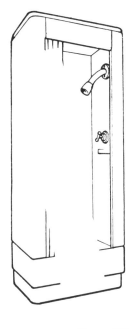

Figure 91
*Built-in shower cubicle*

Figure 92
*Prefabricated shower cabinet*

sufficiently long to fall inside the receiving tray. Curtains are now available in plastics, in a large range of attractive colours and patterns. Shower enclosures can also be built of glass panels with metal framework.

The shower fitting itself can either be of the 'overhead' or 'shoulder height' type, the latter allowing a person to take a shower without necessarily wetting the hair, or adjustable-height shower heads are available.

Completely prefabricated shower cabinets with plinth, receiving tray, front curtains, mixing valve and shower head are available. These can be set anywhere in the house – even on a bedroom carpet – and only require connecting up to hot and cold supplies and waste pipe. No building work of any kind is required. They can be purchased in dismantled sections, allowing them to be taken upstairs and through narrow doorways, to where they can easily and quickly be assembled. It is preferable that cabinets of this type be provided with a top to them, as this helps to confine the vapour that rises from a shower. It is also important that they should be rustproof. For this reason the use of aluminium is of great advantage for it cannot rust and is very light to handle. This type of cabinet is illustrated in Figure 92.

The absence of a domestic hot-water supply system does not rule out a shower. Showers can be operated from certain types of gas and electric water heaters, and can then utilize pressure direct from the cold-water main. Mixing arrangements are available for such showers, and, as both hot and cold come direct from the main, regulations are not contravened.

One maker of self-contained shower cabinets supplies them complete with either gas or electric water heater, and a tapping is often taken from the same heater to supply hot water to a nearby washbasin.

Children almost invariably love showers, but in the case of very young infants it is advisable to have the waste of the receiving tray fitted with a tubular 'standing' overflow which will allow the water to build up to the level of the top of this tube before overflowing. This makes a very satisfactory bath for infants. One make of aluminium shower cabinet on the market is fitted with this type of standing overflow which permits a depth of approximately four inches of water to build up in the receiving tray.

## Impulse showers

These are very much in line with the development of hydrotherapy baths, where water jets have been introduced to the design to provide stimulation or relaxation of body muscles. Impulse showers can provide an interesting variety of sprays and jets to invigorate or soothe, or both.

Belco produce a range of variable heads for their pumped showers that give an exciting choice of functions which can transform showering into an exhilarating activity. The multi-head system produces everything from a silky soft foam, a tingling fresh fine spray or a direct jet to a vigorous, pulsating, pump-driven spray. And there are six different combinations of shower heads as standard supply, or an infinite variety if you choose to invent your own.

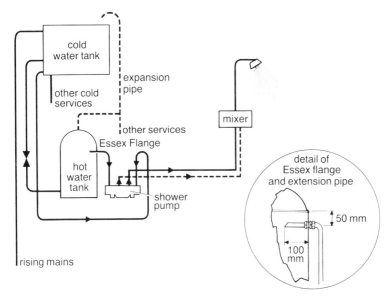

Figure 93   *Impulse shower installation*

The shower systems are designed to use stored hot and cold water. (Shower booster pumps must never be connected directly to the mains-water supply. Where both hot- and cold-water systems in a dwelling are pressurized and mains fed, a separate hot-water storage tank and cold-water storage cistern must be installed to supply the booster pump unit. However, both the mixer valve and the shower handset and hose are suitable for use on mains-water supply when booster pumps are not used.)

To avoid the possibility of fluctuating water supply to the shower, independent supplies should be run from the hot-water cylinder and cold-water storage cistern to the pump (see Figure 93). The hot water must be connected in the top section of the cylinder no more than a third of its height down from the top. The connection is by Essex flange and is simply made. The inner part of the flange is hinged across its centre and will fold to pass through the hole that the installer drills in the cylinder. (Indirect cylinders will have a connection already formed, and this may be used if a secondary return loop has not been fitted to the system.) The folding flange is inserted on a retaining tool which holds it in place while the outer section of the fitting is screwed in and, with internal and external washers in place, a watertight joint will be formed. The pipe connection should extend through the flange by at least 100 mm.

The cold-water connection to the cistern must be made as shown.

To avoid vibration, the pump, which must be fitted upright, should be screwed to the mounting surface leaving $\frac{1}{16}$ in between screws and rubber absorption pad. The hot and cold water must be connected to the pump as shown in Figure 93, and the runs should be kept as short as possible. Elbows and restrictive-flow fittings must not be used. All changes of direction must be by long-radius bends, and all valves should be of the full-way gate type.

The pump simulates a 15 m (50 ft) head and has a normal delivery of 13 litres of mixed water a minute (3 gallons) at a pressure of 22 p.s.i. Water temperature should be in the range of 1°C to 63°C (33°F to 145°F). Higher temperatures up to 77°C (170°F) can be used, but occasionally this may cause aeration, which can induce malfunction at the shower head.

More than one pump may be used, depending on the system selected or designed, in which case electrical relays are required to synchronize the pump operation. Figure 94 shows the plumbing layout for the six standard arrangements. The pumps can supply a continuous or alternating pulsing flow of water, and the heads can be adjusted for the type of spray required. Pressurized water is mixed and then directed to the various shower head outlets via a three- or five-way diverter valve. The type required is determined by the number of shower heads in the system selected.

Clearly, these are not ordinary showers but examples of sophisticated plumbing engineering and, therefore, it is essential that these systems are installed only by people qualified to do so.

The minimum head of water required for the operation of standard showers does not apply to pumped impulse showers of the type described here.

# Installing a shower

A shower can be installed in a space as small as 760 mm square. In fact, this often makes it worth while installing a shower as an extra washing facility.

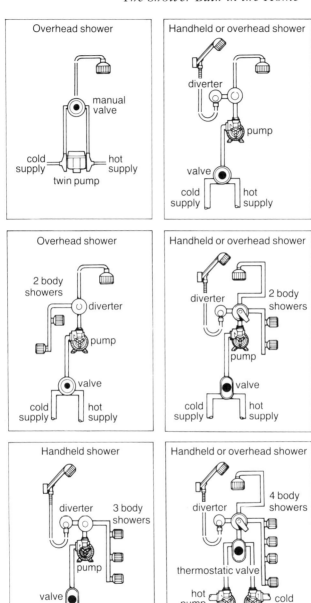

Figure 94 *Impulse shower plumbing arrangement*

## The 'head' or pressure of water

If a 'U' tube is fed from the underside of a water cistern (Figure 95) and the open end of the 'U' tube is at the same level as the level of the tank, no water will flow. If a metre is cut from the open end of the 'U' tube then the water will flow and a small fountain of water will spray from the end of the 'U' tube. If we now cut 3 m from the open end of the 'U' tube it can be appreciated that water will try to reach its own level and create a much higher fountain.

The amount that is cut from the tube is known as the 'head' or pressure. In the first instance we would have had a 1-metre head and in the second instance a 3-metre head, and the greater the head the faster the flow and the more water available.

## Installation

No shower fitting can work satisfactorily unless the installation is right. Careful attention to the following simple requirements is needed only once, and will ensure many years of trouble-free service.

Figure 95   *'Head' or pressure of water*

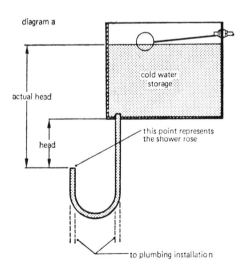

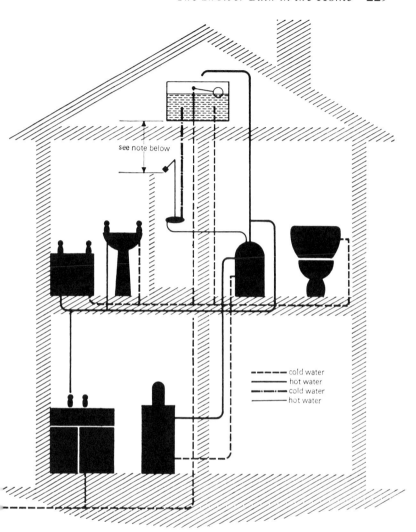

see note below

cold water
hot water
cold water
hot water

Figure 96  *Recommended 'head'*

## Measure the head

Make sure that there is sufficient head or pressure available. You must position the shower rose at a minimum distance of 1 m below the base of the cold-water cistern (Figure 96). (You can ignore the position of the hot-water cylinder on the hot supply; it is its source, as cold water, that matters.) This is the absolute minimum figure and will probably only be acceptable where pipe runs are short and a gentle wetting shower is acceptable.

Normally the figure should be 1.5 m or more which should provide a spray of 4.5–6.5 litres per minute. However, where even the figure of 1 m is impossible to achieve a booster can be installed.

Where the gravity flow is insufficient, a shower booster is the answer (see Figure 90).

*Equal pressures*

Hot- and cold-water supply pressures to the shower controller need to be about equal. If, as is most likely, the hot-water system is fed from a storage cistern, then the cold-water supply to the controller **must** come from a cistern. It is technically wrong and dangerous, and contrary to the byelaws of water authorities, to connect the hot-water side of the controller to the cistern and the cold-water side to the mains supply.

*Get the flows right*

Eliminate long lengths of pipes in which static hot water rapidly cools and that infuriating wait while tepid water issues from the shower rose.

You should also note that the connections with existing pipe runs which feed other taps or draw-offs could lead to intermittent water starvation and so to fluctuations in the shower temperature. Ideally it is better to run independent hot- and cold-water supplies to the controller from the hot-water storage cylinder and the cold-water cistern. The elements of a satisfactory household system are shown, with the pipe runs to the shower.

All controllers are fitted with a maximum temperature limiting device which will enable you to set the maximum temperature of the spray to suit your particular requirements. Hot-water boilers can be set at different temperatures for various purposes and this will affect the shower temperature. The maximum temperature limiting device is an essential safety feature when boilers installed for the dual purpose of central heating and water supply are set at maximum temperature.

NOTE: 1.5 m is the recommended height from the underside of the cistern to the shower rose. If the pipe runs are short this may be reduced to a minimum of 1 m.
NOTE: For elderly or infirm users, or for children, the recommended maximum temperature for showers is 38°C. Shower controls can be purchased with an automatic stop at this setting. An over-ride button is provided for other users.

# 10

# Soil- and Waste-Pipe Systems

The occupier of every dwelling should be conversant with the system of waste and soil disposal from the premises. Single-occupancy dwellings such as houses, bungalows, flats, and caravans are normally straightforward though, of course, problems can and do arise, particularly when the basic design principles are ignored. However, it is in flats and similar buildings (guest houses, hostels, etc.) where trouble can be expected.

But first things first; let us establish what we are talking about.

## Definitions

What is soil? And what is waste?

Soil is human waste products: excreta and urine, which are normally passed through a w.c. pan. Some readers of this book, however, may have use of other fittings, in private residential homes for the elderly, for example, where slop sinks, bed pan washers, urinals, etc. may be used. These are all 'soil fittings' and must connect either to a drain point (ground-floor locations only) or to a 'soil' pipe (often referred to as a soil stack).

Waste is the 'used' water in ablutionary and domestic appliances such as baths, basins, showers, sinks, bidets, and washing machines.

Modern-day sanitation systems allow all these branch discharge pipes, both soil and waste, to discharge into the main soil pipe. The conditions governing these connections are detailed in the section on single-stack plumbing.

## Exclusion of foul air

Despite the fact that present-day medical evidence discounts the

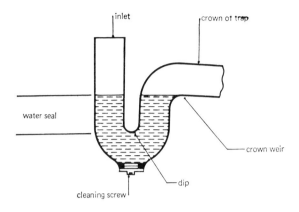

Figure 97   *Details of a P-trap*

once predominant opinion that drain gas can give rise to epidemics and is detrimental to health, there is no person who would want foul air to penetrate his home. The smell of drains is obnoxious and it is imperative that it should be sealed off at all the appliances used for excremental, ablutionary and domestic purposes. Protection against drain gas infiltration is attained by that simple appliance called a trap. A trap is formed by a depression or a U-bend which will retain water in the trap but not interfere with the flow of water through the pipes. Traps may be separate fittings or embodied in the appliance itself. In Figure 97 a P-trap is illustrated. The important part of the trap is the water seal, which forms the barrier against the passage of drain air through the trap. While that seal is maintained all will be well but if the water level is depressed below the point marked 'dip' on the illustration, then drain gas can infiltrate into the house. Traps are fixed to kitchen sinks, washbasins, bidets and baths and are an integral part of the w.c. pan.

## Loss of water seal of a trap

The loss of the vital water seal of a trap may be due to one or more of the following reasons:

1 Self-siphonage.
2 Induced siphonage.
3 Evaporation.

The chief problems are to avoid self-siphonage, by which individual appliances suck out their own seals when they discharge, and induced siphonage by which the discharge of one fitting 'pulls' out the seal of another fitting.

In long spells of hot, dry weather the evaporation of a trap may occur if a house is left unoccupied for any length of time. The only remedy is to arrange for someone to flush the appliances from time to time.

## Single-stack plumbing

Most sanitary plumbing installations today are installed on the single-stack principle, so called because all appliances in a building can discharge into one main pipe. Providing the basic principles are observed there is no need for anti-siphon pipes.

The sole purpose of the design is to control the speed and depth of water flowing along any branch pipe to the main discharge stack. A pipe which runs nearly full will cause the trap on the fitting to siphon, while a pipe that runs no more than half-full will not (see Figures 98A and B).

The steeper gradient of the pipe in Figure 98A causes the water to run faster, thereby increasing its depth and thus preventing the free flow of air back up the pipe to maintain atmospheric pressure at point X. A discharge in a sufficiently long and steep waste pipe will, therefore, cause a minus pressure at point X which atmospheric pressure on the inlet side of the trap will immediately

Figure 98    *Waste pipe gradient and siphonage*

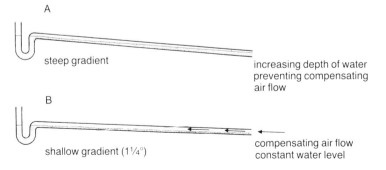

attempt to balance. To do this, the pressure of the air will push the water round the trap and into the waste pipe and will continue until the air pressures inside and outside the pipe are equalized. The most common symptom of this happening is a gurgling noise following the discharge of water from any fitting.

In Figure 98B the problem does not arise, because the flat gradient of the pipe slows the water discharge rate, thereby limiting its depth and allowing adequate space for replacement air to flow freely up the pipe against the flow of the water to maintain equilibrium in air pressure. This point is easily demonstrated by anyone who suffers from a waste appliance that gurgles noisily after discharge. Simply place a 2-pence coin on the recessed grating of the waste outlet fitting, put in the plug and fill the appliance, and then pull out the plug, leaving the coin in place. Because of the restricted flow the fitting will take longer to empty and, consequently, the depth and velocity of the water in the waste pipe will be reduced, with the result that there will be no gurgling siphonic action at the end of the discharge.

Induced siphonage is not a great problem either, providing that the main discharge stack is of adequate size, and that the branch waste pipes are not too long.

Maximum water velocity in vertical main discharge stacks is reached within 3 m to 5 m (10 ft to 16 ft), depending on the smoothness of the bore of the pipe. In a uPVC stack the terminal velocity of 4.6 m per second (15 ft per second) is achieved within 3 m.

Descending water is limited to this speed because of our old friend the displaced air. As the plug of water drops into the stack it tends to compress the air below it, thereby setting up a plus pressure point. The air pressure reacts by forcing its way through the centre of the plug of water and the fluid is, therefore, pushed out against the sides of the pipe. It is a combination of the air pressure pushing upwards and the frictional resistance of the pipe walls that controls the speed of the descending water.

Taking all these factors into consideration we can predict the behaviour of a single-stack installation providing the following guidelines are observed:

1  Wastes of 32 mm from basins must not exceed 1.68 m in overall length or have a fall greater than 1½° from horizontal. For basin waste pipes that need to be longer than 1.68 m the diameter of the entire waste must be increased to 40 mm to a maximum length of 3 m.

2 Waste pipes of 40 mm from baths, sinks, showers, washing machines and dishwashers must not exceed 2.4 m in length with a maximum fall of 5° from the horizontal. These wastes may also be extended to 3 m maximum length providing the diameter is increased to 50 mm.

3 Sinks fitted with macerator waste-disposal units must have a 40 mm waste with a fall of 7½° and a maximum length of 2.4 m.

4 Any waste pipe longer than 3 m must be vented from a point close to the trap of the sanitary fitting and run upwards to a safe outlet (see on termination of stack).

5 It is bad practice to install over-long waste pipes, whether they are vented or not. They are noisy in operation and, because of sediment deposits, prone to blockage. If the main discharge stack is too far away then the fitting should be resited or the waste connected to a waste stack, or to a rainwater pipe providing that it is of a suitable size, is constructed of approved waste-pipe weight materials, and terminates at a safe outlet.

6 All sanitary fittings (waste) must be provided with a 75 mm deep-seal trap. (For the reasons already explained, these must be P-traps.)

7 Each waste to each fitting must connect separately to the main discharge stack. (Combined wastes do work, and may be acceptable, if the collecting waste is of a sufficiently large diameter. In the average dwelling, however, the situation should not arise where this is necessary.)

8 Bends in waste pipes must be kept to a minimum, and those that are used must have a radius of at least 75 mm. An excessive number of bends on even a short length of pipe, will cause self-siphonage because of the air pressure resistance at each bend which will, eventually, hold up the water long enough to fill the pipe. If the bends cannot be avoided, and the fitting cannot be resited, then the waste will have to be vented.

9 Waste pipes must be run in the horizontal plane, and vertical, or raking, drops must be avoided as these increase the velocity of water and result in self-siphonage. Where they do have to be used to avoid obstructions then the diameter of the pipe must be increased and the drop should be on a properly formed upstand (Figure 99).

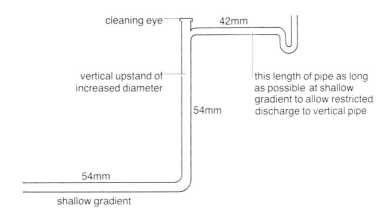

Figure 99    *Vertical upstand*

10  Access points should be provided on all waste branches, particularly at any change of direction.

11  W.c. branches should be swept in the direction of the flow with a minimum radius sweep of 50 mm measured at the throat. W.c. branch pipe connections up to 6 m long have been used successfully when laid to very shallow falls.

## The main discharge stack

This is normally a 100 mm-diameter pipe; only on buildings where a high loading can be expected is it likely to be 150 mm. A 100 mm-diameter pipe is adequate for all the waste and soil discharge from, say, ten flats because the pipe is sized on the probability of usage factor and not on the capacity required if every fitting were to be discharged at the same time. The probability factor assesses the percentage number of fittings that will be discharged at the same time during peak periods of use and the pipe is sized accordingly. It follows, therefore, that a 100 mm-diameter pipe will serve more than ten flats.

For single-occupancy buildings it is more than adequate. The stack is connected to the drain at ground level, and rises vertically to roof level, where its open end forms a vent to the drainage system. This ventilation is important as all drainage is subject to

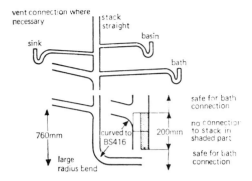

Figure 100   *Design of single-stack system – main features*

varying pressures which are constantly fluctuating, and the free movement of air through the system controls this situation.

## Safe outlet

The vent must discharge to fresh air at least 1 m above or 3 m from the highest opening of the building. It must be stressed that this is to provide ventilation to the drainage system. Where there is adequate ventilation already provided the stack may terminate at any convenient point above the highest fitting with an air admittance valve. This valve is shut under normal and plus pressures within the stack but opens to admit air to counter any minus pressure caused by the discharge of a fitting, or by normal fluctuation within the system.

As these are mechanical valves and liable to malfunction there is considerable debate in the industry on the desirability of siting such fittings in habitable areas or, indeed, in the roof space, where the water in the storage cisterns can absorb any gases given off through a valve that has jammed open. The best advice, probably, is to compromise and restrict their use to external pipework, although the Building Regulations allow them other than for ventilating pipes.

## Offsets

The stack must be vertical from the bottom to the top of the highest branch connection. Offsets in the main pipe cause the hazard of resistance air pressure and should not be used. Again, if they are unavoidable, the offset may have to be vented to relieve any pressure build up.

On stacks with low loading factors local authorities may allow offsets made with high-angle bends (minimum 135°) providing that the topmost bend of the offset is at least 750 mm below the branch immediately above it.

Offsets above the topmost fitting are, of course, permitted.

## Access

Access doors should be located at each 100-mm-branch to the stack and at the end of every waste branch. Access at the foot of the stack is necessary unless there is a drain manhole within 3 m.

## Shared soil stacks

These are particularly applicable to flats, either in blocks or in houses that have been converted into two, three, four or five dwellings according to the number of floors in the building. Sometimes the units are quite small and two dwellings or even three may be arranged on each floor of a reasonably proportioned building.

A clever designer can arrange the dwellings so that they all share a common stack. It is not unusual to have ten to fifteen flats discharging kitchen and bathroom waste into a central, internal soil vent pipe. There is nothing wrong in that as long as the installation is properly done. There are, however, problems arising from shared drainage of which every flat occupier should be aware.

Depending upon the layout of the building and the method of division, the stacks may be internal or external. For multi-dwelling conversions or developments, designers usually opt for internal soil stacks because they are more economical. For that reason we shall consider a building with an internal stack.

It is important that the ground-floor flats have their own separate connection to the drain and do not connect to the stack serving the flats on the floors above. Equally important, the drain should be a separate connection to the manhole from that collecting the soil stack.

Rainwater must not discharge into the soil stack. This is an elementary point but it is often overlooked, and that can bring disaster should there be a blockage in the stack while it is raining.

Internal stacks are usually run in plumbing ducts. If this is the case in any reader's dwelling, make sure there is adequate access to the duct and, in turn, to the stack. Plumbing fittings are usually fixed to the duct face and access is either limited or very difficult.

Ground-floor dwellers should check to see if there is an access door to the main stack in their flat. If there is, and there shouldn't be, do not permit its use in the event of a blockage to the stack. If the blockage is in the drain they will get all the back-up water and mess over their floor when the cover is removed. If it is above they will still get the mess as the rods push the obstruction down the pipe. Blockages should be rodded either from the manhole or from a point above the obstruction. The limit of the back-up water can be checked from the height of the water in the w.c. pan trap. A rodding access should be provided in every flat.


## Backsurge

The most dreaded word for any flat occupier. Unfortunately it is a product of the times; it comes without warning, and its effects are horrifying.

Backsurge is the effect of air pressure within the stack forcing a descending discharge to back up through a branch pipe connection and into the sanitary fitting. If the discharge is of sufficient quantity, or there is a succession of discharges, then the mess will gush up through the fitting outlet, flood the fitting, and spill over on to the floor. It can happen so fast that areas of flats have been several inches deep in filthy water within minutes and certainly before the occupiers have realized what was happening, let alone been able to do anything about it.

It is a complaint that was always associated with those ground-floor flats unlucky enough to be connected to the main discharge stack. The bend to the drain at the bottom of the stack formed a major resistance to heavy discharge, causing the water to inundate the ground-floor fittings.

Today it can happen on any floor. There are cases of backsurge on the 11th and 12th floors of high rise buildings, and it is common on 4th, 5th and 6th floors. The principal cause appears to be deposits of phosphates from washing powders on the walls of the pipe. This encrustation in turn collects solidifying grease and, over a period of time, the pipe diameter can be dramatically reduced to the point where the upflowing air holds back the descending water and backsurge occurs. The deposits are often irregular and are not continuous, so that some parts of a stack are affected and others are not. This situation can only be made worse if rainwater discharges into the stack. Prolonged heavy rain into an affected stack has, in known cases, resulted in extensive flooding of apartments lasting several hours at a time.

This problem can be avoided by regular maintenance and cleaning of both internal and external stacks. High-pressure water jets and coring drills are used to remove the hardened deposits. The operation needs to be repeated at least every two years and, in extreme cases, more often. Occupiers should insist that this work is written into shared responsibility agreements and the managing agents should see that the preventative work is carried out to a satisfactory standard.

## Extensions

In these days of escalating house prices it is often cheaper for families seeking larger accommodation to extend the property they already occupy. That way they are more likely to get what they want as opposed to what's on offer.

The most popular extension is the kitchen/bathroom, and this makes good sense because it offers greater scope for the use of the living space, which is increased in area with the removal of these two utilities.

It is at this point that occupiers become involved with drainage, so it is important that the basic principles of this too-often-overlooked branch of plumbing are explained.

## Household drainage

Again the description 'household' is a blanket term, though there are obvious difficulties in providing extensions for flats (other than those on the ground floor), caravans, etc.

A drain is a pipe, usually underground, that conveys waste and soil to a sewer. Where a combined system of drainage is used the drain will carry everything including rainwater to a common pipe called a sewer; where a dual system is used the rainwater is carried to a separate pipe from the waste and soil.

A sewer is a pipe collecting drains from two or more properties. These are often referred to as 'shared drains'. In Inner London boroughs, any shared drain constructed before 1965 is the responsibility of the local authority; in all other areas those shared drains constructed before 1937 are the responsibility of local councils. This means that only the local authority may carry out works to the sewers, or shared drains.

A blockage in the shared drain will be cleared by the council, who may make a charge to recover their costs; but often this charge is waived. Any defect in the shared drain is repaired by the council after they have served notice on all the properties served by that drain. On completion of the work the costs are divided among the affected properties on that sewer and the owners are charged. Thereafter, it is the council's responsibility to maintain at its own cost that section of drain repaired or renewed.

There is often some doubt about the definition of 'affected' property. The common drain running from house number 1 to house number 6 is clearly a sewer because it is 'shared' or common to all six properties. However, if the drain were defective between houses 1 and 2 or houses 5 and 6, would the cost be shared between all the owners?

The generally accepted answer is no. Both houses number 1 and number 6 are, in effect, on single-line drains because each of these sections of drain serves one dwelling only. Therefore any blockage or breakage to those single-line drains would be the responsibility of the owners of houses 1 and 6 because none of the others is affected.

If, however, the breakage were between houses 4 and 5 then the owner of number 6 would have to pay a share of the cost because the property connects to a shared drain and would, therefore, be affected. In the example given in Figure 101 the houses numbered 1, 2, and 3 would not have to contribute, because the breakage between numbers 4 and 5 would not affect them.

Should the breakage occur on the pipe from the manhole to the sewer then all six properties would bear the cost.

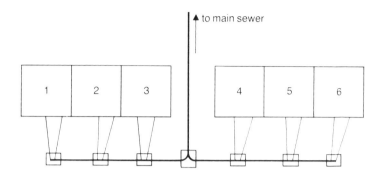

Figure 101   *Shared drain*

Interpretation may vary from borough to borough, and readers who occupy properties that are at the head of a shared drain should seek clarification of their position from the local council in the event of any problem.

## Building over a sewer

Frequently the shared drain, or sewer, is close to the rear of properties and may pass under any extension. If this is the case the permission of the local authority must be obtained before building, as specific conditions may be applied to building over a sewer.

Because it is a shared drain, rodding access to it at all times must be maintained, and the sewer must be protected from the effects of any building constructed over it. The requirements are usually:

1  The existing pipe be taken out and replaced with drain-weight cast iron pipe surrounded in concrete.
2  A manhole be constructed either side of the building extension (see Figure 102).
3  Concrete bridging of the pipe may have to be provided where there is likelihood of building settlement or ground movement (Figure 103).

Bridging is normally required for shallow sewers, and the bridge should extend the length of the building and be formed in reinforced concrete.

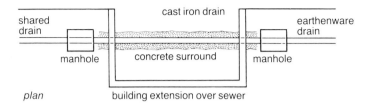

Figure 102 *Building over sewer*

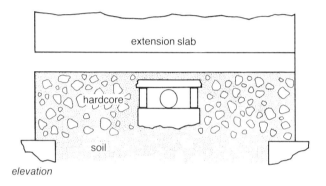

Figure 103 *Bridging over sewer*

The local authority need to inspect the work, and they must be given access at reasonable times to do so. Permission is granted for essential building only; that is, the rooms to be created must be for purposes essential to the property, such as a bathroom or kitchen. Bedrooms or extensions to living rooms are not considered essential. Neither, for that matter, are garages, but these are often allowed because, in the event of problems, the floor slab of a garage may be broken up without causing undue inconvenience to the occupier of the building.

## Drainage layout

In planning an extension, or any change to the existing services within the building that necessitates an alteration to the drainage system, the local authority should be asked for details of the existing drainage layout. These are normally given free of charge, but the accuracy of the records cannot be guaranteed as builders may not have installed work precisely to the approved drawings. For many older buildings records may not exist.

Many detached properties will drain individually to the main sewer, and alterations and additions to these systems offer fewer complications than the 'shared' method.

## Manholes

These are chambers for access to the drainage system. They are normally brick built on a concrete base and fitted with a cast iron or pressed steel cover. A manhole should be provided at every acute change of direction or at the junction of one or more pipes to a main discharge pipe.

There are, however, many instances, especially on older-type properties, where manholes have not been provided, branch connections have been made with Y-junctions, and rodding eyes have been provided at the head of long runs. These systems work well enough and, with today's modern methods, can be cleaned adequately, but there can be problems tracing the run of drains. Usually it is a question of digging until you find it.

Assuming that the drain has been located and that it is a 'shared' drain, a manhole should be provided at the point of connections. This will benefit the individual property, and also assist the local council in any work they have to do on the drain.

Brick-built manholes should be constructed of 225 mm semi-engineering brickwork using a sand and cement mortar of 3:1. Shallow chambers (up to 1 m deep) may be 600 mm × 450 mm internal dimensions providing there are no more than two branch connections on each side of the channel. For each additional 100 mm branch the manhole length must be extended by 300 mm. Thus four branches on any one side requires a manhole 1200 mm long.

At depths greater than 1 m the minimum chamber size (internal) is 1200 mm × 600 mm and galvanized iron steps must be fitted for safe access. The final size of the manhole depends on the number of branches.

Alternatively concrete rings or squares may be used to form chambers. These are purpose-made sections that interlock and are grouted together.

For shallow access chambers polypropylene (plastics)

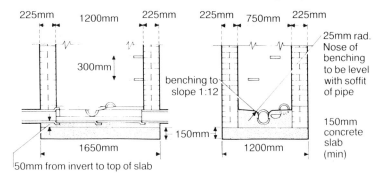

Figure 104A    *Manhole (brick)*

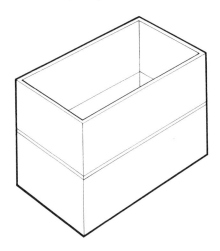

Figure 104B    *Manhole (concrete)*

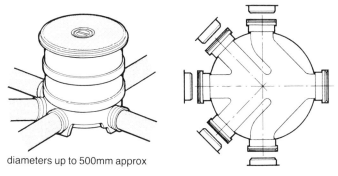

diameters up to 500mm approx

Figure 104C    *Manhole (polypropylene)*

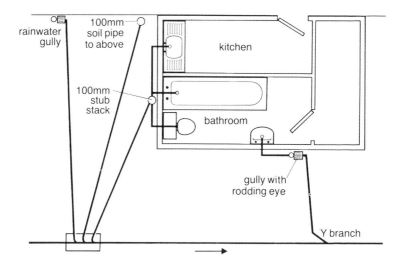

Figure 105   *Typical drainage layout to extension*

chambers may be used. These have branch connections (two per side) moulded in and are suitable for depths up to 750 mm (see Figure 104A, B, C).

Figure 105 shows a typical drainage layout to a bathroom and kitchen extension.

Manholes built on shared drains should be in brick. In the example shown, a drain is run to a 100 mm stub stack to collect wastes from the bath, basin, w.c., sink and washing machine, each of which connect separately to the stack.

## Stub stack

A stub stack is a length of soil pipe which extends 300 mm above the topmost connection, and terminates in a screwed access cap, or an air-inlet valve. This drain is not trapped (Figure 106). Not all fittings should discharge to a trapped gully; if they did, it would act as a solidifying grease trap. If it is not possible to arrange the layout to connect all fittings to the stub stack then arrange for the bath and basin to discharge to a gully or, of course, provide two stub stacks. The gully is necessary for the collection of rainwater and surface drainage.

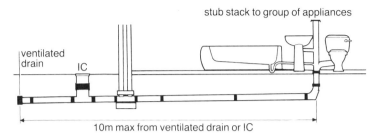

Figure 106 *Stub stack*

Branch drains of over 10 m in length must be vented at their head. This must be by an open vent pipe terminated at a 'safe' outlet.

## Manholes or Y-branches

Figure 105 shows a straightforward arrangement of bathroom and kitchen, but such a layout is not always possible. Often the kitchen, or bathroom, is located in another part of the building; or the work may include the conversion of the property into flats, which involves additional soil and rainwater pipes. In such cases it may be necessary to provide an additional manhole nearer to the point of collection of discharge pipes and fittings. You are permitted to put in as many manholes as you consider you require, but it is sensible to rationalize them because they are expensive items to build.

To economize on connections to manholes there is a temptation to connect the drain from a stub stack to the branch drain from a nearby soil pipe. Avoid this sort of situation, especially in the case of a conversion to flats, but also even if you are simply adding an extra toilet to the ground floor of a house because, in the event of a blockage in the drain downstream of the branch, water will back up the connection and flood over the ground-floor fittings.

## Permitted branch connections and gullies

Branch connections to soil drains are permitted when both pipes are connecting either to soil stacks or to stub stacks. Drains carrying discharge from rainwater pipes may also connect to soil, or waste, or other rainwater drains providing an open-grating gully is fitted at ground level. This is to prevent any back-up in the drain flooding over an internal fitting. Figure 107A illustrates a typical gully. Discharge stacks and waste pipes connect to the back and/or side inlet branches on the raising pieces which are supplied with from one to four branch connections. Because the gully is the lowest open-to-air connection on the system, any back-up in the drains will overflow at this point, thus protecting the internal rooms of the property. This arrangement is important for basement rooms where there is an external drainable area.

Pipes discharging to gullies not provided with side-inlet connections must discharge below the grating level of the gully. For this the grating must be cut to allow the pipe to pass through the grating. The pipe must terminate above the water level in the trap of the gully, and care must be taken to ensure that the trap of the gully is accessible for cleaning. If the discharge pipe obstructs access then a short bottom section should be fitted so that it is easily removable and replaceable to facilitate cleaning.

Open-grating gullies should not be fitted within buildings other than as wash-down points for cleaning or draining floors, or showers for handicapped people.

Figure 107A   *Drain gully*

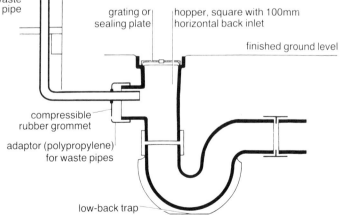

Figure 107B   *Y-branch*

External gullies must not be fitted with sealed plates in place of the grating. Internal gullies may have sealed plates, in which case the gullies must be vented to fresh air by a pipe which may also serve as a waste stack or rainwater pipe. Soil stacks or soil fittings must *not* be connected to gullies. All soil discharge must be directly connected to a drain without any intervening trap.

### Y-branch connections

All branch connections to a drain, if not via a manhole, must be made at an angle of 135° to the direction of flow. These branches are usually referred to as Y-branches. Sharper angles must not be used, as they may limit severely the scope of rodding for drain clearing.

## Materials

Drain pipe materials are generally cast or spun irons, vitrified clayware, and uPVC (plastics). The choice of material depends upon the type of ground in which the drain is to be laid, and the depth of the drain below the ground surface.

## Flexibility

Flexibility in drains is vital where movement is likely to occur. It is generally accepted these days that, save for the most extreme cases, all drains should be flexible so that they may resist any pressure loads to which they may be subjected.

Where ground is unstable because of high water content or inherent soft spots – such as deposits of peat – or its level has been 'made up' from imported tipping, the advice of the local authority's building control officer should be sought on the most suitable method for installation.

Drains should not be laid in unstable ground. Normally, trenches must be excavated to a sound bottom and the levels made up by back filling and consolidating with graded materials such as hoggin before drains can be laid. Where this is not possible, a reinforced concrete beam supported by short piles is provided as a base for drains. Obviously this is a very expensive procedure and would be adopted only on large contracts.

## Plastics

UPVC is accepted by most local authorities as a suitable material for drainage. Trenches must be cleanly cut and have self-supporting sides and a reasonably level bottom. A layer of 100 mm of 9 mm-granular material (pea shingle) should be spread along the bottom of the trench as a bed upon which to lay the drain pipe. Plastics pipes may be fitted in 6 m lengths without problem because the material itself provides all the necessary

Figure 108A/B   *Distorted UPVC pipe/consolidated fill*

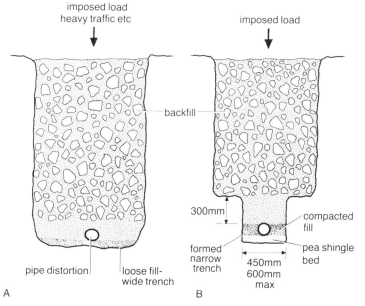

flexibility. After successful testing the trench may be backfilled. Care should be taken to consolidate the granular fill around and above the pipe before filling with graded earth.

The compacting of the granular surround between the pipe and the walls of the trench is very important because any super-imposed weight on the trench could distort the pipe by forcing the top downwards, thus reducing the effective depth of the bore (Figure 108A).

Properly compacted granular surround will support the side walls of the pipe, thus preventing distortion. The trench must not be too wide at pipe depth; no more than 450 mm to 600 mm. If the sides of the trench are not self-supporting then they should be shored to a height of at least 300 mm above the crown of the pipe (Figure 108B).

*Vitrified clayway*
This is a strong, hard-wearing material which is well suited to most drainage installations. Though it is a rigid material it is easily jointed with plastic couplings, which give the system a degree of flexibility which is adequate for all but the most extreme cases of unstable ground conditions.

The critical points for sheer fractures are where the drain passes through, or joins to, a structure. At these points a flexible coupling must be fitted within 150 mm of a wall or its foundation, with a second coupling within 600 mm of the first. This provides a fulcrum 600 mm long which can pivot to accommodate any movement of the drain. Structures include manholes, and this arrangement for flexibility must be provided on each connection to a manhole. Where the length between a manhole and the wall of a building is no more than 2 m, a flexible coupling within 150 mm from each wall with a third in the centre of the run will be sufficient provision for flexibility.

All flexible drainage runs should be laid in granular bedding material. However, very shallow drains may present problems, especially in areas such as gardens, where they may suffer damage from people digging. Some authorities may require the drain to be surrounded in concrete, while others will be happy with a slab of concrete laid across the top of the trench and supported by the infill and rebates cut into the sides of the trench.

Concrete surround to a drain does little but increase an already adequate pipe wall strength and add considerably to the weight.

It will not protect a pipe from sheering because of stress loading. UPVC drains should never be encased in concrete as that would destroy the flexible characteristics of the material.

*Cast iron*

This once widely used material is losing favour because of its cost. It is expensive to buy and even more costly to fit. Though it is heavy it is no stronger in effect than vitrified clayway; and it suffers the disadvantage of deteriorating internally through rust. Corrosion can form stalactites which, in turn, cause blockages when solids, especially papers, catch on them in discharge. It is not a material the average occupier is likely to consider for use.

## Gradients

All drain runs must, as far as is practicable, be run in straight lines, and any bends that are required should be fitted close to manholes. Every drain must fall in the direction of its flow. The question is, what degree of fall is necessary?

In recent years there has been a rethink on the traditional drain gradients of 1 in 40 for 100 mm, 1 in 60 for 150 mm and 1 in 90 for 225 mm. These falls are too steep for any but short-length drain runs, and today's practice is to lay 100 mm at 1 in 80 to 100, 150 mm at 1 in 120 to 150, and 225 mm at 1 in 180 to 200. The effect for these flatter angles is to slow the discharge rate of water in the drain. Water in a 100 mm drain should travel at between 0.6 m/s and 1.0 m/s. This ensures the maintenance of an acceptable flow depth to support solid materials contained in the discharge, thus preventing separation and deposit of solids on the drain floor which, in turn, would trap further solids and result in the blockage of the pipe; and reduces turbulence in the air displacement caused by high-velocity discharges.

Over the years there have been radical changes in the use of domestic drainage systems. Take a look at the stuff that you, or your family, flush through your drains each day compared with the average family's discharge of, say, forty years ago. Waste disposal units churn out a sludge to deposit in the pipes; washing machines add detergents; cooking oils and fats are flushed away for easy disposal; mothers use disposable absorbent nappies and towels and get rid of them through the w.c. pan; but probably the

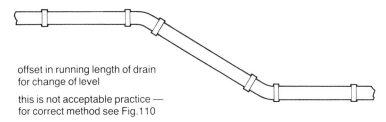

offset in running length of drain
for change of level

this is not acceptable practice —
for correct method see Fig.110

Figure 109 *Offset in running length*

worst offender of all is soft, absorbent toilet paper, which must by now be used in virtually every home. Forty years ago little of this type of material found its way into the drainage system. Toilet paper was the shiny stuff that floated; cooking was by solidifying fat that was put in the dustbin; washing machines and detergents were a Utopian dream; and only the lucky few had a waste disposal unit. In addition, many of the soil stacks were of the one-or two-pipe systems and had anti-siphon pipes to provide a measure of pressure relief from the air turbulence from the drains.

So the changing use requires an improved performance from the drainage system, and an improvement in the quality of materials which the industry has produced. But change is always with us, and drainage design is one of those factors that will always be under constant review.

The lengthy explanation is to underline the need to adopt the new standards in all drainage work. Steep falls increase the discharge capacity of a pipe; they also increase the displacement air pressures within those pipes which may be the cause of induced siphonage in ground-floor sanitary fittings, and gullies; and contribute to problems of backsurge.

## Changes of level

For the reasons stated above, any change of level in a drain must be made at a manhole and not by an offset in the running length (Figure 110A and B).

Short lengths of drain up to 3 m from ground-floor sanitary fittings, stub stacks, or soil stacks may have steeper falls, but only if they are single drains and do not have branch connections to other discharge points.

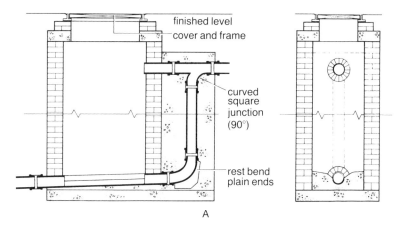

Figure 110A

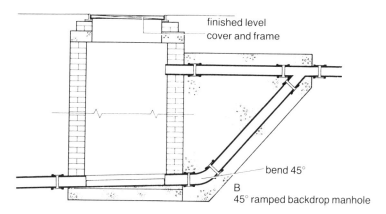

Figure 110B   *Backdrop to manhole*

Steep-angle falls or vertical drops are permissible on the downstream end of a drain immediately before a manhole or at the junction with a sewer. Figure 110 shows a typical vertical backdrop which is formed outside a manhole but within 150 mm of its wall. The vertical length of pipe must be shuttered and concreted, and the concrete must be 'keyed' into the brickwork of the manhole construction to support the imposed extra weight. It is impracticable to surround vertical or steeply inclined pipes in granular material as this cannot be retained, and the tendency is for the pea shingle to drop away, leaving the pipe only partially supported.

In forming the backdrop, the horizontal drain line must be accessible for rodding from within the manhole through the rodding access provided by the open end of the branch which is extended through the manhole wall. It is not customary to cap this open end, but of course should a blockage form in the lower section of the backdrop, this access point will become the discharge point of the drain.

Backdrops are normally used on 'stepped' drainage – where the site is steeply inclined and, therefore, the drain has to be laid in short stretches, and dropped to the required level for the next stretch. The manhole is then built up to the required depth.

They are also used where a main collecting drain, or a sewer, is deep. It is much more economical to cut shallow trenches for the drainage system of a site than to run all the drains at the level of the sewer. Where several runs of drains are involved, these would normally be connected to a shallow manhole, and a backdrop on the outlet connection of that chamber would connect to the sewer. If the manhole were built on the sewer then each drain would have a backdrop connection to the manhole.

## Shared drains and main sewers

It is necessary to distinguish between these two pipes as both can be referred to as sewers – which, of course, they are.

Manholes and Y-branch connections to 'shared-drain' sewers may normally be made by the contractor working for the property owner, providing that connection is on the client's property. The client's contractor *cannot* make any connection to a main sewer. This pipe is normally located in the road and is the responsibility of the local water undertaking for whom the local authority usually act as agents. Only the Water company or their agent may excavate the highway and footpath and make, or repair, the connection to a main sewer. They will run a connecting pipe to within the curtilage of the client's property to which the contractor may connect, usually via a manhole. The cost of these works is the responsibility of the property owner.

## New connections to sewers

A property is entitled to be drained to a sewer providing there is a sewer within 100 ft (30 m) of the property. It can be a greater distance if the local authority is prepared to extend an existing sewer to within the required distance and 'undertake to bear so much of the expenses reasonably incurred in constructing, and maintaining, and repairing the drain . . .' (the Building Act 1984).

Connection to a shared drain, providing that the levels permit, is permissible within the above parameters subject to entitlement to use the drain and, in the event of having to cross other property to make any connection, providing that permission has been obtained. This is of particular importance to readers who live in country districts and those planning to move to and possibly build in rural areas. Guidance on these matters should always be sought from the local authority.

Finally, all drainage and sanitation works other than repair of damaged drain pipes (as distinct from sewer pipes) and above-ground sanitation and rainwater pipes and gutters and the replacement of sanitary fittings require to be notified to the building control officer; as indeed do any building construction works with the exception of 'exempted buildings' (exempted buildings include porches, loggias and garages). Most councils will provide leaflets detailing procedures to be followed for building control. Basically, any works must comply with the new Building Regulations 1985. These are a simplified version of the former regulations and, by their very simplicity, may baffle many applicants. Instead of specific and detailed requirements they are performance regulations which state in the case of, say, drainage, that a building will be adequately drained. The term 'adequately' here means 'effectively' – or that whatever system is installed, it will work.

There are approved documents for guidance on acceptable practices, and such publications as the BS Codes of Practice 8301 for drainage and the BS COP 5572 for above-ground sanitation will be accepted as approved methods.

There is no obligation to follow the precepts expressed in these, but any system which deviates from the basic design principles (as outlined in this book) may be questioned by a building control officer, and it will be up to the designer and installer to prove that the system is 'adequate'. Traditionally, the system of building control operates by negotiation and agreement, and building control officers are invariably prepared to offer advice and guidance on any problems that may arise.

The local authority must be notified prior to the start of works. There are two methods that may be employed:

1 Full plan application, where all layout drawings are sent to the building control officer together with the necessary fee. The plans will be scrutinized and will either be 'approved' (with or without conditions) or rejected. Reasons must be given for rejection.

   Drawings may then be amended to comply with the Building Regulations (1985) and resubmitted with another fee to cover rechecking of plans.

   'Approved' drawings provide a safeguard to the client inasmuch as work installed in compliance with those drawings cannot be rejected by the local authority. However, the client may depart from the 'approved' drawings, in which case that part of the work is not 'approved' and may not be accepted by the local authority.

2 Building notice, which is sent to the local authority prior to the commencement of works giving sufficient information for the council to be able to identify the site and the nature and extent of the works to be undertaken. A block plan (1:1250) is required. The council may ask for additional plans, but there is no obligation to provide them. Any plans that are submitted are for 'information only' and will not be approved. Work is inspected as it progresses, and the systems should be mutually agreed and confirmed in writing before installation.

   Should the building control officer refuse to accept any part of the work the decision may be tested in court if the client so desires. Then it is up to the council to establish that the systems installed are 'inadequate'.

   These should be extreme cases. As has already been stated both parties will meet, discuss and agree, and, if the past years are any guide, there will be very few disputes considering the vast numbers of building projects which are undertaken every year.

There is a third method of building control which hasn't really taken off yet but is likely to in the near future. It is private certification, where a person approved by the Minister may take over the approval and inspection duties of the council. There may be a difference in the fees charged, and this form of building control may be attractive to readers who are planning fairly extensive contracts. Lists of 'approved' private certification inspectors will be available at town halls.

Other than for exempted works and buildings, all construction and conversion works and all drainage, above-ground sanitation and rainwater works *must* be notified to the local authority prior to commencement of contract. If a private certificator is employed then he or she will send to the council an initial notice giving all the required details on behalf of the client.

## BS 5503

The production of w.c. pans has been rationalized to provide a level spigot outlet. This saves manufacturers having to produce many variations of each model: P-trap straight; P-trap left-hand turn; P-trap right-hand turn; S-trap; and so on.

The modern level-outlet pan is connected to the branch soil pipe by means of either a 90° bend connected to form either an S-trap or side turn outlet, or a 104° connector to form the traditional P-trap pan.

In the case of a P-trap or side turn pan the BS requires a 14° fall from the outlet of the pan and care should be taken to ensure that the appropriate adaptor is fitted to the proper angle.

Many level-outlet pans are incorrectly jointed with straight connectors, which may result in washback of the pan's contents after flushing.

# Comprehensive designing based on practical research

The Marley Plumbing team who carried out practical experiments and developed their findings into practical designs and fittings, have given valuable advice to plumbers through the media of lectures and publications.

## The collar boss

One intriguing development in single-stack plumbing is the

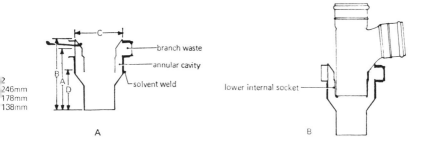

Figure 111   *The Marley Collar Boss*

Marley Collar Boss. This soil-pipe fitting has been designed to overcome a number of different installation problems which occurred when the Building Regulations required all soil pipes in new construction to be located inside buildings.

BS COP 5572 recommends that small-diameter branch wastes with orifices of connections exposed to the w.c. discharge do not join the soil pipe in the 200 mm area below the centre of the w.c. branch (see Figure 111). This often means that the bath waste pipework has to offset through the floor and enter the stack via a boss branch fitted below or in the ceiling space.

Apart from increasing the labour content of the plumbing installation a bath waste passing down through the floor can create structural difficulites for other building trades.

The collar boss has an annular cavity in the main body which receives water from the branch wastes and this is deflected down and around the sloping shoulders into the vertical stack. Air always present in the annular chamber removes any tendency for self-siphonage to occur while the effluent is flowing from the branch waste and the normal rate of discharge from the sanitary fitment is unaffected. Discharge from the w.c. is prevented from making contact with the annular space or boss connections by the wall of the internal socket. Details of the collar boss are given in Figure 111A.

## Installation of the collar boss

When the collar boss has to be fitted high up under the throat of a 100 mm branch the spigot of the branch may be solvent-welded to the lower internal socket (Figure 111B).

Figure 112   *Complete installation of collar boss*

*The intermediate pipe clip is an injection moulded uPVC component. This acts as a guide for the vertical pipe. Support for the soil system is provided by the mild steel plastic coated socket clip. The length of pipe in the vertical stack and horizontal branches will vary with different contracts. The appropriate dimensions may be obtained from the construction drawings in each case.*

*The local ring seal joint on the boss branch allows for movement when hot-water waste is discharging into the stack, and the anchor rib on the socket locating the clip enusres that the pipework is adquately supported.*

*If required, a straight access pipe may be fitted in the vertical stack.*

*It is important to provide an expanded expansion joint between fixed points on all uPVC soil and waste pipes. Manufacturers' instruction on method and position should be followed closely.*

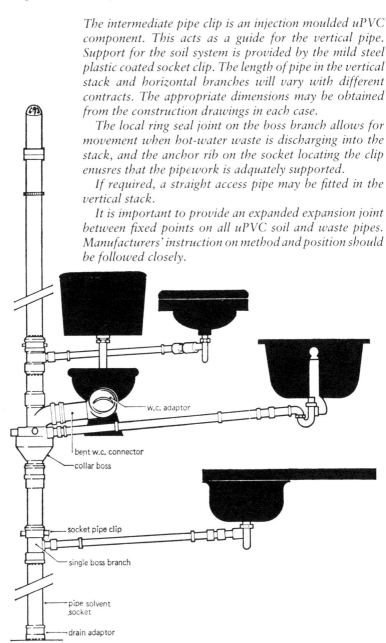

w.c. adaptor

bent w.c. connector

collar boss

socket pipe clip

single boss branch

pipe solvent socket

drain adaptor

Care must be taken when using the collar boss in conjunction with any of the 100 mm boss branch fittings in the soil-pipe range not to close up (by shortening the spigot end of the junction) the centre-to-centre dimension of the opposing bosses to less than 110 mm for branch wastes up to 50 mm, or to less than 200 mm for 100 mm branches.

In Figure 112 a typical domestic installation is shown. Detailed diagrams and catalogue about the fittings may be obtained from Marley Extrusions Ltd, Lenham, Maidstone, Kent ME17 2DE.

Council approval must be obtained before using the collar boss system. Some authorities, especially those in Inner London, may not approve a fitting that is not readily accessible for cleaning, while others may need to be satisfied that alternative direct connections to stack are not possible.

# 11

# Rainwater Disposal

In years gone by the house-builder had little regard for rainwater pipes or gutters. They were necessary however, and the main thing was to get them fixed as cheaply as possible – after all, you could hardly sell a house on its rainwater pipes and gutters! Even on better-class, architect-designed properties, very little thought was given to the position size or design of rainwater pipes and gutters. Many a house having a commanding or attractive elevation has been spoiled by a festoon of pipes and gutters.

Cheap materials, bad sizing, and inferior fixing of rainwater gutters and pipes has caused damage to property. Leaking joints, pipes and metal gutters fixed without painting, and in a position so that painting the back of them has been impossible, has caused them to rust away after a relatively short period of time.

## Need for care in fixing

The purpose of a rainwater gutter is to catch all the rain falling on the roof during the heavier downfall and to convey it to the outlets, where it empties into the down pipe, which in turn should be capable of conducting all the water to the drain, without any spilling out of the joints and soaking the brickwork.

All joints must be made properly and if the pipes and gutters are of metal they must be painted. They should be fixed in such a manner that it is possible to clean them and repaint them at regular intervals. Gutters must have an adequate fall to take the water to the outlets and to make them self-cleaning. It is essential that the outlets of the gutters should be protected with wire balloons to prevent leaves and other matter from choking the downpipe.

## Plastics rainwater goods

Possibly the most progressive development has been the design and supply of plastics rainwater goods, which provide many advantages over those made from other materials.

By using plastics materials it has been possible to employ greatly improved design techniques resulting in a considerably improved appearance and substantial savings in erection costs. Guttering is simply snapped into a bracket which has a moulded-in clip joint and a butyl rubber strip provides a 100 per cent watertight seal. In this way the need for gutter bolts has been removed.

Plastics have eliminated corrosion problems – a constant worry with cast iron. Hence there is no need for surface protection and for this reason the guttering and downpiping can be self-coloured.

A comprehensive guide to rainwater gutter and downpipe installation follows. It is intended for the installer and the householder, explaining step by step the procedure and techniques. For simplicity we have restricted the instruction to one type only manufactured by Marley Plumbing Ltd.

The most serious losses occasioned by a failure of conventional guttering and downpiping are due not only to corrosion but to accidents through storage and transportation, and breakage during fitting. The percentage of breakages with plastics rainwater goods is negligible, and their lightness in weight makes transportation and erection on site a simple and trouble-free job.

# Gutter installation

The Marley gutter joint with separate jointing strap located between notches on spigot and socket is shown in Figure 113. The strap compresses the spigot down against the synthetic rubber seal which is secured in every socket before the products leave the factory. When correctly assembled the joint cannot pull apart, and it will absorb the expansion and contraction of the gutter while maintaining a watertight seal.

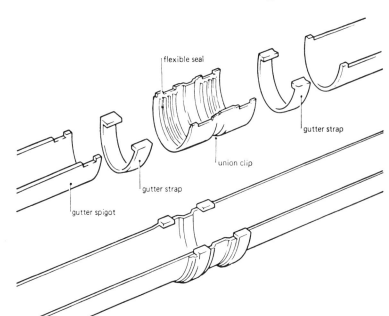

Figure 113   *Plastic gutter joints*

## Position of the underground drain

The location of the underground drain is an important factor in setting out a gutter installation. The trapped gulley or drain socket at ground level automatically determines the centre line of the gutter outlet which is normally immediately above. This is shown in Figure 114.

## Position of rainwater pipes

Considerations affecting the position of rainwater pipes are:

1 Architectural requirements.
2 Maximum flow capacity of the gutter.
3 Underground drainage design.

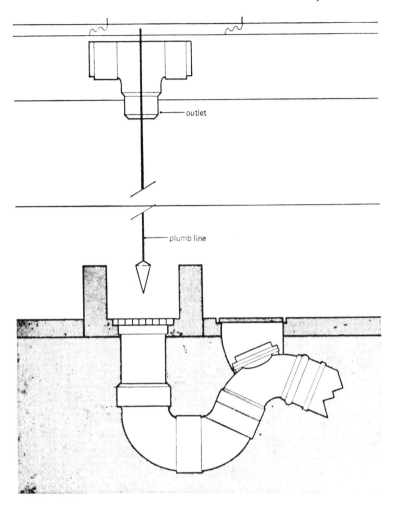

outlet

plumb line

Figure 114 *Positioning gutter outlet*

4 The accuracy with which the timber fascia is fixed to the rafters.

Item 4 is particularly important yet often overlooked. Fascia boards that are not level cause a large gap to develop between the gutter and the eaves' course of tiles (see Figure 115). This occurs when the plumber is fitting to gradients which are opposed to the slope of the fascia.

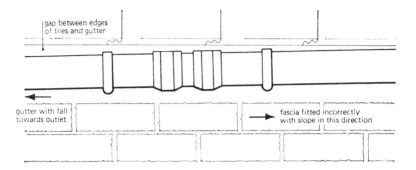

Figure 115

## Fixing the brackets to a timber fascia

Plumbers occasionally fix the brackets and install the gutter before the roof is tiled. There is a risk of damage to the PVC gutters during the roof tiling operation as well as a great accumulation of debris collecting in the gutter. It is advised that the sequence of events be arranged that the roof is tiled and the final painting of the fascia board completed before the plumber fixes the brackets and installs the gutter while the scaffolding is still in position. A good plumber can be relied upon not to damage the finished paintwork while fixing the gutter. The brackets may be fixed in the usual way with a string line acting as a guide to alignment for brackets between the extreme end of the installation and the outlet of the gutter (Figure 116).

Figure 116

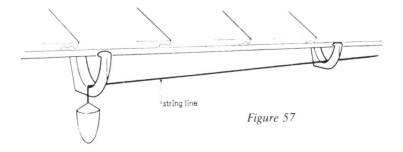

*Figure 57*

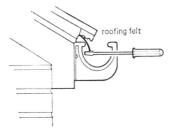

roofing felt

Figure 117

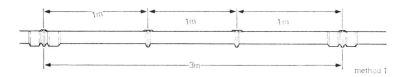

Figure 118

When fitting brackets to a fall, the end bracket at the high point should be secured as close as possible to the underside of the roofing felt and projecting eaves' course of tiles. The intermediate brackets are then screwed to the fascia with zinc plated or sheradized round head screws at a maximum of 1 m centres (Figure 117).

## Position of gutter brackets

Gutter is supplied in 3 m lengths and on long straight runs the arrangement of brackets should be as indicated in Figure 118. The gutter union has a centre portion to accommodate the fascia bracket and this feature in combination with the 3 m double spigot lengths of gutter, provides the method of arranging the support brackets. Careful attention to detail is necessary because the union bracket has to be accurately located taking into account the small tolerance on every gutter length.

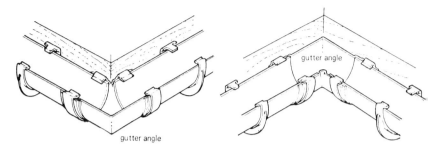

Figure 119

## Angle

External and internal angles should have close supporting brackets on each side of the joints as shown in Figure 119.

## Outlets

Gutter outlets should also have brackets fitted on each side of the joints to the gutter (Figure 120). The stopend outlet is designed to suit the fascia bracket and this type should always be installed so that the rainwater pipe may be correctly engaged with the nozzle of the outlet.

Figure 120

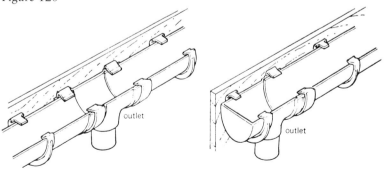

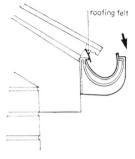

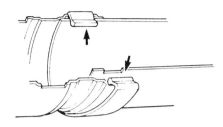

Figure 121                                                    Figure 122

## Fitting and jointing the gutter

Lengths of gutter are introduced into the brackets as illustrated in Figure 121 and clipped into place under the projection at the front of the fascia brackets. As the gutter is installed the rear edge should turn into the brackets under the roofing felt in order that the gap between gutter and tiles is weathered. This prevents the rainwater from being blown against the fascia as it runs from the tiles into the gutter.

To assemble a joint, clip the gutter strap around the socket of a fitting between the notches. Turn the spigot end of the gutter into the socket, under the back edge of the strap, so that the retaining projection fits into the notch (see Figure 122). Ease the front edge of the gutter spigot down until it snaps under the strap. This now compresses the gutter against the pre-fixed synthetic rubber seal to form a watertight joint.

Finally line up the notches on the spigot and socket so that the strap is in the centre (Figure 123).

## Cutting and notching the gutter

Occasionally it will be necessary to cut a length of gutter. A fine tooth saw should be used for this purpose taking care to cut straight at 90 degrees to the axis of the gutter (Figure 124). The notches must then be cut or filed into the edges of the spigot end. A tool is available from the Marley Company for cutting notches

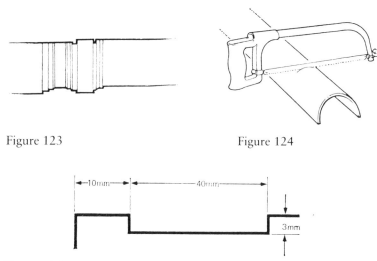

Figure 123                         Figure 124

Figure 125

but they can be done quite easily using a file. The dimensions of the notch are given in Figure 125.

The notches must always be formed before attempting to complete a joint.

# Circular pipe installation

### Connection to the gutter outlet

When the gutter outlet is positioned directly above the drain, the offset must be of the correct projection passing straight back under the soffit to engage with the rainwater pipe. Ideally a ring seal should be located in the socket recess of the offset to secure and seal the connection of the two fittings (Figure 126).

### Solvent-welded offsets

An offset may be fabricated on site from an offset socket, offset spigot and an offcut of pipe. The procedure is as follows:

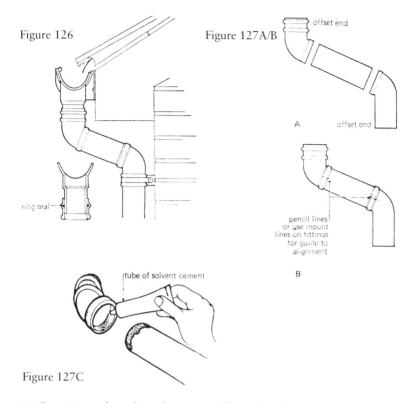

Figure 126

Figure 127A/B

Figure 127C

1 Cut pipe to length and remove all rough edges (Figure 127A).
2 Internal surfaces of solvent-weld sockets and outside of pipe ends should be wiped perfectly clean with a dry cloth.
3 Assemble the offset dry and draw pencil lines along the pipe and fittings (Figure 127B) to ensure correct alignment.
4 Remove pipe from fittings. Apply solvent cement evenly around the spigots and inside sockets from the tube (Figure 127C).
5 Press pipe and fittings quickly and firmly together taking care to line up with pencil guide lines.
6 Leave the offset for several minutes before fitting into position in order that the joints may set properly.

## Connection of offset to rainwater pipe

The offset spigot is 112 mm long. This allows the socket of the

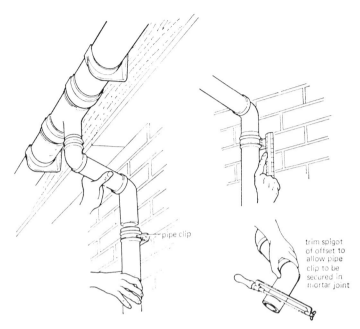

Figure 128   *Assembling offset*

offset to be pushed fully on to the nozzle of the outlet, while providing some facility for adjusting the first pipe clip. The clip is fastened around the socket, then the offset and first length of pipe are placed in position (Figure 128).

If the holes in the pipe bracket backplate fail to come in line with a mortar joint, *do not* lower the offset on the nozzle of the outlet. Instead, measure the amount of spigot to be cut off, in order that the pipe clip may be fixed in the next joint up.

## Location of rainwater pipe clips

Pipe clips are provided to fit both the rainwater pipe and the pipe socket.

The vertical centres of pipe clips are usually marked on the wall with the aid of a plumb line suspended from the top pipe-clip position.

Pipe-clip backplates, or in the case of the one piece fitting, the clip itself, are secured to the structure with two 38 or 32 mm × 10

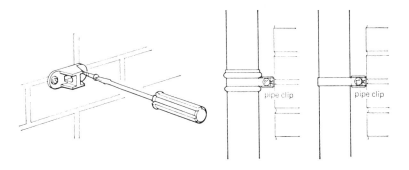

Figure 129 *Positioning and fixing brackets*

gauge zinc plated or sheradized round-head steel screws. Purpose-made fibre or plastics plugs should be inserted into the fixing holes when they have been drilled. The use of handmade softwood plugs should be avoided (Figure 129).

The pipe clips are supplied with nuts and bolts to fasten the uPVC ring to the backplate. Every rainwater pipe should have a clip located at the socket to support the pipework system. Intermediate pipe clips should then be provided in the centre of each pipe length where it exceeds 2 m.

*An expansion gap of 10 mm should be left between the end of each pipe and the bottom of the socket* (Figure 130).

Figure 130 *Expansion gap*

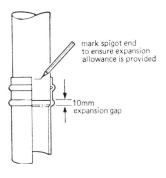

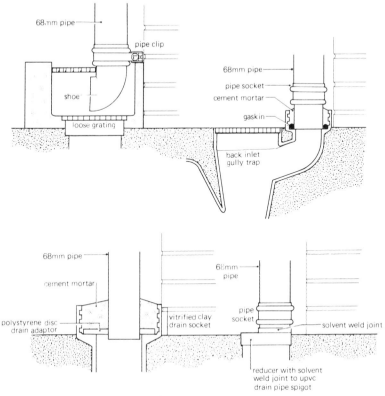

Figure 131   *Connection to drain*

## Connection to the underground drain

Depending on the design of the system of buried drainage, rainwater pipes may terminate as follows:

1  Below the grating level of a trapped gully, providing access to the gully is not obstructed for cleaning purposes. This problem can be overcome if a short length of pipe is removable immediately above the gully mouth. The grating should be cut to fit snugly to the pipe, which must be terminated above the water line of the trap.

2  Connected to the back or side inlet of the gully with a 2:1 sand and cement joint.

3  Connected direct to an untrapped bend with a 2:1 sand and

cement joint or with an adaptor. This is permissible only if the gutter outlet discharges to air in a 'safe' position: 900 mm above or 3 m from the highest opening in the building. The gutter (half-round) described in this chapter is only one of many designs available. The range includes Deep Flow, an elliptical gutter $110 \times 75$ mm deep, which, when running full, has a capacity equal to a 150 mm half-round gutter.

Fixed level with an outlet at one end, it has a flow capacity of 1.83 l.p.s.; fixed level with an outlet in the centre, its flow capacity is 3.43 l.p.s. Flow capacity is increased by at least 20 per cent when fixed at gradients of 1:600 or more.

Assuming the maximum rainfall intensity at 75 mm per hour, a Deep Flow gutter fixed level with an outlet at one end will drain a roof of 87 sq. m (167 sq. m with an outlet in the centre). Fixed with a gradient of 1:600 and an outlet at one end, it will drain a roof of 105 sq. m (200 sq. m with an outlet in the centre).

Therefore, a typical terrace of five houses, having a frontage of 37.5 m and a roof pitch of 5 m, can be adequately drained by a rainwater pipe front and back sited in the centre. This gutter may be used in conjunction with a Deep Flow Box Eaves unit and either 68 mm diameter round rainwater pipe or 65 mm square pipe.

For full details of fittings range, capacities, discharge rates, etc., the appropriate catalogues issued by Marley Extrusions Ltd should be consulted.

A few years ago it was the policy for all pipes, often including rainwater pipes, to be fixed on internal walls within plumbing ducts. The main reason was to avoid freezing during severe winters and, though the only pipes likely to be affected were soil and waste stacks, it was held by many architects that any pipe on an external wall was an unnecessary blemish.

Any rainwater pipe fixed internally must be of soil weight, and must be jointed so as to be air- and watertight. It is important for occupiers of flats, especially in tall blocks, and even houses, to be aware that waste pipes from additional fittings such as washing machines must not be connected to an internal rainwater pipe no matter how conveniently it may be placed for the fitting in question. Discharge into a rainwater pipe can be heavy during periods of high-intensity rainfall, and back pressures can develop that may cause backsurge through a waste pipe and consequent flooding of both the sanitary fitting and the floor.

In flats and converted houses both the gutters and the rainwater pipes will come under shared-responsibility agreements. It should be written into these contracts that waste connections to rainwater pipes are prohibited.

There are many properties in this country where rainwater and surface water do not discharge to drain because main drainage is not available. Rainwater should not discharge to cesspits for obvious reasons. Soakaways are acceptable providing that they are properly constructed and are sited at a safe distance from any part of the structure of the property. This is normally 10 m, but a building control officer may agree to a lesser distance if this is not practical.

Soakaways should not be constructed in heavy clay soil. To do so effectively would mean penetrating the clay strata into the 'deep' water table from which the local water undertaking may take water, or into which other people in the neighbourhood may have sank wells to obtain their drinking water supply. If you are faced with this problem, seek the advice of your local water board.

In drainable soil, a soakaway should be cut to a depth determined by the local authority (usually from 2 m to 3 m) by 1 m in diameter. The sides should be supported by building blocks or other suitable means (to be agreed with the building control officer) and the soakaway formed by filling with random rubble to within 0.6 m of the ground surface. Rainwater and surface water drains should be discharged into the rubble area. The capacity of the soakaway is determined by the area to be drained into it.

From time to time a soakaway will need to be cleaned if any surface soil has washed down into it; and neither waste pipes nor soil pipes must be allowed to discharge into a soakaway at any time.

It is a standard part of the 'search' by a conveyancer at the time of purchase of a property to check the method of drainage. Any new owner, therefore, will be made aware of the existence of soakaway drainage.

In many rural areas rainwater and surface water may be discharged into nearby natural water courses such as rivers and streams. Again waste products from human habitation must not be connected to these systems. To do so would pollute the watercourse and adversely affect the habitat of the indigenous wildlife population.

# 12

# Plastics Plumbing

Plastics, although with a history of over a hundred years, is a comparatively new material in the plumbing world. Because of its lower cost in both material and labour it has moved in rather rapidly, with the result that information relating to these materials has not been digested quickly enough.

Another danger that has arisen is that various types of plastics can be used for the same application, but require different techniques for installation and jointing, just as do copper and stainless steel. Therefore, it is essential for the plumber to recognize these new plastics materials.

The plastics range of material today is vast, but, for practical purposes, only the materials that are used for plumbing products are our real concern. The main emphasis must be on the plastics that make up the pipe and fittings of the installation and not so much the plastics materials of the appliance to which the system has to be connected. The reason being that individual items under the categories of storage and flushing cisterns, taps, basins and baths, generally have their own specific fixing instructions attached.

## Five groups of plastics

The plastics that are used in the manufacture of pipes and fittings for above and below ground drainage and services, can be placed into five basic groups.

1  Polyvinyl chloride (uPVC and CPVC).
2  Styrene based (ABS).
3  Polyolefin (polyethylene and polypropylene).
4  Glass reinforced plastics.
5  Nylon.

Group 1 is used for rainwater, soil, waste, overflow below ground drainage, cold-water services and pressure pipe installations. Has a hard, smooth finish with a specific gravity of approximately 1.4.

Group 2 is used for waste runs generally of 35 mm, 42 mm and 54 mm nominal bore diameters, overflow pipes and water services. Is being used in the US for soil installations, but not in the UK. Similar appearance and feel to the plastics in Group 1, but with a specific gravity of approximately 1.1.

Group 3 is used for waste runs including laboratory work, overflow, water services and internal rainwater systems. Has a 'waxy' feel about it, and a specific gravity of 0.9 to 0.96.

Group 4 is used for rainwater roof outlets, valley type gutters and special fittings for large-diameter pipework. Can be recognized by the glass fibre reinforcements embedded in the material. Its specific gravity is 1–2 or more, depending on the glass content.

Group 5 is used sometimes for 'minibore' central heating tube and pressure pipework. Has a similar feel and appearance to the polyolefins and a specific gravity of approximately 1.1.

## Identification of plastics

It will be observed that out of these five groups, only the polyolefins (Group 3) has a specific gravity of less than 1.0. Hence by placing a fitting, or small offcut from the pipe in fresh water, only the items made from material in this group will float. It is essential that no air is trapped in the components when carrying out this procedure.

Both the components from Groups 1 and 2 will not float, but they can be distinguished apart by offering small shavings of the materials to a flame. The polyvinyl chloride in Group 1 will be self-extinguishing when taken away from the flame, while the styrene based material in Group 2 will continue to burn.

As already mentioned the glass reinforced plastics in Group 4 can be identified by the glass fibres embedded in the material, but as a further test press a hot metal point on its surface. Resin glass material will only char slightly whereas the effects on Groups 1, 2, 3 and 5 will be similar, only in a lesser degree, to a hot metal point pressed on to sealing wax.

The nylon plastics can be distinguished from Group 3 because they will sink in water and not burn so readily. The vapour smell when burnt is akin to burning hair.

Identification of all these plastics components by their colour is not possible, because depending on the pigments used in manufacture, a variety of colours can be produced.

It is important to be able to identify these plastics materials that are used for pipes and fittings, for each group has certain individual characteristics. For instance, chemical resistance, temperature limitation, weathering ability and coefficient of expansion present each group with a different specification, which must be taken into consideration. Identification is also important to ensure that the correct method of jointing is applied.

In practice it has been proved that all joints of recognized design which incorporate a seal ring are suitable for making an air- or watertight joint with all plastics piping. But the method of making a joint by using a solvent to fuse the materials together is limited to specific plastics.

The polyolefins and nylon plastics cannot be solvent-welded, whereas the styrene based and polyvinyl chloride materials can. Different formulations of solvent cements are supplied for the two latter groups and should be used in accordance with the manufacturers' instructions.

With the exception of the comment on nylon, we have refrained from identifying the materials by burning and smelling the vapour, for it is felt that some experience in this field is required to ascertain positive results. Also any foreign matter in the burnt plastics could mislead one's sense of smell. It must also be noted that inhaling any vapour given off from smouldering plastics may be injurious to health.

In constant association with these materials the plumber will quickly be able to recognize the polyolefins and resin glass easily by the appearance, feel and the manner in which the saw cuts them. Distinguishing between the styrene based and polyvinyl chloride is a little more difficult and very often the experienced person has to apply a basic identification test to confirm the result.

Once the identification of the plastics materials is established the recognized methods of working can be applied.

## Allowance for expansion

If expansion is not allowed for in rigid plastics pipework, there could be a high percentage of failure in the installation, but the degree of failure could depend upon the use to which the system is put.

For instance, if the ambient and flow temperature of the pipe varies by say, only 10°C, it would be debatable whether the installation would suffer any damage, even if the length of the rigid pipe run was 1.5 or 2 m.

In practice it is very seldom that these conditions can be guaranteed for the life of the installation. Therefore, maximum temperature conditions relating to the purpose of the system should always be assured.

When a rapid and a reasonable amount of expansion is taking place, the cause is generally due to very hot fluid flowing through the pipe. In these conditions plastics pipe would be more vulnerable to deformation, and unless adequate allowance is made for expansion, the pipe is likely to buckle. It could also damage or disturb the fittings locating the pipe.

Changes in surrounding temperatures also create thermal movement, especially with outside pipe and gutter installations.

# Plastics plumbing installation

Manufacturers of plastics pipe and fittings systems issue their own fixing instructions and it is always advisable to conform to their recommendations. The allowances for thermal movement have been established, not only by theoretical calculations, but by sound practical testing.

A question that concerns many is that if an installation could be constantly moving throughout its life, surely this would be detrimental to the system? The answer is simply that if the system has been fitted to give adequate allowance for freedom of movement then under its normal working conditions for which it was designed no strain will be taking place, and the material will not be subjected to fatigue.

Obviously there will also be expansion and contraction movement in the width of the pipe work. But as this is so slight it can be disregarded for practical purposes.

With plastics piping there is a considerable temperature difference between the discharge and the outside wall of the pipe.

A clear example of this is illustrated in the British Standards discharge cycling test for uPVC soil pipes. This shows that when 35 litres of water at 91°C are discharged into a 3.17-mm-thick uPVC soil stack from a waste entry, over a period of 90 seconds, the hottest point of the outside pipe wall will be in the region of 70°C. Because the material has low heat transmission, the expansion of the pipe is not so great as one would expect in relation to the high temperature of the discharge. It is for this reason that plastics systems will withstand intermittent discharges of higher temperatures than the melting point of the material.

It will be seen from the foregoing that the main concern about thermal movement in plastics is related to rigid materials, which are being widely used for above surface drainage.

## Soil and waste pipes

We are going to deal only with soil, waste and drain pipes because it is in this area of plumbing that most progress has been made in the use of plastics. The tried and tested material used is unplasticized polyvinyl chloride which we will now refer to as uPVC. These pipes have been widely used in the UK for some years now and they are accepted by almost every local authority. Changes and improvements in design of components and materials are constantly taking place and the wise plumber will keep abreast with these changes by maintaining regular communication with manufacturers and trade bodies through technical literature and meetings. He should also concern himself with British Standard Code of Practice for the material and the Digests published by the Building Research Station. For comprehensive information of a practical nature he can obtain publications from the Institute of Plumbing: 64 Station Lane, Hornchurch, Essex RM12 6NB.

# Types of systems

The uPVC systems for soil pipes are classified by their methods of jointing and are placed in two groups: (1) joint ring and (2) solvent weld. The joint ring systems may include fittings in the range where a solvent weld is required and similarly solvent weld will require expansion joints in the form of joint ring sockets to allow for thermal movement. A typical joint ring system is illustrated in Figure 73. There are a few other types all of which are effective and suitable.

## Joint ring systems

The joint ring illustrated fits in the annular space of the pipe socket. When the other pipe is inserted in the socket, a coupling nut locks the ring on the socket and spigot surfaces, forming a gas and watertight seal.

It is important to know that the design of ring seals differs from one to another manufacturer and they are seldom interchange-able. It is essential that the correct ring be used and that the manufacturer's instructions be carefully followed. Even when the joint rings are despatched from the manufacturer already fitted into the sockets, the plumber should carefully check to see that the ring is correctly engaged and undamaged before he makes the joint.

When the ring is supplied separately it should be cleaned before being inserted in the recess in the socket, which of course should also be cleaned.

Figure 132   *Joint assembly*

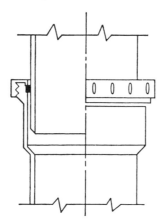

*Joint assembly*

There is a very wide range of soil- and waste-pipe fittings available in the plastics industry and most manufacturers can provide the plumber with lavish brochures showing their complete range and giving detailed dimensions and fixing instructions.

One general point which must never be overlooked in assembling plastics pipes and fittings is the maker's instructions giving the depth to which the spigot should be inserted in the socket. These instructions are in some cases given on an adhesive tape attached to the spigot of the fitting. In other cases the depth is indicated by a mark on the spigot end.

In all installations the spigot end of a pipe secured by a joint ring should always be directed in the same line as the flow of water from the appliance.

Spigot ends must be chamfered to permit easy assembly. Moulded fittings have their spigot ends already chamfered but the plumber must prepare pipe ends himself.

Plastics pipes can be cut with a hacksaw, or better still, a fine-toothed saw. With the latter it is less difficult to make the absolutely square cut so important in correct assembly of pipes and fittings.

When the pipe has been cut a pencil guide line should be made around the pipe about 7 mm from the end. Then with a fine rasp or a coarse file a chamfer can be formed working from the guide line to the end of the pipe, avoiding making a sharp edge.

The pipe must be inserted in the fitting to the correct depth and this can be achieved by marking with a pencil the depth recommended by the manufacturer or, alternatively, the pipe may be inserted to the full depth, marked with the pencil and then withdrawn 10 mm. A bold line is then drawn round the pipe at the top of the socket (see Figure 133). This method provides a better guide line for preparing the pipe for assembly with the socket.

*Making the joint*

The chamfer on the spigot is lubricated generously witth silicone grease, and with the clean joint ring in place in the cleaned socket, the spigot is lined up with the socket. With a slight twisting motion the spigot is pushed firmly past the joint ring and into the socket until the insertion depth mark is level with the face of the socket.

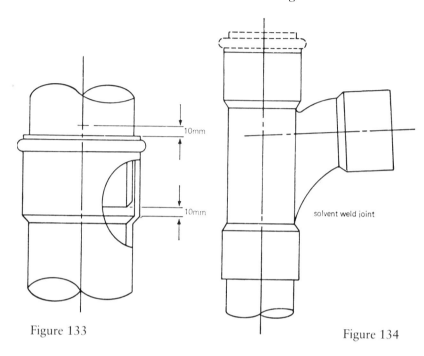

Figure 133

solvent weld joint

Figure 134

*Coupling-nut compression type joint seal*

The compression type of joint is made by a locknut which is slipped on to the spigot end after which the joint ring is also put on the pipe end. The spigot is then entered in the socket to the prescribed depth and the joint completed by pushing the rubber ring into the socket and tightening the locknut. The manufacturers of this type of joint issue explicit instructions which must be followed in all assembly work.

## Solvent-weld system

The solvent-weld system is satisfactory providing that due allowance is made for thermal movement in the installation. This is achieved by the use of expansion joints of the ring seal type at strategic points.

In a solvent-weld joint the spigot should fit very closely with the socket. In some cases it will be found that when pushed together dry, the spigot will enter the socket only to about half its depth but when the solvent is applied its effect will allow penetration of the spigot to full depth.

With the solvent-weld system it is permissible to make a joint against the direction of the flow in vertical and horizontal pipework installations (see Figure 134). There are all-socketed fittings and fittings with spigot ends to which the pipes are attached by using loose sockets. When properly made the joint is homogeneous and rigid with the spigot butted against the internal shoulder of the socket, leaving a smooth, full and uninterrupted pipe bore.

Care must be taken to make a solvent weld correctly and the procedure is as follows:

1  Remove any dust and swarf from the pipe end and the socket, both of which should be cleaned thoroughly. The manufacturers of plastics supply a special cleaning fluid which acts as a degreasing agent and removes the glossy surface from uPVC in readiness for the solvent welding operation.
2  If a pipe has to be cut the end should be square and even and all rough edges smoothed before applying solvent.
3  Apply one coat of uPVC solvent cement to the external surface of the spigot and the internal surface of the socket.
4  Push the spigot into the socket with a slight twisting movement until it reaches the full depth of the socket.
5  Wipe off any surplus solvent cement immediately.

With careful treatment it should be possible to handle the joint in two or three minutes. If possible, however, the system should be left to stand for 24 hours before being put into operation.

Some manufacturers recommend the application of two coats of solvent cement.

*Plastics pipes used for water services* must comply with the following:

Unplasticized Polyvinylchloride (uPVC) pipe for cold-water services must comply with the requirements of BS 3505. If laid in the ground the uPVC pipe must be of the appropriate class for the maximum working pressure. Pipes of a nominal size 75 mm or less for the conveyance of potable water must be coloured blue for identification purposes.

*Joints and fittings for use with uPVC pressure pipes* must comply with BS 4346.

*Polyethylene pipe* to BS 6572

Blue polyethylene pipes up to a nominal size of 63 mm are for below-ground use for cold potable water. These pipes have been specially developed for services laid in the ground.There is one class designed for a working pressure of 12 bar at 20°C. The pipes may be used above ground providing they are not exposed to direct sunlight. Compression fittings for polyethylene pipes must be to BS 864. If laid in the ground, copper alloy fittings should be made of gunmetal or material to BS 2872 or BS 2874 CZ 132.

# 13

# Copper Tubes

All copper tubes for water, gas and sanitation must comply with BS 2871. Copper tube to this standard is designed to be jointed by compression or capillary fittings, or brazing. All copper tubes should bear either a BS kite mark or evidence acceptable to the water board that it has been properly cleaned during or after production.

For above-ground installation, tube to Table X or Z may be used (note: Table-Z tube must not be bent, and only capillary or non-manipulative type compression fittings may be used). If installed below ground, Table-Y tube must be used. This can be obtained with a polyethylene coating which some water authorities may require.

*Joints and fittings for BS 2781 pipes* must be to BS 864: Part 2. Copper alloy fittings must be made from gunmetal BS 2872 or 2874 material CZ 132 (which means they are resistant to dezincification). Under no circumstances can adhesives be used to make any joint to copper tube in the ground.

The resistance of copper to corrosion is due to the formation by natural processes of a protective film which in nearly all cases renders the metal safe from attack by the atmosphere and from any water, gas or soil with which it may be in contact. The film is primarily an oxidized layer which forms a protective skin on both the outside and inside of copper tubes and ensures not only a long life for the pipe, but also that it will not contaminate drinking water or require any additional treatment for protection when installed in contact with the usual building materials or normal types of soil.

Copper tubes cannot rust and do not require painting, which saves cost and, in the case of hot-water pipes, avoids the unpleasant smell of warm paint. In certain cases where the pipes are run on the surface the attractive appearance of the metal can be exploited to fit in with the surrounding decorative features. The trend in modern plumbing is to conceal pipes as much as possible, with the result that they are installed in chases or are buried in walls and floors. Concrete, lime and lime plasters and cement mortar have no harmful effect on copper but there are certain acid soils and materials which are known to be corrosive to all metals.

In addition to their corrosion-resisting properties, copper tubes possess a combination of physical characteristics. The ductility of the metal enables them to be manipulated with ease, while the strength of even light gauge tubes ensures that they will withstand pressures far higher than those to be found in normal pipe services. They will withstand considerable internal and external pressures and adjust themselves to irregularities and settlements in soils or buildings without risk of fractures occurring.

In certain cases, tubes are subject to expansion and contraction due to changes in temperature, and restraint of the consequent movement at various points in the installation may set up stresses in the pipes. Copper combines sufficient strength and elasticity to prevent any permanent deformation such as that which occurs in tubes of softer metals under similar conditions. In the case of heating installations carried out in copper tubes, there is economy in the amount of metal used, with a consequent saving in cost, weight and space, a smaller mass of metal to be heated, less radiation surface for heat loss, thereby effecting a saving in fuel. The ease with which the tubes can be handled, manipulated and jointed means lower labour costs and reduction in the number of fittings required.

The very smooth surface of a solid drawn copper tube is an important feature particularly in a water pipe, because of the low frictional resistance it offers to the flow of the water, and in waste pipes because it reduces the risk of blockages to a minimum. In hard-water districts the calcium carbonate deposits do not adhere so quickly or firmly to the smooth interior surface of a copper tube and therefore the removal of scale that might form is a simple matter.

From a decorative point of view, the smooth non-rusting exterior surface has much to commend it and it can be polished easily and it readily takes a plated finish. The small diameter tubes and fittings give a neat and unobtrusive appearance.

A point of some importance arising from the smooth bore of a copper pipe is that, in conjunction with the strength and ductility of copper, it gives a measure of protection against frost bursting.

It is of course not claimed by the manufacturers of copper tubes that they will not burst under extreme conditions. A good plumber would never expose any tube installation to extreme conditions.

An important development came with the manufacture of long-length copper tubes in 'dead soft' temper. These tubes are supplied in coils of 20 m.

# Jointing copper tubes

The present widespread use of copper for all forms of pipework in plumbing is a result of the development of suitable means of jointing light gauge tubes. The joints commonly used today in house plumbing are manipulative and non-manipulative compression fittings and capillary joints.

British Standard 864, part 2: 1971 'Capillary Fittings and Compression Fittings of Copper and Copper Alloy, for Use with Light Gauge Copper Tube' gives the general dimensions and classifies them as non-manipulative compression fittings Type A, manipulative compression fittings Type B, and capillary soldered fittings, and states that the fittings shall be of copper or a suitable corrosion resisting alloy. A table sets out the allowable hydraulic working pressures and temperatures for these forms of joints, but it may be of interest that many of the fittings, both capillary and compression, can be used at higher temperatures and pressures. Under such conditions, however, the manufacturers should be consulted regarding any special requirements necessary to ensure their products give satisfactory service.

In the past some confusion has arisen over the method of stating the sizes of tees or crosses. To overcome this a standard method has now been adopted by all manufacturers as follows:

28 × 15 × 22 mm        35 × 22 × 28 × 15 mm

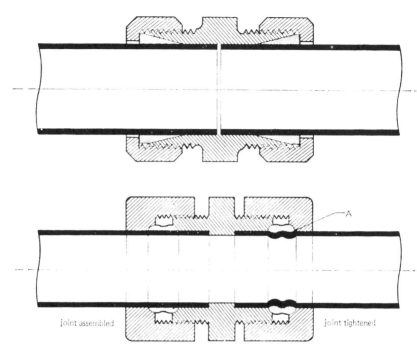

Figure 135　*Non-manipulative compression joints*

A good type of joint should not in any way restrict the bore of the tube and in addition should preferably be so made as to allow easy dismantling for maintenance or other purposes.

## Compression joints

The non-manipulative compression joint, as the name implies, does not require any working of the tube end other than cutting it square. The joint is made tight by means of a loose ring or sleeve which grips the outside wall of the tube when the coupling nut is tightened.

In the manipulative type of compression joint the end of the tube is flared, cupped or belled with special forming tools and is compressed by means of a coupling nut against the shaped end of corresponding section on the fitting or a loose thimble.

Figure 135 shows typical joints of the non-manipulative type.

A joint of this type is made by slipping the coupling nut and compression ring on to the squared end of the tube and inserting it into the mouth of the fitting up to the internal shoulder. The coupling nut is then screwed up tight with a spanner, causing the edge, or edges, of the compression ring to bite into the copper tube. The effect (A) is shown in exaggerated form.

In Figure 136 are shown three main types of manipulative compression joints. Joint No. 1 is prepared by cutting the tube to length, squaring off the end and, after slipping the coupling nut on, a special expanding tool is inserted into the tube. A tommy-bar in the tool is then turned in its housing to the stop; by this action the steel balls in the tool are forced outwards and at the

Figure 136   *Manipulative compression joints*

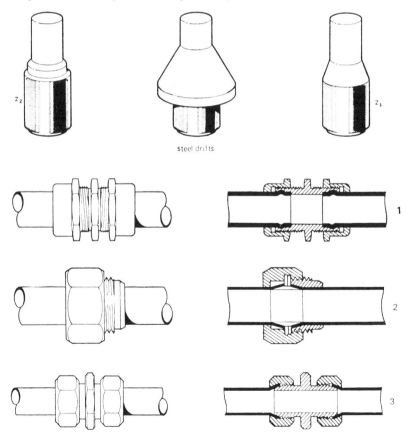

steel drifts

same time are rotated, thereby swageing a bead in the tube wall. The tool is removed from the tube by bringing the tommy-bar back to its original position. The tube is then inserted in the mouth of the fitting and the joint completed by screwing up the coupling nut.

In joint No. 2, the centre ferrule is machined from copper, bronze and brass and the angle or degree of taper matches that formed on the tube end after it has been expanded by the steel drift. The mouth of the male portion of the fitting and the friction ring inside the coupling nut are similarly machined, so that the jointing faces all marry up. The union is assembled by screwing up the coupling nut with a spanner, the body of the fitting being held at the same time with another spanner.

In preparing joint No. 3, the coupling nut is first slipped over the tube end, a split collar die is placed on the tube and secured by tightening up the side nuts; the tube end is then opened by the drift Z and after withdrawing this, the second drift Z is used to form the belled or cupped mouth as shown. The collar is removed by unbolting and the tube end pulled up tight to the body by screwing up the coupling nut, thus making a mechanically sound joint.

## Capillary-soldered joints

Since the soldered or sweated joints – or as they should be called – capillary joints were introduced in this country, development has been taken up on a considerable scale and now the joint has come to be generally accepted as neat, sound and economical. Capillary fittings are suitable for hot- and cold-water services and waste pipes. They are made from copper and copper alloys.

Capillary fittings are constructed upon the basic principle of capillary attraction, which provides the means by which molten solder is drawn into the narrow space between the two closely fitting metal surfaces of the exterior of the tube ends and the interior of the jointing piece. The joint can be made either in the horizontal or the vertical position. The closeness of the fit is the main factor in ensuring capillary attraction, and it is therefore of the greatest importance that the fittings are those intended for the exact gauges and diameters of the tubes being used.

The certainty of an exact fit is provided for by the British

Standard for Light Gauge Copper Tubes (BS 2871: Part 1 and BS 864: Part 2) which specifies both wall thicknesses and external diameters and states the permissible tolerances; and is still further assured by BS 864, part 2: 1971 'Capillary Fittings and Compression Fittings for use with Light Gauge Copper Tubes', which similarly specifies the dimensions of fittings.

It was thought at one time that there might be a likelihood of corrosion due to electrolytic action taking place between the copper of the tubes or fittings and the jointing solder. This fear was unfounded, however, for it is most unlikely that any appreciable action could take place with normal waters and a properly made joint, since the amount of solder left exposed to the action of the water inside the pipe, or to condensation on the outside, is so small as to be negligible. If the water is likely to be of such a corrosive nature that there is a danger of electrolytic action, it may be assumed that it is sufficiently corrosive to act upon plain metal and should therefore be submitted to preliminary examination no matter what type of joint is used.

However, the presence of other dissimilar metals in the system may produce electrolysis, which may make otherwise acceptable water aggressive. One effect of this could be an attack on the lead content of any solder accessible to the water, which could raise the lead content of the water above the safe levels. For this reason lead-free solders, for instance tin/silver, must be used. The publication of a British Standard on lead-free solders is pending. Any system which is installed using solder containing lead may be accepted if tests show that the lead levels in the water are acceptable. In the case of an existing system found by an inspector to have been jointed by solder containing lead, the owner/occupier of the premises may be advised about the potential risk. This will be without prejudice to any other course of action which may be open to the water undertakers.

Years of experience have now proved that capillary joints are perfectly satisfactory for hot water and heating installations. Where especially long pipe runs are encountered in such installations, provision should be made to take up the movement due to temperature variations, by means of expansion bends or expansion joints. These are hardly ever likely to be required for installations in the ordinary dwelling house.

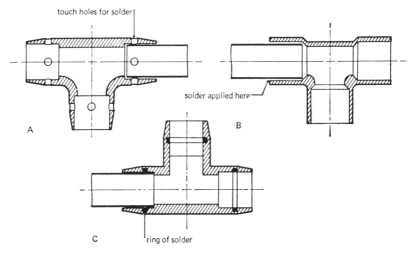

Figure 137   *Capillary joints for copper tubes*

## Assembling capillary joints

The assembly of any type of capillary joint consists, briefly, of cutting square the tube ends, thoroughly cleaning them and the inside of the fitting, fluxing, inserting the tubes in the fitting and heating with a blowlamp. When heat is applied, solder is fed into the joint from solder wire applied (A) at a touch hole in the fitting, (B) at the mouth of the fitting, or (C) from a reservoir of solder already within the fitting. These fittings are illustrated in Figure 137. As an alternative to feeding solder in by these means, the joint can be made with solder paint, applied evenly to the tube after cleaning and prior to inserting in the fitting.

Much emphasis is placed on the need for close attention to every detail in making capillary joints even though it appears to be a very simple process. The steps are as follows:

1  The tube must be cut square to sit evenly on the shoulder at the bottom of the socket, and all rough edges formed by the sawing operation should be removed by file or reamer. For sawing, a special vice is obtainable which has interchangeable jaws to hold tubes of all sizes. The vice holds any length of tube, and because the saw blade moves between close guides,

there is less burr to be removed and no trueing up is required after the cut is made.

2  The exterior surface of the tube at its ends and the interior surface of the fittings must be scoured to remove all traces of dirt and oxide, which could prevent the solder from adhering to the metal. This operation should be carried out with steel wool or sandpaper but emery paper or emery cloth should not be used.

3  The metal surfaces to be united on both tube and fitting are next evenly coated with flux to prevent the surfaces from oxidizing when heat is applied. It is most important that the flux used should be one approved by the fittings manufacturer.

4  The tube ends are then inserted in the fitting and it is important that their ends bed squarely on the socket shoulders.

5  Heat is applied by playing the flame of a blowlamp upon the outside of the socket until it has reached an even temperature all round to melt the solder evenly. The temperature may be determined when applying the solder externally (Fig. 137A and B), by watching for flux vapours. When these appear it is time to apply the solder at the touch hole (type A) or at the mouth of the socket (type B). The socket should not be overheated, as overheating could break down the flux, oxidize the cleaned surfaces and burn the solder. In type A, if the solder does not run freely into the touch hole and does not appear at the mouth of the socket, or if in type B does not disappear freely into the socket before it finally floods up to the mouth, the joint should be regarded with suspicion and it would be advisable to re-make it.

When using type C it is only necessary to apply heat after having completed carefully the cleaning and fluxing operations. The joint should be closely inspected to check that the solder has crept out to the mouth of the socket, forming a complete and even ring of solder there.

# Bending copper tubes

One of the advantages in the use of copper tubes for building services is the ease with which they can be bent either by bending machine or spring, and in the case of larger-diameter tubes, by means of sand filling, resin filling, low melting-point filler alloys or mandrel bending machines.

For a proper understanding of what is involved in bending, the reader should clearly understand what deformations take place when a copper tube is bent. The walls of a straight tube are parallel and must remain parallel after bending if the true round section of the tube is to be maintained in the bend. The original

Figure 138A   *Bending techniques*

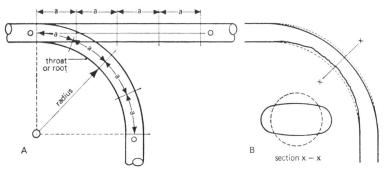

theory of bending

True and deformed bends
A True bend.Each division a represents a 'throw' in making the bend.
B Deformation of bend in unsupported tubes.

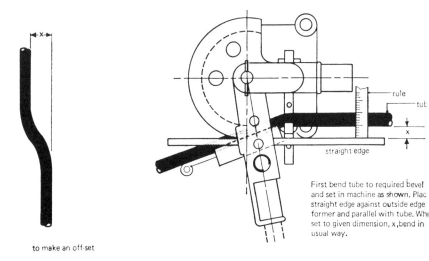

to make an off-set

First bend tube to required bevel and set in machine as shown. Plac straight edge against outside edge former and parallel with tube. Wh set to given dimension, x ,bend in usual way.

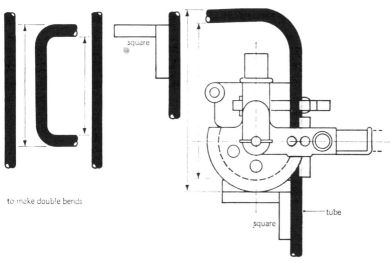

to make double bends

To bend to inside measurement, v.mark tube as shown. Place square on mark and insert in bending machine so that the square touches the inside of the groove of the former. Bend as usual.

To bend to outside measurement, z.mark the tube as shown. Place square on mark and insert in bending machine so that the square touches the outside edge of the former. Bend as usual.

Figure 138B   *Bending techniques*

length of the tube o–o remains unaltered after bending only along the centre line of the tube. It follows that the inside, or throat, of the bend is shortened and compressed and the outside, or back, is lengthened and stretched (see Figure 138). From this it will be seen that the tube will collapse in the bend unless precautions are taken to prevent it. Therefore, it is necessary to support the tube while bending takes place. This support is provided by filling or loading the tube by the material just mentioned or by the use of a bending machine – of which there are many on the market – which will prove an economic proposition, particularly for sizes of tube up to 54 mm diameter. These machines work by hand power or through a ratchet action or gear and employ special formers and back guides to ensure that the tube, when pulled to the necessary angle, maintains its true diameter and shape throughout the length of the bend. In using any machine, the formers and guides should be maintained in good condition and well lubricated. This also applies to bending springs.

# Fitting copper tubes

Advantages of light gauge copper tubes are the ease with which they can be installed and their neat appearance. These points can be appreciated where numerous tubes run parallel on walls or ceilings. They should always be accurately lined up, be parallel and plumb and kept equidistant if at all possible. The use of purpose-made fittings and bends makes this an easy matter. Where pipes change direction through 90 degrees, or are offset to pass some break or obstruction in the building, it is generally better to use bends rather than sharp elbows.

Where several pipes are running together, they should be left far enough apart to allow sufficient clearance for the securing of fixing clips.

In setting out bends or offsets, it is always worthwhile making a full sized drawing, on the bench or floor, to which the bending points on the straight pipes can be set to obtain the correct angles easily and quickly.

One additional advantage of using light gauge copper tubes is the ease with which off-site prefabrication can be done. This means a considerable saving in labour as such units can be assembled in jigs, easily transported to the site, and call for a minimum of site labour for fixing.

Copper and brass fixing clips for use with light gauge copper tubes are made in a variety of patterns.

The coefficient of thermal expansion of copper is $16.6 \times 10^{-6}°C$, that is to say a length increase of approximately 3.5 mm for every 3 m run of tube for a temperature rise of 50°C. While this amount is slightly greater than that of iron, it is considerably less than that of lead or plastic tubing. In the general run of heating and hot-water installations, the many bends and offsets which occur accommodate the amount of thermal movement that will take place due to temperature variations.

Occasional complaints of noise transmission arise as a result of high water pressures, faulty ball valves or other terminal points, or where pumps or boosters are installed. The trouble can be overcome by using flexible connectors, called vibration eliminators, at terminal ends and on pump inlets and outlets. In some cases, however, noise transmission may occur as a result of inadequate use of fixing or spacing clips. Taking the Imperial measurements given in the British Standard Code of Practice CP 310: 1965 and converting these into metric terms, the fixing spaces for light gauge copper tubes are as follows:

| Diameter mm | Horizontal run m | Vertical run m |
|---|---|---|
| 12 | 1.2 | 1.5 |
| 15 | 1.2 | 1.5 |
| 18 | 1.2 | 1.5 |
| 22 | 2.0 | 2.5 |
| 28 | 2.0 | 2.5 |
| 35 | 2.5 | 3.0 |

Where these dimensions are adhered to, noise transmission will not occur under normal service conditions.

# 14

# Screwed Pipes and Fittings

All iron barrel pipes must be to BS 1387, and all wrought steel pipe fittings to BS 1740: Part 1.

If these pipes are to be installed below ground, both pipes and fittings are to be heavy-gauge only, and protected by the methods set out in BS 534, section 30 for external protection. Galvanizing is normally sufficient for internal protection, but it is not sufficient for external protection.

When fixed above ground, all pipes and fittings are to be:

1 Heavy- or medium-gauge tube.
2 Galvanized internally.
3 Coated externally in addition to galvanized (as described below).
4 If screwed-thread joints are used, PTFE tape or paste must be used as the jointing compound.

The weights of pipes to BS 1387 are easily identified by a ring of paint denoting the class colour:

Brown = light gauge*
Blue = medium gauge
Red = heavy gauge.

* Light-gauge barrel should be used only on installations such as fire sprinkler systems from which no water is drawn or used for other purposes.

## Protection

Unprotected iron and steel pipes are liable to severe corrosion by some waters and internal encrustation may in time be formed which will entirely close the bore of small-diameter pipes. Discoloration of the water might also occur with certain waters. All pipes should be galvanized, and where they are in contact with the soil be also coated with bitumen and wrapped with a spiral wrapping of glass tissue impregnated with bitumen. Pipes should never be fixed in contact with magnesium oxychloride flooring or with Keene's cement.

## Pipe threads

The screw threads on pipes are referred to as gas threads, and the manufacturers make them to the requirements of British Standard Specification No. 21.

The screw threads on the pipes or, for that matter, all external threads are termed 'male' while the internal screw threads of pipe fittings are referred to as 'female'. It is important to use these terms when ordering fittings for any kind of plumbing work.

## Pipe fittings

A very wide range of pipe fittings is available and they are manufactured in wrought iron and in malleable cast iron.

Wrought-iron fittings are products of a special process from which semi-molten metal, mixed with slag, is passed through squeezers and rolled to the desired section, from which the fittings are produced.

Malleable cast-iron fittings are cast from white iron and subsequently annealed. This is a heat-treatment process which gives the fitting a certain elasticity. Such fittings are easily recognized by the strengthening bead round the edge of the fitting. They are of pleasing appearance and because they are cheaper than wrought-iron fittings they are widely used in the plumbing trade.

In Figure 139 the range of pipe fittings available is illustrated. Those with the beads are malleable fittings. The letter M refers to male and the letter F to female. This is the method of description employed by the trade as stated earlier.

## Rules for reading

It is important to know how to 'read' sizes of tee-pieces, crosses and side outlet fittings, etc.

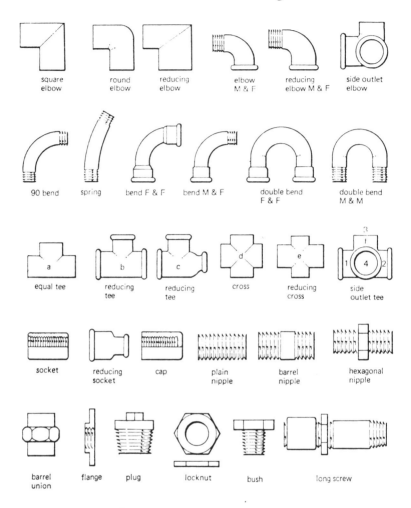

Figure 139　*Pipe fittings*

Tee-pieces: When one size is specified it applies to each outlet, i.e. an equal tee is illustrated at A in Figure 139.

When two sizes are specified, the first applies to both ends of the barrel and the second to the branch (see B).

When three sizes are specified the first two apply to the ends of the barrel, the larger end being specified first.

Crosses: When one size is specified it applies to all the ends of the cross.

When two sizes are specified the first applies to one pair of opposite ends, the second to the other pair, the larger pair being specified first. When four sizes are specified the first two apply to one pair of opposite ends and the second two to the other pair, the larger size being specified first. It should be remembered that a cross should never be described by only three sizes.

Side outlets: When fittings have a side outlet, their ends should be specified as for normal fittings and then the size of the side outlet should be given. F in Figure 139 indicates the sequence of the size. For unequal fittings it is best to provide a sketch and indicate whether the side outlet is left or right hand in relation to the other outlets.

# Pipe fitting

In actual practice pipe fitting consists of measuring, cutting, threading, assembling and securing lengths of pipe and fittings. Special tools are required, particularly for threading the pipes, and it is hardly likely that the do-it-yourselfer will wish to

Figure 140 *Measuring for pipework*

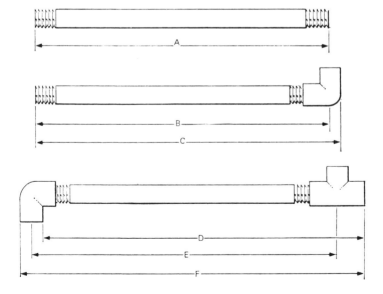

purchase them because they are expensive and are not adaptable for many other purposes. It might be possible to hire tools and equipment from a tool hire firm.

## Measuring for pipework

Iron pipes should be fixed about 28 mm clear of the plaster or tiles and due allowance should be made for this when measuring.

There are several methods of measuring and these are illustrated in Figure 140.

A    End of thread to end of thread.
B    End of thread to centre of fitting.
C    End of thread to back of fitting.
D    Back of fitting to inside of fitting.
E    Centre of fitting to centre of fitting.
F    Back of fitting to end of fitting.

In all cases of measuring due allowance must be made for the engagement of the thread on to the fitting.

## Cutting the pipes

The easiest way to cut iron pipe is by using special wheel cutters but the pipe should never be cut completely through with this tool. It is better to make the final severance with a hacksaw thus eliminating the internal burr. For pipes of small diameter a good hacksaw has many advantages. The wheel cutters by their spreading action leave a distinct burr on both the inside and outside of the pipe and these must be removed by using a file on the outside and a reamer or rat-tail on the inside. Pipes should never be fixed without first removing the inside burr. The hacksaw cut leaves no burrs, but be careful when sawing – the blades break easily when doing this job.

## Threading the pipes

There are a number of excellent stocks and dies available for threading pipe and although the finished thread made by each tool is identical, the methods of setting, adjusting and operating them differ.

It may be necessary to file a slight taper on the end of the pipe to be threaded in order to engage the dies, and good 'push-on' pressure is required as the stock is turned. Once the dies start to cut they draw themselves on to the pipe.

It is important, of course, that the dies be engaged perfectly square to the pipe so that the thread will be truly aligned. A thin-oil lubricant should be applied while the thread is being cut.

After a little experience it will be possible to decide at a glance the correct length of thread.

## Connecting

Considerable care is required in assembling pipes and fittings, because a faulty joint could give a great deal of trouble and might even mean dismantling the entire system.

Before assembling, the pipes should be inspected to see that the interior is clean and free from any obstruction. If a thread has been cut then be sure that no metal cuttings remain on or inside the pipe. A sharp blow with a hammer will usually dislodge the cuttings.

To make the joint, wipe the oil from the thread with a piece of waste then, starting at the beginning of the thread, wind PTFE tape clockwise round and up the length of the threaded section, making sure that the tape is pulled taut throughout the operation, and that it is pulled well down into the valley between each thread. Snap off when the length of the thread is wrapped and smooth off with the fingers. Jointing paste is not required when PTFE tape is used.

On joints where paste is required – mating faces of barrel unions, tank connectors, etc. – use only approved jointing materials such as Boss Blue.

Next, inspect the fitting to ensure that it is clean and is undamaged and it is a good idea to paint a little of the jointing paste on the thread.

The fitting must engage the pipe thread freely and it should be possible for the first few turns to be made by hand without difficulty. Then a pipe wrench should be used finally to tighten the fitting to the pipe. Gradually increase the pressure on the wrench until the fitting is really tight, but avoid over-tightening, otherwise the fitting might split.

In assembly work some fittings can be assembled in the pipe vice: others must be fixed in the location, in which case two pipe wrenches might be required, one 'holding against' the other.

Beware of a crossed thread in assembly work. This occurs when a fitting is not properly engaged with the pipe. It is easily detected by the sudden tightening of the fitting before more than a thread or two have been engaged.

## Pipe supports

All pipework should be supported by projecting clips commonly called 'holderbats'. The back of the holderbat may have a plate with two holes for attaching to a wood ground or may have a tail for building into the wall. The spacing of the supports should be such that there will be no sagging of the pipe, nor any possibility of it swinging on a fitting under its own weight or of being pulled by anyone.

# 15

# Stainless Steel for Domestic Water Services

Stainless steel pipes must comply with BS 4127: Part 2. This tube is suitable for use with BS 864: Part 2 capillary or compression fittings. If laid in the ground the pipe should be of the class capable of withstanding a pressure of at least 12 bar for sizes up to and including 63 mm diameter. Adhesives are not permitted for making joints. Pipes fitted above the ground should be of a class capable of withstanding at least 1.5 times the maximum working pressure.

Stainless steel tube for plumbing and domestic central heating has now been in regular use since 1966 and to date many millions of feet of tubes of varying sizes have been installed.

Stainless steel is generally accepted as one of the most corrosion resisting metals available. This resistance is due to the hard, adherent and transparent oxide film that covers the surface of the metal and which re-forms instantaneously if the metal is scratched or abraded. The experience now gained in domestic plumbing confirms that the metal will remain unaffected when in contact with most types of potable water.

The tube is particularly resistant to damage because of its hardness and high strength and it requires fewer fixing clips and supports than other materials.

The clean attractive appearance of stainless steel tubing and fittings is an important advantage where they have to be fixed in view, although they may be painted without difficulty to blend with any particular colour scheme.

## Dimensions and weights of tube

Stainless steel tube for domestic water installations is fabricated by the continuous welding of stainless steel strip. The material

*Dimensions and Weights of Stainless Steel Tube (BS 4127: Part 2)*

| Size of tube mm | Outside diameter max mm | min mm | Nominal thickness mm | Weight per metre kg | Approx. No. metres per 1,000 kg |
|---|---|---|---|---|---|
| 6 | 6·045 | 5·940 | 0·6 | 0·081 | 12,305 |
| 8 | 8·045 | 7·940 | 0·6 | 0·110 | 8,965 |
| 10 | 10·045 | 9·940 | 0·6 | 0·140 | 7,050 |
| 12 | 12·045 | 11·940 | 0·6 | 0·170 | 5,823 |
| 15 | 15·045 | 14·940 | 0·6 | 0·220 | 4,601 |
| 18 | 18·045 | 17·940 | 0·7 | 0·310 | 3,283 |
| 22 | 22·055 | 21·950 | 0·7 | 0·370 | 2,668 |
| 28 | 28·055 | 27·950 | 0·8 | 0·550 | 1,829 |

used is a stainless steel containing about 18 per cent chromium and 9 per cent nickel.

## Fittings

The outside diameters of the tubes are such that they can be used in conjunction with fittings specified for the standard copper tube. These fittings are manufactured from copper or copper alloy in accordance with BS 864, Part 2. Stainless steel tubes are suitable for use with capillary joints, except on drinking water services and types A and B compression fittings included in this standard. In those parts of the country where dezincification of brass fittings is liable to occur, copper or gunmetal fittings should be used and will be quite satisfactory with stainless steel. As the thermal expansion of stainless steel is very similar to that of copper there is no danger of the joints being weakened through unequal rates of expansion. Where appearance is important chromium or nickelplated copper fittings can be used.

# Installation techniques

## Stainless steel in contact with other metals

Care should be taken if using stainless steel in conjunction with other materials such as copper cylinders or galvanized tanks. Although, in the past, it has been generally accepted as suitable for use with other metals, some water authorities now either prohibit or discourage its use.

As with all materials used in water services, the approval of the local water undertaking should be obtained before any work is started.

## Cutting the tubes

A fine-toothed hacksaw (32 teeth per 25 mm) should be used for cutting stainless steel tubes. Standard wheel pipe cutters are also suitable.

## Bending

Because of its ductility the grade of stainless steel tube used for domestic water supply can be bent quite easily by an experienced plumber. The 15-mm tube can be bent by the spring method using the same technique as for copper tubes. The spring should be lightly greased to facilitate its removal after the tube has been bent.

Generally speaking, most bending machines suitable for light gauge copper tube can be used with stainless steel but experience has shown that the higher strength stainless steel requires the use of a sturdier machine than would be necessary for copper tube of similar diameters. For 15- and 22-mm stainless steel tubes it is advisable to employ the bending machines designed for copper tubes of 22 and 28 mm respectively. In case of doubt the manufacturers of bending machines will be ready to advise.

# Jointing

## Capillary joints

The procedure is the same as that for copper tubes and fittings (see chapter 13) but because the flux could cause skin irritation it should be applied with a spatula. Also it should be known that the thermal conductivity of stainless steel is low so heat should be applied to the fitting and not the tube.

## The choice of a flux

The extremely high corrosion resistance of stainless steel depends upon its naturally occurring oxide film which re-forms immediately when damaged by abrasion. To remove it by chemical means demands a flux which must be highly corrosive at the moment when the solder is required to wet the steel to make the joint. However, the flux residues remaining after the joint has been made must not be corrosive, and therefore the acid chloride fluxes sometimes used for soldering stainless steel metalwork are not suitable for making capillary joints in stainless steel tube.

The correct fluxes are those based on phosphoric acid. This acid is sufficiently corrosive towards stainless steel at soldering temperatures to provide solder wetting but innocuous after the joint has cooled. These phosphoric acid-based fluxes in paste form, specially prepared for making capillary joints with stainless steel tubes and copper or copper alloy fittings may be obtained from builders' and plumbers' merchants.

## Compression joints

Both type A and type B compression fittings can be used with stainless steel tube and the methods of jointing are explained in the chapter on jointing copper tubes.

# 16

# Roof Weathering

The roofs of homes in this country are usually covered with tiles or slates. Not many new homes have slated roofs because of the very high costs involved. The plumber seldom fixes the roof tiles but he has an important job to do in making the roof watertight.

He is responsible for what is known as the 'weathering', that is, the gutters, aprons and flashings which render watertight those parts of the roof where the tiles abut brickwork or pipes. On a modern house roof weathering presents few problems because of the simplicity of design. In many cases, there is but one chimney pot which terminates the flue of the central heating plant. The parts to be weathered are the chimney stack and the soil and vent pipe where it emerges through the tiles.

## Weathering a chimney

No matter how closely fitting the tiles may be to the brickwork where the chimney stack emerges through the roof, they cannot be made watertight without the weatherings. At the back of the chimney there must be a gutter to take away the rainwater as it streams down the roof slope. Down each side of the stack there must be flashings and soakers to keep the driving rain from striking the brickwork and running down into the roof space. The soakers also prevent the discharge from the backgutter from getting through to the roof space, by directing or channelling it towards the roof slope and on its way to the rainwater gutters at the eaves. The front apron protects the face of the chimney stack where it comes through the tiles. Although side flashings with soakers are the most effective method of weathering the sides of the chimney stack, the flashing can continue in one piece from the brickwork on to the tiles. The illustrations show the arrangement of weathering a chimney, which applies no matter what material is used for the weathering.

The work of preparing and fixing roof weathering is a highly skilled job. The householder should see to it that they are done properly by a skilled plumber because a leaking roof can cause serious damage to property. Do not allow the builder to use cement fillets as a substitute for weathering materials.

Where a soil and vent pipe or a flue pipe penetrates the tiles a weathering is made by means of sleeve, or 'slate', as it is usually called by plumbers. Once again it is stressed that a cement fillet is not suitable.

## Materials used for roof weathering

Sheet copper, lead, zinc and aluminium are all suitable metals for roof weathering. An asphalt bonded asbestos sheet of laminate construction called Nuralite is now widely used by plumbers. It is highly resistant to atmospheric corrosion and being non-metallic it is not subject to electrolytic decomposition. It is an excellent material for weathering and it costs less than the traditional metals.

The principles adopted in weathering a chimney are the same whatever material is used. The techniques employed in manipulating the materials differ somewhat. For instance sheet lead can be 'bossed' into required shapes by a skilled plumber or it can be cut and welded. Copper can be welded or brazed. Nuralite is manipulated by simple methods and the Nuralite Company Limited, Higham, nr Rochester, Kent, will send an excellent instruction manual to any plumber on application.

Zinc is a traditional metal for roof weathering and it is now produced in convenient 10 m rolls in standard widths of 150, 240, 300, 480, 600 mm. It can be worked quite easily and soldered without difficulty. It has been given a trade name of 'Zincon'. The descriptions of the various roof weathering applications are for Zincon but the general principles are similar for all materials.

The weathering applications are shown in Figures 141 to 148.

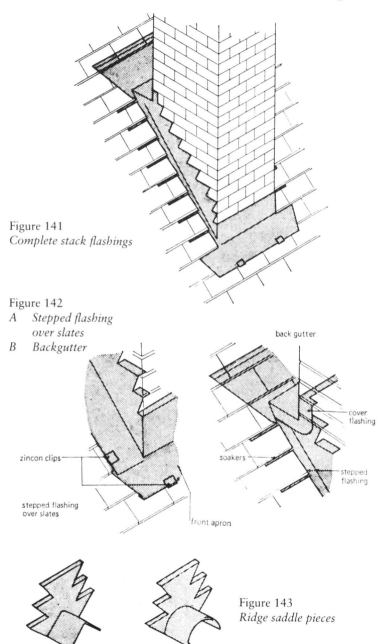

Figure 141
*Complete stack flashings*

Figure 142
A   *Stepped flashing
    over slates*
B   *Backgutter*

back gutter

cover
flashing

zincon clips

soakers

stepped
flashing

stepped flashing
over slates

front apron

Figure 143
*Ridge saddle pieces*

A

B

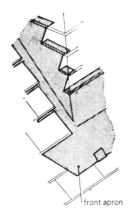

*Figure 144*
*Stepped flashing*
*over soakers*

front apron

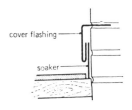

cover flashing

soaker

*Figure 145*
*Soaker detail*

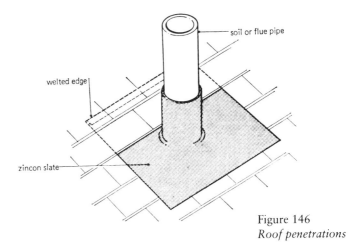

soil or flue pipe

welted edge

zincon slate

Figure 146
*Roof penetrations*

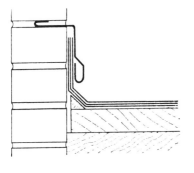

Figure 147
*Cover flashing to felt roof*

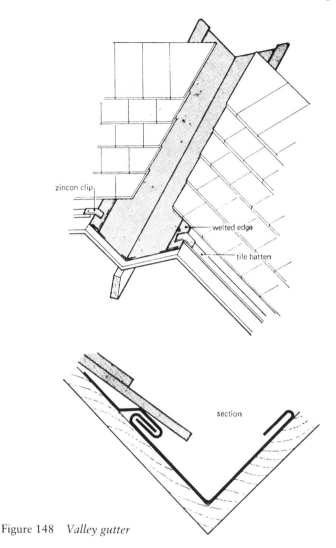

Figure 148   *Valley gutter*

## Stack flashings

The soft malleable temper of Zincon flashing strip makes stack flashing easy as well as economic. Cover flashings, stepped flashings and front aprons are made in the normal way. Backgutters can be cut and soldered together with no weak spots.

Wedges for joints should be cut from the flashing strip and galvanized nails should be used. No treatment to the surface is needed when bedding the material in mortar joints. Where profiled tiles are used, Zincon can usually be formed into the profile of the tile. Allowance should be made for extra material needed to take up this profile in the case of front aprons.

For deeply profiled tiles it is necessary to cut the strip and tuck it into the profile.

Where chimney stack penetrates the roof at a ridge, the side flashings are jointed with a saddle piece. This is formed with a lapped and soldered joint.

Side flashings fixed to brickwork are cut with steps, each step being turned into a joint, wedged, and pointed in. The distance between the internal angle of the step and the line of the roof should not be less than 50 mm and, if the roof covering is plain tiles or slates, the side flashing laps over the upstands of soakers coursed in with the tiles or slates. The soakers are folded to turn up at least 75 mm against the side of the stack and to extend 100 to 125 mm under the tiles or slates.

The free edge of the flashing is stiffened with a 25 mm fold. Where the roof covering is single-lap tiling or sheet material the flashing extends on to the roof covering 100 to 125 mm. The free edge is secured with 40 mm wide Zincon clips spaced at 300 mm centres and nailed to roof timbers.

Where soil vent pipes or flue pipes penetrate roofs, slates can be easily formed to provide the weather-proofing. The slate is cut to course in with the tile or slate module and a short length of pipe soldered in at the appropriate angle. This length of pipe can be cut and soldered from flat strip. This technique need not be limited to pipe sections and can be extended to roof penetrations of any outline. In the case of flat roofs the same technique should be used except that the slate should be laid over the first layer of felt and under the second two layers.

*Felt roofing*
Zincon can be used as a cover flashing where a felt roof abuts a wall.

## Valleys, gutters and ridge tiles

In new work or repairs it is possible to site form Zincon into valleys and ridges to give a long-lasting job with a pleasing appearance. Valley gutters should be formed over timber battens, using a wooden dressing tool. They should be fixed with clips and galvanized nails at 300 mm centres along the edge under the tile or slate. Ridge tiles should also be fixed with clips at 300 mm centres. Overlaps should be 300 mm minimum.

# 17

# Frost Precautions in the Home

This chapter describes how water pipes and other fittings, including cisterns, should be installed in new houses to be safe from damage by freezing. To improve on existing installations, certain recommendations are given and these, although general, should be practicable in most houses.

## How to prevent pipes from freezing

Obviously prevention is better than cure and the prevention of frost damage to water pipes is not difficult or expensive. If it is understood from the start that if the house is heated the pipes cannot freeze and that if water pipes outside the house are laid in the ground below the penetration level of frost they will not be affected, it is clear that the cheapest and most effective method of avoiding frost damage is:

(a) Keep the house warm throughout.
(b) Run pipes in protected places wherever possible.
(c) If pipes have to be exposed to cold or draughts see that they are protected by efficient lagging.

It should be understood that lagging a pipe in an exposed place is inferior to fixing the pipe unlagged in a warm area because it does not matter how thick the lagging, it can only give a limited protection against continued hard frost.

All pipes should be fixed with proper falls so they can be emptied of water when a building is left vacant. Where there is a dip in the pipework that cannot be drained then a draintap should be provided at the lowest point.

## Why some British plumbing is vulnerable to frost

In most parts of Great Britain the temperature does not fall low

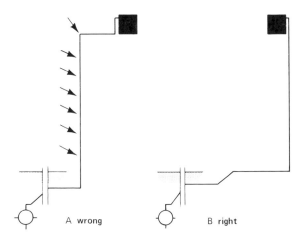

Figure 149 *Protecting the rising main from frost*

enough every winter to give rise to trouble from burst pipes, and we never have long periods of exceptionally low temperature such as occur regularly in Canada or the United States of America. Nevertheless, burst pipes in America are a far less frequent occurrence than in this country, a state of affairs arising only in part from the greater use of central heating throughout that continent, since full central heating is by no means universal in poorer class property. Much of the difference arises from the fact that it is customary to take the rising main up an inside wall (generally that of the central chimney stack) and to place the cold-water storage cistern with one side in contact with the kitchen or sitting-room chimney flue. This precaution does not necessitate appreciably increased installation costs, for it will be seen from Figures 149A and B that the length of supply pipes is similar in both American and English practice. (In Figures 149–153 the heavy arrows indicate the vulnerable area.) Occasionally it is less convenient for branch mains, but with a little ingenuity in designing the pipe layout this can usually be overcome.

The only difficulty likely to arise is the branch to the kitchen sink. In houses with suspended wooden ground floors, the 15-mm branch from the main may be run in the void beneath the floor to the sink unit, but care must be taken to lag all pipework in this void to protect it from the through draught from the air bricks at the front and back of the building. Do not, under any circumstances, block the air bricks: through ventilation is essential to prevent musty smells in ground-floor rooms and, worse, dry rot.

A drain-off cock must be fitted in an accessible position.

In many properties the ground floors are solid concrete and the water main enters the building through a pipe duct. As access is not possible under the slab, the supply to the kitchen sink should be taken through the first-floor void and brought down, if possible, on an internal wall surface adjacent to the sink.

While it is advocated that cold-water supply pipes should be routed through warm areas wherever possible, care must be taken to ensure that the water is not actually heated. Indeed, cold-water pipes in any warm area should be lagged to prevent condensation.

Where hot- and cold-water pipes are run in pairs horizontally, one above the other, especially on the surface of walls, always ensure that the cold-water pipe is beneath the hot-water pipe and separated by at least 50 mm (preferably 75 mm) to prevent condensation.

## Why pipes burst

A study of the action of ice formation which leads to burst pipes suggests other ways in which damage may be obviated. The formation of ice in a water pipe rarely takes place simultaneously throughout its length, but proceeds progressively from the coldest point towards the warmer points. As is well known, when water freezes its volume increases approximately 9 per cent. If a pipe has one end open and unobstructed, and if ice formation begins at the closed end, it is possible for freezing to continue steadily towards the open end without increasing the pressure on the walls of the pipe (Figure 151A). Indeed, such a pipe may be repeatedly frozen solid in this way without the slightest risk of fracture. If, however, the freezing begins at the open end (see Figure 151B) a plug is formed, and as the water cools towards the closed end, pressure is built up until after repeated freezings a burst is inevitable, no matter what thickness of material is used for the walls of the pipe.

In the case of the normal domestic service pipe, the main in the street practically never freezes and so acts as the open end or relief

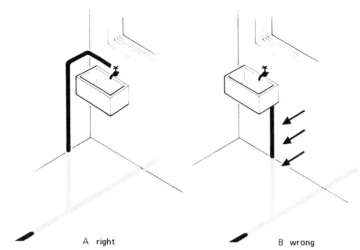

A right                     B wrong

Figure 150    *The position of the cold water supply to the sink*

Figure 151    *Cause of frost burst*

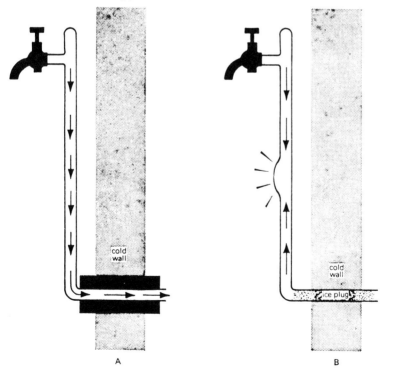

valve, provided always that freezing starts at the remote end. If, however, freezing starts at some intermediate point, and there forms a plug of ice, trouble is likely to be serious between that point and the house end of the pipe. For this reason particular care should be taken where it enters the house. It is generally considered in this country that a pipe buried 0.760 m deep in ordinary streets or garden ground is below the limit of frost action, even in severe weather. Again, in the case of a pipe passing over a series of windows or into and out of buildings, there is more than one point likely to freeze and form a plug at a comparatively early stage. In all such cases relatively high pressures will be built up as freezing proceeds from the plug towards the dead end of the pipe and sooner or later a burst will occur.

A pipe buried in an external wall is more likely to freeze than one fixed on the internal surface of that wall since, apart from other reasons, there will be less thickness of wall to protect it. Naturally, too, if it should burst, the damage done to the structure and the cost of repair will be greater.

Pipes which are exposed to cold draughts tend to lose heat rapidly and thus run an increased risk of freezing. Thus, pipes in roof spaces can be protected to a considerable extent simply by covering them with any material which will protect them from draught. Actually, the most vulnerable position for a pipe in a house of normal type occurs at the point where it is carried up the outer wall and passes unprotected close to an open eave, where it is exposed to continual draughts (Figure 152).

Figure 152   *Exposure at eaves*

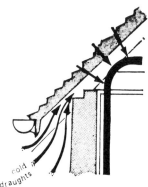

# Insulation

There are on the market at the moment a great variety of insulating materials, most of which are satisfactory for their purpose. It should be remembered, however, that even the best insulating material must allow for some heat loss, and that during prolonged spells of cold weather it is only a matter of time before the temperature of the pipe falls to a dangerous limit, unless, of course, fresh warmer water is passed through it from time to time. For this reason, therefore, a pipe placed in a wholly exposed position, even after insulation with the best possible material, is not so safe as an uninsulated pipe placed in a room or against a chimney the temperature of which never falls to freezing point for appreciable periods. Of course, it cannot be guaranteed that the house will not from time to time be left uninhabited, but when this is the case, precautions can and should be taken to see that the pipes are emptied. The boxing-in of pipes in a properly insulated chase generally gives more protection than casual insulation wrapped round the pipe.

## Pipes in exposed positions

Particular care should be taken when the pipes are placed in exposed positions and protected in insulation to see that all points in the length of the pipe are equally and fully protected, for any part less protected than the rest provides a point at which a plug of ice may form. If freezing continues and a volume of water is entrapped between the pipe and a closed end or even another ice plug, increased pressure must occur and there is a risk of bursting.

## Protecting the cold-water cistern

The means commonly taken to protect the cold-water storage tank show many examples of wrongly applied insulation. It is common for such cisterns to be protected with an ordinary boarded casing filled with sawdust or some better insulator, but with the feed pipe far less adequately lagged (Figure 153A). Even if the cistern were to freeze solid, which would take a long time,

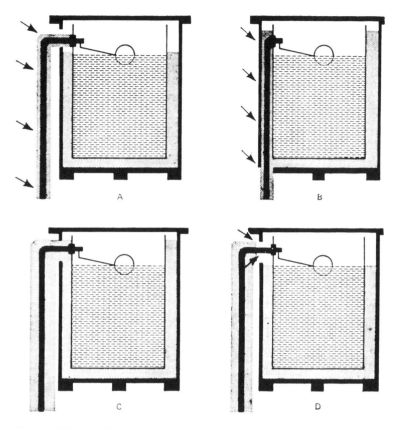

Figure 153   *Insulating the cistern*

there would probably be no actual splitting of the metal. The small volume of water in the feed pipe will, however, not only tend to freeze more quickly, but after several freezings will almost certainly burst the pipe. This, therefore, needs more and not less careful protection than the tank.

Perhaps the commonest mistake where cisterns are thoughtlessly protected is to box-in the feed pipes in the same casing. To some extent, of course, the volume of water in the cistern tends to keep the feed warm, but it will be seen from Figure 153B that in most cases the amount of effective insulation for the pipe is less than one half that which it has been thought necessary to provide for the cistern. Either the pipe should be separately treated

(Figure 153c) or else an extra space in the boxing of the cistern should be allowed on the pipe side.

Again, it is very common to cut through the casing for a feed pipe without any precautions being taken to insulate the pipe where it passes through the boards or sheeting (Figure 153d). Such an open hole through the casing and round the pipe may also permit the passage of a considerable draught. This is a very undesirable condition, because, as has been said before, cold air in movement is much more dangerous than air that is completely stationary, which, by the way, is one of the best possible insulating media.

Where any form of organic insulation has been used and trouble is experienced with mice or rats, some protection can be given by wrapping the outside of the insulating materials with thin bitumen felt. It is not an absolute safeguard, but appears to be distasteful to most rodents. Moreover, it reduces the passage of air through the insulating material, and prevents accidental wetting, thus giving increased efficiency.

A further point in connection with the use of makeshift insulating materials is in connection with the covering of external waste pipes, particularly from baths and lavatory basins. It is quite common in the country to see such wastes covered with a sack, perhaps straw filled, nailed to the wall above and beneath. When dry this may give some protection. When wet, it is probably worse than useless as the pipe will be surrounded by actual ice, but be effectively shut off from the warmth of the sun in the middle of the day. All insulation must be kept absolutely dry, preferably by boxing-in with a carefully jointed waterproof casing. If this is impossible, then wrapping with waterproof felt will help.

However perfect the insulating material, it is practically valueless when wet, and even when only damp suffers a considerable loss of efficiency.

## Thawing out

Where through lack of protection lead pipes have been frozen, care is necessary in thawing them out. Even if a burst has not occurred at once because the expansion on cooling has been accommodated by the stretching or give of the pipe, it is quite possible for the trouble to arise later from careless thawing. The warming should be done slowly, starting at the open end of the pipe so that increased pressures are automatically relieved.

# Hints to the householder

It is essential that you should be familiar with your plumbing system, particularly the hot- and cold-water services. A study of the chapters on these services in this book should enable the householder to cope with an emergency, but if there is any doubt about the draining of the system or if it is safe to use the boiler, then the advice of a qualified plumber should be sought.

## The golden rules at all times are:

1  Find out where the stopvalve is located.
2  See that it will shut off the main supply.
3  Locate and label any other stopvalves in the house.
4  Repair all leaking taps.
5  Check up on the ball valves of the w.c. cistern and the storage cistern in the roof. See that they are not leaking and that they work properly. It will be as well to ensure that the overflow pipes from the cistern are not obstructed.

## When there is a likelihood of a severe frost lasting some days:

Adequate precautions depend upon individual circumstances. If, for example, your house is warmed by central heating, your pipes routed on internal walls and properly lagged in any danger areas, then you have taken all the precautions necessary.

If, on the other hand, you have no general heating and there are very cold spots in the house, then it is advisable to turn off and drain the cold-water rising main, which is simple enough to do. More difficult are the other services, such as the cold feed and cold-water down service from the cold-water storage cistern. It is impracticable to drain the entire system every night, quite apart from wasting water – and possibly dangerous if you use a boiler and forget to turn on the cold-feed valve.

This is a problem particularly affecting elderly people living in older-type properties, who cannot afford to install a heating system or, even if the system is installed, cannot afford the fuel to run it. Anybody in this situation should consult their local town hall for guidance and possible financial assistance.

## If a pipe in the house freezes:

1 Shut off the main stopvalve – or if it is controlled by an adjacent stopvalve, shut that off. If the pipe is a distributing pipe from the storage cistern and is not controlled by a valve, inspect it first to see that it has not burst before attempting to thaw it out.
2 Try to thaw the pipe by using cloths soaked in hot water or safe portable heaters. A blowlamp may be used if the householder is accustomed to its operation. Always start thawing at the nearest open tap on the pipe and work away from it.

## If a pipe bursts:

1 If the burst is discovered before the thaw begins shut off the main stopvalve; this will stop flooding if the burst is on the main pipe. If the burst is on a distributing pipe from the cistern, close the control stopvalve if there is one. Otherwise open all the cold-water taps being fed from the cistern to drain it off as quickly as possible. The main stopvalve must be closed, of course, to cut off the feed.
2 Call in a qualified plumber as soon as possible.

## The hot-water system in frosty weather

Many householders get worried in freezing weather about the hot-water system of the house, particularly if it is an installation with a boiler. They have heard of boiler explosions in other people's houses. There is little cause for alarm, however, providing normal precautions are taken. In fact it is advisable to keep the hot-water system working in frosty weather because the fire – and the pipes – can give that essential background warmth which might well prevent the plumbing becoming frozen.

The essential thing is that the system is full of water and that none of the pipes is frozen.

If the cold feed to the hot-water cylinder is blocked by ice *do not light the boiler.*

If it is already lit, the first signs of trouble will be no water at hot-water taps, but there is no immediate danger if your boiler is controlled by a thermostat.

The greatest danger is from an open fire with a back boiler which has no heat control system. If this fire is burning, it can rapidly boil the water out of the cylinder. At best, the cylinder will collapse under excessive external pressure. At worst, the cold feed may thaw, allowing cold water into a red-hot boiler jacket – which is likely to explode. There are, however, early warning signs: loud banging from the hot-water cylinder and hot water discharging from the cold-water tank overflow. If this happens, put out the fire immediately and let the system cool. Do not interfere with anything. Call a plumber without delay.

It is not advisable for the householder to drain his hot-water system without expert advice. Unfortunately, it is not possible to give any general instructions about draining systems, because many have been installed by incompetent persons and an inspection would be necessary before a decision could be made – even by an expert.

If the water from a copper hot-water storage cylinder was drained when the vent pipe was frozen, the cold feedvalve closed, and the taps at the fitments closed, the cylinder might well collapse like a tin can crushed by a heavy boot. A partial vacuum is caused in the cylinder. When this reduction in internal pressure takes place, the external atmospheric pressure is such that the material from which the cylinder is constructed is not sufficiently strong to withstand the enormous external pressure exerted on the cylinder, with the result that the body of the cylinder is crushed in – or more simply, the cylinder collapses.

# 18

# Water Softening in the Home

As rain sinks into the ground it begins to dissolve some of the minerals in the earth, so that when water comes from a spring or from a well – depending to a large extent upon the nature of earth through which it passed originally – it can have dissolved in it a good many different things.

Generally speaking, water that has gone through chalky soils is hard while that which has gone through sandy soils is likely to be soft.

It is the presence of calcium and magnesium elements in water that hardens it and prevents lather being formed easily. The fat in the soap acts upon these calcium and magnesium elements – upon the hardness – and combines to form an insoluble scum of white curds that float on the water. Put soap in hard water and after a few rubs the water is milky in colour. It gets milkier according to the amount of hardness in the water and number of rubs you give the soap until soap scum – decomposed soap or greasy curdled fat – forms. A lather forms when, and only when, the hardness has been neutralized, but the hardness is still in the water.

This scum, because of its sticky nature, clogs the pores of the skin, mats the hair, clings to and discolours clothes and fabrics washed in it and sticks to dishes, silverware and glass. It sticks round washbasins, kitchen bowls, kitchen sinks and baths.

There are two forms of hardness in water – temporary and permanent. It is necessary to explain the term temporary.

When hard water is heated, some of the hardness is thrown down and evidence of this can be seen in the domestic kettles of homes in hard-water areas. That 'fur', or 'scale', is temporary hardness. There are minerals that cannot be removed in this way and substances left dissolved in the water, even after boiling, cause what is called 'permanent' hardness.

When a kettle or a boiler becomes coated with this 'fur', or 'scale', which is a very bad conductor of heat, the water takes longer to boil or requires a great deal more fuel to boil.

Just as 'fur' forms in kettles so it will form around an immersion heater in a hot-water tank, in a back-fire boiler or in the more conventional free-standing boiler whether gas fired, oil fired, or solid-fuel fired. So also, will it form in the coils of a water heater.

If the hardness is allowed to continue depositing, the immersion heater may well burn itself out or if a complaint is made that the heater has lost efficiency and so has to be removed for descaling, it may well be found that the extent of the scale formation is such that the heater cannot be withdrawn from the tank through the hole originally cut for it, which may well mean the replacement of the hot-water tank.

The first sign of trouble is often a complaint from one of the family that the water does not get as hot as it used to or not as quickly as it did. How can it when more and more scale has to be heated before the water itself is heated? In boilers and hot-water pipes the scale can thicken and thicken until it chokes off the flow of water and cleaning by a chemical process or complete replacement becomes necessary – an expensive business.

Hard water wastes time, soap and fuel, causes hard work and can in certain circumstances impair health.

## The benefits of soft water

Softened water saves soap because only a touch of soap is needed to produce ample lather.

It preserves beauty because it keeps skin soft and supple, as nature intended, keeps pores clean and free, allowing the skin to breathe and improves complexion by eliminating hard-water blemishes and prevents 'dishpan hands'.

Softened water improves home laundering because it washes clothes soft and clean, and it is essential for obtaining perfect results with washing machines. It simplifies washing up because it quickly removes grease, and the dishes can be drained clean without wiping. Glassware and silver drain dry to a high polish.

If softened water is used the burden of housework is eased because floors, woodwork, tiles, baths and sinks are quickly cleaned without hard scouring.

Softened water saves tea and coffee because less tea and coffee are needed to obtain the true full flavour and colour.

Plumbing repairs are reduced by soft water because there is no 'scale' to choke the flow in boilers, pipes and radiators – even in car radiators – while heated coils last their full life.

# The water softener

By passing hard water through a water softener, hardness-free water can be obtained. The water from one tap can be softened by using a small portable unit, but for household purposes the ideal unit is one which is connected into the cold main-water supply pipe at a point after the drinking water draw-off to the sink, so that all the water to every other tap in the dwelling is softened.

Water that is to be used for drinking purposes should *not* be softened. There is some evidence to support a claim that softened water may be hazardous when used with certain milk products for babies' feeds. Water board guidelines advise that at least one tap should remain connected to the hard-water supply for all water that is to be drunk.

A water softener is simple to install and maintain and once the softening material in the equipment becomes saturated with hardness, all that needs to be done to bring it back into its original efficiency is to pass ordinary common salt through it. In some models the salt is poured into the container in its ordinary dry form while in the other models – the semi-automatic and the automatic models – the salt is introduced as a brine solution. In either case the salt is rinsed through the softener and once all the salt has gone down the drain the water softener is again ready to give its rated output of hardness-free water. This process is known as regeneration and so long as the water softener is regularly regenerated it will for many years give thoroughly satisfactory service.

The size and type of unit required depends on the degree of hardness of the water requiring to be softened, the number of people using water – for this determines the amount used – and, of course, the space available for the positioning of the unit. They are installed in kitchens, in cloakrooms, in larders, in cupboards under stairs, in garages – in fact in any reasonably accessible position where regeneration can be carried out without difficulty and where easy access can be obtained to water main and drain.

# The water-softening process

For years household water softening has been undertaken by what is known as the Base Exchange process. The process is virtually the same today, but is becoming more widely referred to as the Ion Exchange method of softening.

A number of ion exchangers are produced in this country. One, a unifunctional polystyrene resin, is known as Zeo-Karb 225. These ion exchangers have replaced the earlier natural greensand and synthetic materials but the principle of operation remains the same.

Zeo-Karb 225 in its sodium form is used for water softening. A quantity of this material, which is of a golden brown colour and spheroid in shape, is filled into a container and hard water passes through it – generally in a downward direction. The softening material has the unique property of changing its sodium content for the hardness content in the water. In other words, the calcium and magnesium hardness-forming elements in the water are changed into their equivalent sodium elements – nothing more – so that the water contains exactly the same quantity of elements as originally but in another form – in a sodium form. Household water softening is in fact just as simple as that.

Hard water is passed through the resin until it is saturated with calcium and magnesium – saturated with hardness – whereupon the water coming out of the container will be as hard as that going in. The resin is exhausted but as a proof of the further simplicity of household water softening the resin can be brought back to its original condition – to its full water-softening power – by a process known as 'regeneration'.

Sodium must be put back into the resin and what easier way than by passing ordinary common salt – sodium chloride – through it.

Exactly the reverse action to that described takes place. The calcium and magnesium hardness-forming elements are thrown out of the resin which takes up sodium from the salt. The hardness in chloride form is washed down the drain.

# Water-softening equipment

*The portable unit*

The most simple form of household water softener is the portable unit available from good plumbers' merchants and from Permutit Ltd. This is a hard plastics container with polythene handle cap, inlet bend, and outlet spout. A rubber hose is attached to the inlet bend and a rubber connection is pushed on to the tap from which water is drawn. It can be hot water or cold for neither the resinous softening material nor the hard polythene is affected by water temperature.

The softener is delivered already filled with the resin, so that having attached the hose the tap can be turned on. Water enters through the bend on the side of the container and is spread over the resin by means of a distributor pipe. The hard water passes downward through the resin, the exchange previously described takes place and hardness-free water is collected in a pipe at the bottom of the container and passes from the outlet spout under pressure. Turn off the tap and the flow stops.

The quantity of resin in the unit shown is capable of producing 680 litres of hardness-free water providing the hardness of the water is 16°. If there is more hardness in each litre of the water the number of litres softened will be less and, of course, if there is less hardness the number of litres softened will be more.

When the resin is exhausted – or saturated with hardness – the user removes the handle cap and pours into the container 0.50 kg of salt – ordinary common salt – replaces the handle cap and turns on the tap so that the salt dissolves and rinses through the resin until this is regenerated and returned to its original condition.

The manufacturers supply with this unit – and, in fact, with each of their household water softeners – a small simple testing outfit consisting of a shake bottle marked at 40 cc and a bottle of soap solution with a dripper top. With this it is possible to check if softened water is being obtained, that regeneration needs to be carried out or that all salt has been rinsed off. In other words, that regeneration has been completed.

### Mains-supply unit

The portable appliance is an extremely convenient unit for carrying round but the ideal water softener for the household is a mains-supply unit designed for connecting to the main water supply. In general, the principle of the mains-supply water softener is the same as for the portable unit already described but there are what is known to the manufacturers as dry-salting and wet-salting units.

In recent years the near-monopoly of one company in the supply of mains-supply water softeners for domestic use has ended, and there is now a wide selection of models from UK manufacturers as well as imported models, many at competitive prices. Today most have rust-proof plastic or fibreglass cases and more sophisticated controls. One has an excellent device which senses when regeneration is required. This over-rides the timing clock, so that when little water has been used in the household, needless regeneration is avoided, thus saving the cost of salt.

## Assessing water requirements

A water softener must be considered against the requirements of the particular household. It is advisable to assess the likely consumption of water, which obviously depends upon the number of persons in residence. In a household where a check was made by a water meter it was discovered that the average consumption of water per person per day, over quite a long period, was 159 litres. This was water for every use and in that particular household nothing but softened water was obtainable. The meter was used not only to check water consumption but also to check the efficiency of the water softener installed. There is good reason to believe this is a fair average consumption of water per person per day, but of course there are households in which the average consumption is higher than this and some where it is lower and it is reasonable to work on this basis. Having ascertained the number of people in residence and multiplied this by 159, it is recommended that the figure should be multiplied again by 8 in order to ascertain the weekly consumption of water in litres. Having arrived at this figure and with the knowledge of the hardness of the water as supplied to the residence, it is possible to determine with reasonable accuracy the size of water softener which is capable of producing at least one week's supply of softened water between each regeneration. A water softener of this size is recommended by the manufacturers, for after long experience they have reached the conclusion that, in the case of manually regenerated water softeners, it is better that regeneration should be undertaken at regular intervals rather than at more frequent intervals. It is better to install a water softener capable of softening more than one week's normal requirements for this then takes into account the possibility of guests or visitors who will, if staying for any period of time, increase the consumption of water. There is no doubt a great deal of harm has been done to the cause of water softening by the installation of units which are quite incapable of producing water in quantity to meet the needs of a household.

## Connecting the softener

To connect these mains-supply water softeners, it is necessary to break into the cold main-water inlet pipe and run a hard-water inlet feed to the water softener and bring a return pipe from the water softener to the supply pipe and fit between these two connections a valve which becomes known as the by-pass valve, which is closed when the water softener is in operation. It is recommended that a valve be fitted on both the hard-water inlet and soft-water outlet lines for emergency purposes and to enable the owner of the equipment to isolate the water softener.

Most water companies insist upon the fitting of a non-return valve before the water softener. A waste pipe is required to take the effluent during regeneration away to an outside gully or drain and the size of this waste pipe should be determined by the size of the hard-water inlet pipe and, of course, the length of the run of the waste and whether or not it contains a number of bends and elbows.

# 19

# Flushing Cisterns Explained

A fixed quantity of water must be discharged to cleanse water closets and for this purpose flushing cisterns are used. A cistern is stipulated for the following reasons:

1  To provide sufficient water to flush and cleanse the pan effectively and reseal the trap with fresh water.
2  To prevent waste of water by using a regulated volume to each flushing.
3  To break direct contact between the water supply and the fixture so that, should a stoppage occur in the fixture, the pollution of the water supply by foul water being siphoned back into the main will be prevented.

The flushing cistern generally used is known as a valveless, waste water preventing, siphonic cistern, so called because there is no valve through which water from the cistern can run to waste down the flush pipe and because the discharge of water is due to siphonic action. Although flushing cisterns differ in design and construction, most of them depend upon the principle of siphonage for the discharge of their contents. The cistern has provision made for the supply of water through an automatic ball valve situated either on the right-hand or left-hand side. On the opposite side, provision is made for the connection of an overflow pipe which allows excess water to discharge where it will be noticed, but will not cause a nuisance or damage property. The flush pipe connection is at the bottom of the cistern.

It is only necessary in this description of flushing cisterns to deal with two types: (1) a straight outlet cistern and (2) a low-level cistern, both of which are in common use in normal houses.

## Straight outlet cistern

*Construction*
This type of cistern has the working parts contained in a cast iron

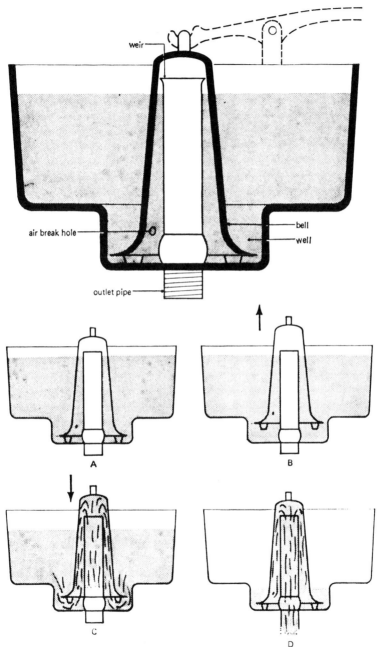

Figure 154   *Flushing cistern action*

vessel, with a cylindrical well in the centre of the bottom. In this well is a vertical outlet pipe with a lip at the weir and an enlargement near the bottom, to assist in the setting up of siphonage. The outlet pipe weir terminates slightly above the normal overflow weir of the cistern.

A heavy cast-iron bell of conical shape, flared out at the bottom, fits over the outlet pipe and stands in the well. It has a diameter at the base which allows it to move up and down freely in the well, but has only a small space between it and the wall of the well.

The bell has a loop at the top to which is attached a lever and a chain, and near the bottom is a small air-break hole. Projecting lugs leave a clear space between the bottom of the bell and the bottom of the cistern.

In this type of cistern, as shown in Figure 154, a simple inverted U-tube is formed, the short leg being the annular space between the outlet pipe and the inside of the bell, and the long leg being the outlet pipe and its continuation as a flush pipe.

Water is supplied through an automatic ball valve which should be adjusted to shut off when the water level is about 25 mm below the overflow weir of the tank.

*Action*

Figure 154A shows the cistern ready for discharge, the bell in its normal position and the automatic ball valve shut off, the water level being the same under the bell as in the cistern. Air which previously filled the space between the bell and outlet pipe has now been expelled through the outlet pipe as the water has risen. The bell is raised by the lever and chain (B), but actual siphonage is not set up until the bell is lowered.

On release of the chain the bell, owing to its weight, drops heavily on the water beneath it, which cannot escape quickly enough through the small space between the bell and the vertical wall of the well. It is compelled to rise inside the bell and flows over the outlet weir and down the long leg of the U-tube, thus setting up siphonic action, as shown in (C). This siphonic action will continue until the level of water is reduced to the air hole in the bell, as shown in (D), when an admission of air breaks the siphon and allows the cistern to fill again.

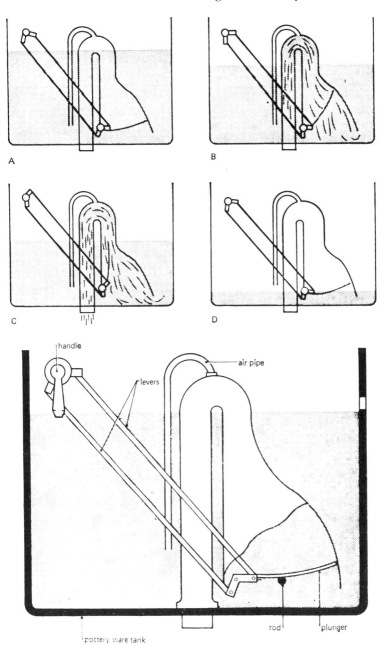

Figure 155  *The low-level cistern*

## Low-level cistern

A low-level cistern is generally part of a suite, consisting of cistern, flush pipe and pan, designed for the efficient working of each part and a relatively silent flush.

*Construction*

The vessel of the low-level cistern, as shown in Figure 155, is of heavy glazed pottery ware. Although it contains the usual quantity of water it has a comparatively small width, thus taking up a minimum of space. An inverted U-tube is formed in the cistern, a straight 45-mm-diameter pipe and the flush pipe forming the long leg.

The short leg is formed by the inlet pipe in the cistern near the bottom. There is no bell in this cistern, but the balanced plunger is fixed inside the inlet to the U-tube and rests on a rubber-coated rod.

The plunger is connected by levers to a small turn handle fixed on the outside of the cistern. All these parts are made of heavily galvanized iron to prevent the formation of rust.

Connected to the crown of the U-tube is a small brass air pipe which terminates about three inches from the bottom of the cistern. Its function is to admit air to stop the siphonic action at the conclusion of the flush. The weir of the U-tube is situated above the overflow weir of the cistern, and in this regard a similarity to the straight outlet type of cistern will be observed.

As the height at which the cistern is fixed has a direct bearing on the proper flushing of the pan, it is important that the length of the flush pipe should not be altered by the plumber when fixing the suite. The loss of head of water by fixing the cistern at a low level is offset by the increased diameter of the flush pipe.

Water is supplied through an automatic ball valve which should be adjusted to shut off when the water is about 25 mm below the overflow weir.

*Action*

As the long leg of the U-tube is open to the atmosphere the water flowing into the cistern will rise in the short leg of the U-tube to the same level as that in the cistern, as shown in Figure 155.

Siphonage is set up by turning the handle on the outside of the cistern. The balanced plunger is thrown upwards, causing a wave motion of the water in the U-tube, as shown at (B).

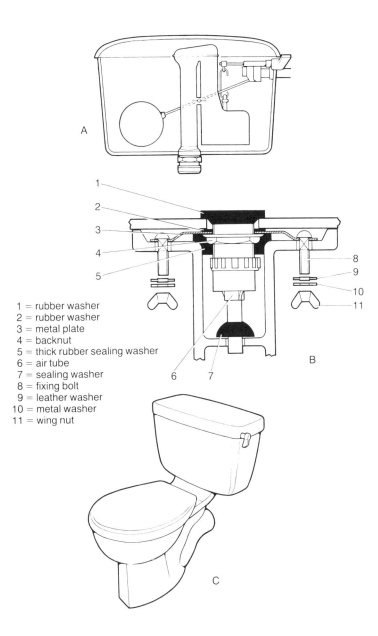

1 = rubber washer
2 = rubber washer
3 = metal plate
4 = backnut
5 = thick rubber sealing washer
6 = air tube
7 = sealing washer
8 = fixing bolt
9 = leather washer
10 = metal washer
11 = wing nut

Figure 156   *Close-coupled w.c. suite*

This results in a quantity of water being forced over the weir of the inverted U-tube, and down the long leg causing siphonic action to be set up, such action continuing as shown at (c).

When the level of water in the cistern has been reduced to the inlet of the air-breaking tube, an admittance of air breaks the siphon, as shown at (d).

Owing to the plunger being balanced, it will remain in an upward position during the time the water is discharging from the cistern. As the discharge finishes, it will slowly come to rest on the rubber-coated rod, in its original position.

These descriptions and illustrations of straight outlet cisterns and low-level cisterns have been retained in this revised edition because it is likely that many dwellings around the country may still be served by such appliances. There is also a growing trend in some areas for property owners to refurbish their premises with old, and where possible, original fittings and, therefore, a description of their working principles may be valuable in their maintenance.

However, the majority of people will be using the modern low-level cistern or the close-coupled suite, where the cistern is bolted to the w.c. pan to form a composite unit (Figure 156a, b and c). The close-coupled suite is produced either as a wash down or a siphonic appliance. Thanks to the design of the flushing rim on the pan the cistern works efficiently on a wash-down suite to clean the pan and to evacuate the contents of the trap.

On the siphonic model an air pipe fitting is inserted into the casting in the pan (on some models it screws to the flush outlet of the cistern), and the cistern is located directly on to it. As the wing nuts are tightened on the captive bolts joining the cistern to the pan the washers are compressed, thus forming an air-tight joint and housing the air pipe securely in place. The air pipe forms a one-way air connection between the flush discharge pipe of the cistern into the flushing rim of the pan and the top of the second trap of the pan. When the cistern is flushed, the water passing across the top of the air tube draws air from the top of the second trap, creating a partial vacuum. The greater (atmospheric) pressure on the exposed surface of the water seal of the first trap displaces both water and any solid content before the bulk of the flush discharge reaches it. This means that the prime function of the flush is to clean the pan, and its bulk does not have to be used to clear away pan contents.

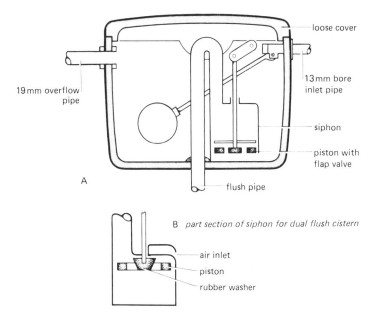

Figure 157 *Dual-flush cistern*

Siphonic pans are silent in use and more efficient than their wash-down counterparts. Generally, the centre of their outlet is lower than in the wash-down pan, which may present problems if occupiers wish to replace existing wash-down pans with siphonic models. However, where alteration of the outlet soil pipe connection is not possible it may be practicable to raise the floor under the pan the few inches necessary to make the connection.

If any w.c. pan is to be fixed to a 'raised' floor for whatever reason it is important that the area of floor raised should extend to the full dimensions necessary for the use of the pan.

## Dual-flush cistern

A recent development is the dual-flush cistern, designed to save water on what is the highest-usage domestic fitting. This device gives the user a choice of either a 4.5-litre flush or a 9-litre flush.

Figure 157 shows at (A) a typical low-level cistern with a direct-lift piston which raises water within the bell over the inverted U-pipe to create the siphonic action to empty the cistern via the flush pipe into the w.c. pan. The siphon is broken when the water level in the cistern falls to the bottom of the siphon and air is admitted to the chamber.

Figure 157 illustrates at (B) the dual-flush adaptation. For a 4.5-litre discharge the handle is depressed and immediately released. When the water level falls to the top of the siphon, air is admitted to the bell through the air inlet and breaks the action. For a 9-litre flush the handle is held down, causing the rubber washer on the piston to be held hard against the seating, making an airtight seal and preventing the premature entry of air. The siphonic action is then broken either when the water level reaches the bottom of the bell or when the handle is released, allowing the washer to drop away from the seating.

# 20

# Fault Finding, Repairs and Maintenance

## Faults in ball valves

| Cause | Remedy |
| --- | --- |
| Rubber washer worn or defective. | Renew rubber washer. |
| A piece of rust or other foreign matter on the rubber washer, preventing the washer from fitting correctly on its seat. | Remove the foreign matter or Rewasher the valve. |
| Ball waterlogged, and instead of floating on the surface of the water remains partly or completely submerged; therefore there is not sufficient power to lever the rubber washer to its seat. | The ball must be drained of water and repaired where defective or Renew the ball. |
| Ball detached from lever. Incorrect adjustment of the lever. | Re-attach ball to the lever. The lever arm should be bent down at the ball end so that the rubber washer is forced to its seating when the water level is lowered. |
| Jamming of the ball on some portion of the cistern. | Free the ball and adjust the lever arm to prevent recurrence of the trouble. |
| The seating of the valve defective and not providing a proper surface for the rubber washer. | Seat of valve may be re-faced or The body of the valve or the complete ball valve replaced. |
| Striking arm of the lever in the plunger worn. | File where bearing or Renew lever arm. |

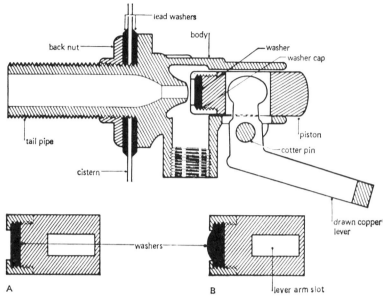

Figure 158   *Re-washering a ball valve*

## Re-washering a ball valve

1   Shut off water supply at the stop tap.

2   Disconnect the union nut between supply pipe and ballcock.

3   Unscrew the lock nut and remove ballcock from cistern. Should the ballcock have a cap piece, as shown in Figure 158, it is unnecessary to remove the ballcock from the cistern as the cap and split-pin may be removed without removing the complete ball valve.

4   Remove the split-pin to release the lever arm and plunger.

5   Disconnect the extension and valve seating from the body, by using a pipe wrench or spanner on the hexagonal shoulder and holding against the pressure with a rod placed in the water outlet.

6   Take the plunger apart by inserting a flat tool in the lever arm slot, and unscrew the cap piece with pliers or a small wrench.

7   Remove the old rubber washer and clean away any rubber adhering to the cap piece or plunger.

8   Cut a piece of rubber to size and insert it in the washer cap piece. When a washer is to be cut, place the cap piece on the

rubber and give it a light tap. This will mark the correct outline of the circle to be cut. Cut the rubber neatly with the wet blade of a knife and then insert in the plunger cap piece.

9   Screw the cap piece on the plunger and tighten. The rubber washer may have a very slightly convex facing to the seat, as shown in Figure 158. If the washer is too thick, or cut too large, the facing will be too convex (B) and the washer will not last long.

Figure 159   *The BRS ball valve illustrated below is manufactured by the Kings Langley Engineering Co. Ltd.*

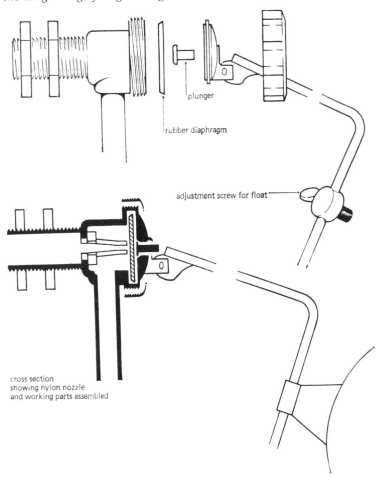

10   File any tool marks off the plunger and place it in the body.
11   Insert the lever arm in the plunger slot, and secure the plunger and lever arms by replacing the split-pin and opening its ends.
12   Screw the extension and valve seat tightly to the body.
13   Replace the ballcock in the cistern.
14   Tighten the lock nut and connect the union nut on the service pipe.
15   Turn on the water supply.

## The BRS ball valve showing working parts

The ball valve illustrated in Figure 159 was designed by the Department of Scientific and Industrial Research (Building Research Station) to fulfil the urgent need for fittings which would give longer, reliable service, and not be prone to the well known weaknesses of earlier types. We refer, of course, to the corrosion or erosion of the metal seatings which results in the familiar 'saw-cut' effect, and to the sticking of the piston of Portsmouth type valves in certain waters. These disadvantages have been fully overcome, and in the latest design several other most desirable features have been included.

The main features of the BRS ball valve are as illustrated, a nylon nozzle shaped to overcome cavitation and a rubber diaphragm which stops the flow of water when pressed against the nozzle by a plunger. This design ensures that the moving parts of the valve are out of water and therefore free from corrosion and incrustation. The movement of the plunger is controlled by the usual float on a hinged arm, which at its free end is bent down at a right-angle. By means of a thumbscrew, the float can be fixed on this part of the arm at any height depending on the water level required in the cistern. It can also be adjusted radially to avoid any obstacle.

## Renewing a tap washer

Step by step

1   Turn off the supply to the tap at the stopvalve.

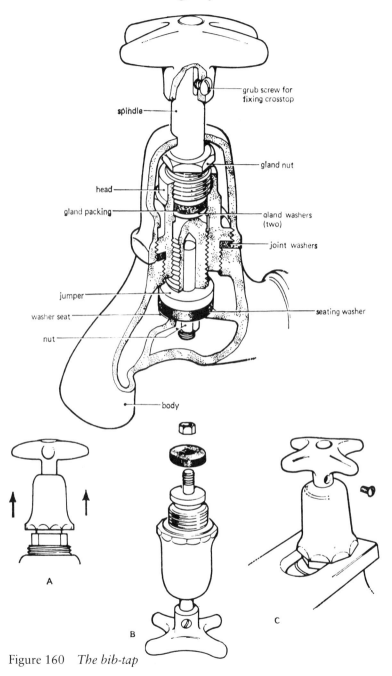

Figure 160   *The bib-tap*

2  Open the tap to its fullest extent and unscrew the easy-clean shield to expose the hexagon on the headpart (Figure 160A).
3  Using a spanner unscrew the headpart from the body of the tap. The body of the tap should be firmly held with the free hand against the pressure exerted by the spanner.
4  Release the worn washer by removing the nut holding the washer to the jumper (Figure 160B).
5  Replace the washer making sure that it is the correct size for the tap jumper, and tighten the retaining nut.
6  Replace the headpart and tighten with spanner, again holding the free hand on the tap against the pressure exerted by the spanner. Make certain that the spindle of the tap is still in the open position, otherwise the washer will engage the seating of the tap and prevent the headpart being screwed tightly on the body.
7  Restore the water supply by opening the stopvalve.

## Repacking the gland

Step by step

1  Remove the grub screw securing the crosstop (see Figure 160C) and turn the tap fully on to expose as much of the spindle as possible.
2  Unscrew the easy-clean shield and raise it to expose the hexagon head of the tap.
3  Insert a piece of wood or two spring type clothes pegs (Figure 160C) to keep the shield in the raised position. Close the tap and the crosstop will be removed by the upward pressure of the easy-clean shield.
4  Unscrew the gland nut, remove the top washer and pick out the defective gland packing.
5  Re-pack the gland with lamp cotton into which vaseline has been worked. Make two or three turns of the cotton around the spindle in a clockwise direction, pressing it down into the gland box.
6  Replace the top washer and screw down the gland nut firmly.
7  Before replacing the easy-clean cover slip on the crosshead and turn on the tap to ensure that the packing is effective. If it leaks a little, take another turn on the nut.

# Faults in screw-down taps

| Defect | Cause | Remedy |
|---|---|---|
| Water flowing or dripping from the tap outlet when shut hard down. | Worn or defective washer. Piece of grit, rust or other foreign matter on the washer. Defective seat of tap. | Re-washer tap. Remove foreign matter or Re-washer tap. Renew tap. |
| Water flowing from around spindle or stuffing box gland. | Defective packing in stuffing box. Gland nut of stuffing box not screwed down tightly. | Renew packing with greased hemp. Tighten stuffing box gland nut. |
| Spindle continually slipping when turned and tap will not shut off. | Spindle thread stripped or badly worn. | Renew tap. Renew packing with greased hemp. |
| Tap hard to turn on and off. | Stuffing box packing too tight. Spindle bent. | Work tallow into stuffing box. Renew tap. |
| Loud noise in the tap when turned on. | Jumper loose on the spindle. Washer loose on valve. | Solder the jumper to the spindle or Renew tap. Renew the jumper or washer or Renew tap. |
| Sudden cessation of the flow of water. | Foreign object caught in the stopcock ferrule, stop tap, or a particular tap. | Shut off water and clean out the obstruction. |
| Stain from water on sanitary fitment. | Stain from leather washer on valve. | Replace leather washer with a fibre washer. |

## Care of chromium plated fittings

Water fittings are usually made from brass, an alloy of 60–65 per cent copper and 35–40 per cent zinc. The component parts are either made from brass rod, brass tube, brass castings or brass forgings. After all the machining operations are carried out the surface is usually ground and polished. Although brass-polished fittings look pleasant this metal tends to tarnish very quickly. In consequence good-quality water fittings are nickel-plated, which is comparable with a good priming or undercoat and subsequently chromium-plated, which is the top high-gloss finishing coat.

Chrome is extremely hard and resistant to most acids. All that is necessary is to wipe the fittings dry immediately after use and if this is done regularly, fittings will last a lifetime.

Many cleaning materials contain abrasives and it stands to reason that frequent use of these will gradually destroy the protective coating and the life of a chromium-plated water fitting.

## Fitting a waste outlet to bath, sink or washbasin

The method of performing this operation is as follows:

1   Remove the lock nut from the thread, and fit a plastics washer over the thread (Figure 161A).

Figure 161   *Fitting a waste outlet*

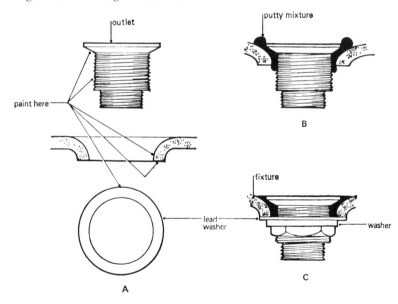

2 Paint the outside of the plug and washer, and around the inside and outside of the outlet hole of the fixture, with white lead paint.

3 Fill the flange of the plug with a mixture of white lead (or white lead oil) and linseed oil putty, and, with a few strands of hemp wound around, insert through the outlet hole (Figure 161B).

4 Paint the washer, and with a little of the putty mixture on it place it over the thread of the plug, and tighten firmly with the lock nut (Figure 161C). When fitting a plug and washer to a fixture with an overflow, a grummet of hemp should be placed between the sink and the washer to prevent the putty mixture being squeezed into the overflow holes of the plug and washer.

5 Adjust the grating bars to a neat finish and clean off surplus putty and paint.

## Stoppages in waste pipes

Stoppages in waste pipes are indicated first by a slowing down of the usual rate of discharge of waste water, and finally by a complete stoppage of the discharge. The position of a stoppage may be at any point between the fixture and the point of discharge to the drain, and is caused generally by a gradual silting up of the pipes with matter carried by the waste water. A stoppage usually occurs at fittings, particularly when the burr has not been removed from the pipe after cutting, and also in long runs of pipe with insufficient fall. If effective gratings are fitted on fixture outlets, stoppages caused by foreign objects in the pipes are rare. If foreign objects do pass the fixture grating, they will generally be found in the fixture trap. The trap may be cleaned by removing the cleaning screw (Figure 162).

In modern plumbing systems the trap beneath the kitchen sink and washbasin in the bathroom will often be of the type that can be dismantled without difficulty. This enables the U part of the trap to be cleansed and also allows access to the waste pipe.

## Clearing stoppages in waste pipes

Choked waste pipes may be cleared either by the application of suction and pressure, or by using wires or canes. Where

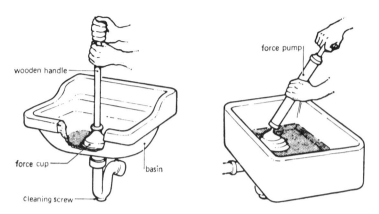

Figure 162    *Clearing a stoppage in a waste pipe*

compressed air is available it may be used to bring direct pressure to bear in clearing stoppages.


## Suction and pressure

Force cups and force pumps are used for creating suction and pressure on stoppages in waste pipes.

### Force cups

A stoppage in a single fixture may be cleared by using a force cup, as shown in Figure 162. A force cup consists of a rubber cup with a wooden handle, and is placed over the outlet of the fixture and worked with a reciprocating action, thus causing suction and pressure in the waste pipe. Force cups are particularly useful for stoppages in lavatory basins.

### Force pumps

A patent force pump with a rubber cup and a pump attached is also used for waste pipework.

# 21

# Home Improvement Grants

Over two million older homes have been modernized, mainly in respect of bathroom facilities, with the aid of home improvement grants since the system was introduced in 1949.

But many homes still lack basic amenities. In fact, it has been estimated that there are over a million homes in England without a bath, let alone an inside w.c.

Assistance for people who want to improve and modernize older buildings in sound condition was increased by the Housing Act 1969, which was superseded by the Housing Act 1974, which, in turn, was amended by the Housing Act 1980. The Housing Act 1985 is a consolidation of the 1974 and the 1980 Acts. The 1980 Act seeks to remove unnecessary statutory and administrative restrictions in the grant system; and to secure a more flexible system that will get resources more effectively to the properties and persons that are in most need of them. The main obstacle, however, is a lack of knowledge by the general public of just what grant aid they possibly are entitled to and how they go about getting it.

There are four types of grant available through local councils: improvement grants; intermediate grants; repairs grants; and special grants.

Grants are intended to help repair, improve, or provide with basic amenities dwellings which were built before 1961 (or, in the case of repairs, before 1919).

There are, of course, conditions and limits on the amounts payable. They may be granted to owner-occupiers, landlords and tenants, and full details can be obtained from your local town hall.

The maximum amounts of the grants and conditions are set by the Department of the Environment and local authorities base their figures on these. The amount of grant you are likely to receive depends on the amount of work you want to do, where you live, and what sort of work is needed. The council will decide whether or not to give you a grant, and how much.

*Improvement grants* are intended to improve homes to a good standard or to provide additional homes through conversions. They are discretionary and are normally paid at 50 per cent of eligible expenses (total cost of agreed works which may include professional services).

*Intermediate grants* are to help meet the cost of providing missing basic amenities – fixed bath or shower, washbasin, sink, hot- and cold-water supply to each, and a w.c., which should normally be inside the dwelling. These grants are mandatory.

*Repair grants* are available only for houses or flats built before 1919, or forming part of buildings built before then, to cover substantial and structural repairs such as roof, walls, floors, and foundations. They do not cover maintenance work such as rewiring or replacement of worn fixtures.

*Special grants* are not available to tenants. They are provided for basic improvements and the provision of means of escape from fire in houses in multiple occupation. Repairs and special grants are both discretionary unless the council has served a notice under Section 189 and 190 of the Housing Act 1985 for the former, or a notice under Sections 352 or Section 366 of the Housing Act 1985 for the latter, in which case a grant payment is mandatory.

As a result of grant aid the condition of the property must be brought up to a standard acceptable to the council and have a further useful life of at least thirty years. Rateable value must not be more than £400 in Greater London or £225 elsewhere.

The following table sets out the limits for eligible expenses and the percentage rate normally paid. It must be understood that the totals shown are not the total payable grants but the cash limit set on work agreed to be done. Any costs over and above these limits must be met from your own resources.

If the property is in need of structural repair, intermediate grants may also include a repairs element of up to £4200 in Greater London and £3000 elsewhere.

| | Typical amounts* | | | Priority | |
|---|---|---|---|---|---|
| Grant | In Greater London | Elsewhere | % | London | Elsewhere |
| Improvement | £ 9000 | £6600 | 50** | £13,800 | £10,200 |
| Intermediate | £ 3005 | £2275 | 90 | | |
| Repairs | £ 6600 | £4800 | 90 | | |
| Special | | | | | |
|   Means of escape | £10,800 | £8100 | 50 | | |
|   Repairs element | £ 4200 | £3000 | 90 | | |
| Standard Amenities | | | | | |
| – depends on number | | | | | |
|   needed | | | 90 | | |

\* Check the current level of grants at your town hall: they change from time to time and almost certainly yearly.

\*\* Priority cases are houses in particularly bad condition (unfit, lacking standard amenities, or in need of substantial and structural repair); houses in housing action areas; improvement of dwellings; and disabled occupants.

A higher percentage (65 per cent) is payable on improvement grants if the property is in a general improvement area or housing action area and can be given in priority cases.

The twelve-month rule which prevented sitting tenants who purchased their homes in housing action areas or general improvement areas from obtaining grants during the first twelve months of ownership has been removed. Grants may now be approved for improvement of dwellings occupied, or to be occupied, by members of the applicant's family. Secure tenants in the public sector and regulated tenants in the private sector can now apply for improvement, intermediate or repairs grants. Landlords should be informed, and you may need their consent to carry out the works.

Councils can 'entertain' applications for grant from prospective purchasers and give provisional approval of grant. This is to assist applicants who have received an offer of mortgage conditional on a grant being available. But formal approval cannot be given until the council is satisfied that the applicant has acquired the necessary interest in the property.

In cases of hardship an increased grant may be payable to applicants who cannot pay their share of the cost of the work. Favourable consideration may be given by councils to applicants who qualify for supplementary benefit or family income supplement (even if these benefits have not been claimed) and, possibly, who are eligible for rate rebate; and applicants whose principal source of income is a state retirement or disability pension.

VAT charges, professional services in the preparation of drawings, etc., may be included in the calculation of eligible expenses in grant applications.

Where a firm of builders carry out grant works to properties which they own their labour costs will be included in the eligible expenses. Where an applicant carries out works to his own dwelling a local authority is not likely to include the value of his labour in the calculation of eligible expenses.

*Conversions*

If you own a property you can apply for a grant to help with the cost of works of conversion (for example, converting a house into two or more flats). If you intend to occupy one of the flats you will not qualify for grant if the rateable value of the house before conversion is more than £600 in Greater London or £350 elsewhere. You will be required to let any other flats you create in the conversion.

The eligible expenses limits (per dwelling provided) for these grants are:

| For conversion of houses of three storeys or more | Greater London £ | Elsewhere £ |
|---|---|---|
| Priority cases | 16,000 | 11,800 |
| Non-priority cases | 10,400 | 7700 |

| | Greater London £ | Elsewhere £ |
|---|---|---|
| *Other conversions* | | |
| Priority cases | 13,800 | 10,200 |
| Non-priority cases | 9000 | 6600 |

*Listed buildings*

Buildings which are of special architectural or historical interest are protected from any alteration that could affect the character and appearance of the building by order of the Secretary of State, and these properties are detailed on lists which denote the grade of the building on the preservation order.

Therefore any improvement work to these buildings, or to any dwelling which is a part of the building, must preserve the specified parts of that building, and this will inevitably involve extra costs for special materials and mouldings, specialist crafts-men, architects, etc. To reflect this higher, eligible expense limits apply to Listed properties.

*Standards*

Those dwellings improved with the help of improvement grants must, on completion of the works, achieve the following standards, though a council may use its discretion and accept a lower standard if it is satisfied that it would be unreasonably expensive for a particular property to meet all the requirements, or that the applicant could not pay for the works in excess of the grant funding. The property must:

1   Have a useful life of at least 30 years.
2   Be in a reasonable state of repair.
3   Have all the standard amenities (bath, basin, inside w.c., etc).
4   Have no rising or penetrating damp.
5   Have adequate natural lighting and ventilation in each habitable room.
6   Have adequate and safe provision throughout for both artificial lighting and power with sufficient electric sockets for domestic appliances.
7   Have an adequate drainage system.
8   Be in a stable structural condition.
9   Have a satisfactory internal rooms arrangement.
10  Have satisfactory facilities for preparing and cooking food.
11  Be provided with adequate facilities for heating.
12  Have proper provision for the storage of fuel (where neces-sary) and for the storage of refuse.
13  Have adequate thermal insulation in the roof space.

Item 13 is, of course, not included in the four grants that have been discussed but is covered by a separate grant for loft insulation. If your loft has not been insulated you should contact your local council for details and the necessary application forms.

Where works are carried out with the aid of an intermediary grant property must usually, on completion of works, be 'fit for human habitation'. Council do have discretion to waive this requirement. Where a repairs grant is given the property must, on completion of works, be brought up to a standard of 'reasonable repair' (as described in Section 519). This requirement may *not* be waived.

### Lead in drinking water

Plumbo solvency, the ability of water to dissolve lead, may affect a considerable number of dwellings which yet remain a small percentage of the total. Water companies normally treat the water to inhibit its plumbo solvency, but the treatment may not be successful. Similarly, other factors such as electrolysis may promote water attack of lead pipes in areas which are normally considered safe.

In the event it is the responsibility of the local authorities to test the quality of water in their areas, and residents who are concerned should contact them. Councils will refer any problem to the water undertaking for possible treatment.

However, if the problem cannot be cured, or is sufficiently urgent for it to be inadvisable to wait for water treatment, or where a household is at particular risk then local authorities can pay improvement grants for the replacement of lead plumbing. As the problem of lead in the environment has been repeatedly stressed it would be a prudent precaution to ask for sample testing in areas where lead plumbing is still used. (Where sections of lead plumbing are renewed it is important that other metals, particularly copper, are not used.)

### Help for the disabled

Grants for work to adapt dwellings for the accommodation, welfare, or employment of a disabled person are available at the highest (priority) rates on all grants. Rateable value limits and restrictions on dates of construction of properties do not apply to these grants.

### General

If you are applying for grant aid it is important not to start any work before your grant is approved by the council.

Grant approval is not the same as building or drainage approval; the appropriate departments of the local authority must be contacted for these approvals and any necessary drawings and forms submitted.

Grants are not available for second, or holiday, homes. On

receiving the grant you will be required to sign an undertaking to occupy or let the premises for five years. If you provide a certificate of owner-occupation it is possible for you to sell the house to another owner-occupier for him and his family to occupy or, after the first year, you can let it. If as a landlord you sign a certificate of availability for letting, you cannot sell the property within the five-year period without causing a breach of grant conditions. If there is a breach of the grant conditions pertaining to either certificate, the council may demand repayment of the grant, or any instalment thereof, together with compound interest.

Grants for insulation of buildings are separate from and in addition to those listed above.

# 22

# Employing Contractors

Whatever the do-it-yourself skills of individual readers there inevitably comes a time when householders need to employ a contractor. It is no secret that, in recent years, employing people to do work for you has become a bigger problem than the job that needs doing. We live in the 'cowboy' era. Too many people have been the victims of unscrupulous operators; others are understandably nervous of obtaining 'professional' assistance.

However, providing readers follow a few basic rules, they will avoid the problems and heartache these people cause, and, if everybody were to adopt this safety-first policy, the 'cowboy' would disappear as quickly as he materialized.

The cowboy flourishes because so many clients suffer from two basic faults:

(a) They know little or nothing about the work they want done.
(b) They settle for the first chap who quotes them what appears to be a low price, especially if they are told there will be no VAT if the client pays promptly in cash.

It's a bit like the old Dutch auction. If you'll fall for that glib line then the cowboy knows you'll fall for anything.

The term 'cowboy' is unfortunate. These characters are more like the outlaws. So beware! The cowboy works on his client's gullibility. Sure he can do the job cheaply, and yes, he can start Monday, and definitely the job will be finished in two weeks, and he comes highly recommended. But before he starts he needs some money up front to buy materials. After all, he doesn't know you, so if he lays out £1500 on materials and labour and you can't or won't pay . . . He's had this sort of trouble before. Of course it's nothing personal, but . . .

The price seems attractive, no VAT and he sounds very competent, so you give him a cheque for £500. It's quite reasonable, surely! It might be except for the fact that you don't know him either. So why is it that you'll trust him with your cash without any work or material to show for it when he won't even unpack his tools without your money in his bank?

From then on you're on the downward slope that so many people have travelled. Each and every one has regretted it, because you'll never nail a cowboy in court. You'll be very lucky to find him after he's finished your job, that is if he gets that far. Often they'll disappear half way through, after another advance, leaving the job in a mess. Those who stay the course (a sort of grade II cowboy) inflate the final bill with a range of extra works you never dreamed possible.

Somehow, the cheap job never works out that way. And, on top of paying through the nose, you're left, at best, with a shabby job that you're simply going to have to pay someone else to put right.

Mercifully, not every contractor is a cowboy. Indeed there are very many honest and competent craftsmen and companies, and, if you're careful, it's not too difficult to sort out the good from the bad. But it is you, the client, who has got to do it. And you will if you take a firm stand on the following points:

1  Understand exactly what you want done. You may not know all the technical problems of the job but, for example, if you want a central heating system installed decide what type of boiler you want, the rooms in which you require radiators and the temperatures you wish to achieve. It is best if you write it all down so that you can give a copy to all prospective contractors.

2  Ask for prices from as many contractors as you can find. Estimates are, in fact, quotes for finished works but, for some reason, they have come to be regarded as approximate costs and any adjustment always appears to be upwards. If a contractor knows exactly what you want he can prepare a design and give you a firm price on that design.

3  Insist that all contractors inspect the site before tendering so that they can see any problems and allow for them. Make it clear that the only extras for which you will pay are the ones that you add to the job. It is normal practice to give instructions in writing for extra works. Make it clear that this is what you intend to do.

4  Employ only qualified craftsmen. Look for membership of an institute (for instance the Institute of Plumbing for plumbers)

or a recognized Association (for instance the National House Builders Confederation – NHBC – for builders). Check with any association (there is only one institute for plumbing, although you may employ a registered heating engineer) that the person in question is a bona fide member.

5  Question contractors at tender stage on any technical aspect you do not fully understand so that you are aware of what he proposes to do to meet your requirements. If you have any doubts (because of conflicting accounts from several tenderers), associations and institutes will invariably answer specific technical questions to resolve your problems.

6  Always confirm your initial requirements in writing in a letter as an instruction. It is important to include any specific start and finish dates and ask for assurances that the work can be completed in that time. Contractors must be given the opportunity to accept or modify time limits because they may be affected by factors beyond their control: delivery of special items of equipment, staff holidays, sickness, etc.

7  When you have received all the estimates you must now select the contractor to do the job. Having met them you will have a guide, in addition to their price, to help you select.

8  The contractor, in turn, will have his conditions, and these are included in the contract he will ask you to sign. *Read it carefully*. It will contain the things you must do to protect your possessions, conditions of payment, etc. Reject anything you find unacceptable. For instance:

(a)  Do not pay any money in advance of any work being done. If the contractor cannot fund the job to the extent of buying materials (and he usually gets a month to pay from the merchant) then you will be well advised to find another contractor.

(b)  Do not accept responsibility for any materials you are asked to store. They are the contractor's responsibility until they are fully and finally fixed.

(c)  Do not pay for any materials delivered to site. Many contractors ask for a payment as part of a valuation in respect of materials. You should arrange to pay for materials, if required, after they are fixed. You are entitled to know that the work has been properly installed, otherwise you may pay twice for material if work has to be altered.

(d) Do not pay up the full amount on completion. Hold at least 10% against possible defects for the length of the contractor's guarantee, but at least for six months.

(e) Ensure that work is carried out in a professional manner and that any works are approved by any appropriate authority. (The gas board, water board, council and so on are not there to supervise work you may have done, but they must be informed of works relevant to them as they may need to inspect and approve.)

(f) Before any contractor starts work in, or on, your property make sure he is fully covered by insurance against any risk to your property, or personal injury to anyone using the property, that may be occasioned by him or his staff.

(g) Get a clear understanding on what constitutes extra works. It is seldom possible for a contractor to see everything, but he should be able to see enough to anticipate any problem and advise you. Therefore, on any quotation you may accept (and don't forget, if the job is reasonably large you may split the work between two or more contractors to take advantage of the cheapest prices for various items such as brickwork, plumbing and plastering) do make sure you know exactly what work the price covers.

(h) Confirm any extra works you require to be done in writing to the contractor and be as specific as possible.

(i) Naturally the contractor will want some assurances about your ability to pay and, normally, a letter from your bank will be sufficient. At least he knows where you live and he has a signed contract, so any difficulty can be resolved in the courts.

(j) If the work is grant-aided he may ask that the grant money be paid by the council to him and, as this will be subject to council inspection, you may agree. A lot of people do this, but do remember that your best safeguard in any contract is the control of the money. Many councils inspect thoroughly, and their officers have a keen eye for workmanship and quality of materials and designs, but some are interested merely in ensuring that the money has been spent on the specified works and they may not be very particular about standards.

## Professional assistance

A reputable contractor will generally accept the conditions outlined here though, of course, attitudes may vary according to experience and it may be necessary to negotiate the points to protect your interests. However, if a contractor tries to apply conditions that leave you unprotected you will be best advised not to employ him.

Ideally, for readers planning large jobs professional guidance should be obtained, and there are many good surveyors available to prepare contracts, drawings and specifications and supervise works. They may charge a fixed fee or a percentage of the cost price of the contract. Many are listed in the Yellow Pages telephone directory or, of course, you can find estate agents and surveyors in your local high street.

If you retain a solicitor then you should consult him on contractual matters if you encounter problems. Good advice can also be obtained from Consumer Centres and Citizens' Advice Bureaux.

## Recommendations

One of the best ways of selecting a contractor is by recommendation from someone you know who has employed him. At least you will know if he's trustworthy and will honour the guarantee on his work. It's worth remembering that the recommendation works two ways: he is recommended to you, and you to him. It's not foolproof; no system is – any more than following the advice in these pages will ensure complete satisfaction – but it is a reasonable safeguard, and it is equally reasonable to assume that if he did a good job for one client he will do the same for you.

## Friends and . . .

This is dangerous ground, but it needs saying. Most of us have friends or relatives who are handy and are always ready to oblige. Obviously it is nice to accept offers of help; it's cheaper, there's no need for contracts and no doubt of their honesty, and so many of them do some very good work.

But very often there are problems and, because of friendship, they are often difficult, if not impossible, to resolve. Guidance cannot be offered on this point; judgement can only be made with a knowledge of the person(s) concerned and the work to be done. All that can be said is that the reader must get his priorities right and put the job first and all other considerations second. A polite refusal in the first instance may avoid an irreparable breach later. On the other hand, of course . . .

No one will avoid all the pitfalls involved in building work. Even hardy experts after a lifetime in the industry can still find trouble simply because there are so many unknown or unpredictable factors involved. These few pages have tried to show a few elementary precautions to protect your own interests; they are not intended as a recipe for a trouble-free contract, for such a recipe does not exist.

# Index